Ellen Who?

 Story of a Secret Love Child

E. O'Neill

WE 3 PRESS
Vail, Colorado

Copyright © 2012 by E. O'Neill

WE 3 PRESS
http://www.alovechild.com

All rights reserved. No part of this book may be reproduced, or transmitted in any form or by any means, electronic or mechanical, including photocopying, recording, or by any information storage and retrieval system, without written permission from the author, except for the inclusion of brief quotations in a review.

The names of people and places and the details of some events have been changed, but the subject has not been misrepresented.

ISBN 978-06155753-6-0 Paperback
ISBN 978-16209501-1-1 Ebook

Library of Congress Cataloging-in-Publication Data available upon request

Published in the United States of America
Interior Design by Dotti Albertine

To We Three

—My Everything

➤ Foreword

This is a work of creative nonfiction. The events are all true and have been rendered as I remember them to the best of my ability. I experienced everything that I present in this story, although I've taken minimal liberties in order to keep the narrative as focused as possible, combining and condensing some conversations and events to best reflect their mood and spirit. Rather than a word-for word documentation, what I present stays true to the essence of the settings and situations, which are all real; I have changed some names and identifying details of individuals to protect their privacy, but every character in my book is aware of this written account.

My goal in writing this book is simple: I hope to help others who have experienced similar *love-child* situations and to inspire people from varied circumstances with the hope and realization that overcoming life's obstacles is possible.

There are many aspects of my story that may seem unbelievable—unexplainable phenomena that connect the dots in my life. Whether or not a person believes in the spirit world, psychics, or mysticism, these types of occurrences have played a strong role in my history. Hopefully, skeptical readers will find such events at least interesting, giving pause for thought. Whatever your spiritual outlook, the immense challenges facing a *love-child* are real, and can be overcome with a mixture of faith, pride, and perseverance.

Acknowledgments

I owe a great debt to my counselor, Sarah Sicliano-Hartt, Ph.D. She has been my steadfast guide, support, sounding board, and co-parent.

Trudi Rossi has been an insightful and integral part of my journey. She is very gifted at what she does as an astrologer and music instructor. (She resides in Pompano Beach, Florida; I'm happy to refer to her by email request.)

Lisa Tener is a writing coach who guided me in this process, along with Rusty Shelton of Shelton Interactive. Both specialize in assisting writers, and can be found online. Thanks to Peggy Lang for developmental and content editing under a time crunch to complete this manuscript; credit to Marta Quest for a later-stage edit; and kudos also to Stuart Horwitz whose Book Architecture method helped tighten and polish my work.

With thanks to the numerous couples who have embraced me and my children along the way from Florida to Michigan to New York to Boston and Colorado. It takes a village.

Heartfelt gratitude to my vast support network "in the rooms." You know who you are.

Special thanks to Dorothy and Shirley, for your nurturing love.

My unending thankfulness for Virginia, my oldest and best friend—always.

Thanks to Tori and Kate, sisters in single-parenting life, and long-standing friends.

Lastly, but far from least, my mother.

I

➤ The Wrong House

My first actual memory is of hearing music playing on the radio, "Moon River," and seeing the brick-red pattern on the shiny linoleum floor. This was the kitchen of our ranch-style house in Rochester, New York, and I was sitting in my highchair. The house seemed calm, so my father must have gone to work. My six-year-old sister Janet was probably at school. Mom was wearing a nice dress, as always, and yellow gloves covered her hands. I watched them reach and grasp and scrub, and I knew that those rubber gloves hid her perfect hands and nails. All her life she protected her perfect manicures, and dressed impeccably. It was a picture of the perfect upper-middle-class suburban setting.

Even as a baby, as odd as it may sound, I understood in that instant that something was very wrong. I had no words for what I felt so strongly inside, but I knew one thing for sure: I was in the wrong house.

2

➤ The Secret Closet

What I felt, even in my earliest moments as a newborn babe in October of 1961, was the anger that filled my house. Tension simmered along with the pots on the stove. Resentment and hostility raged throughout every room, more piercing than my baby wails for attention. I swallowed it down with my formula, and then I was weaned on it. Yet I never got used to it.

Amazingly, even toddlers can seek escape in the form of mind-altering chemicals. One of my earliest memories is of enjoying the smell of gasoline at service stations when my parents filled their vehicles' tanks. I soon figured out that if I woke up before anyone else, I could wiggle my feet into my furry slippers and creep out of my bedroom, no one the wiser. I crossed the red-brick linoleum of the kitchen floor, turned the door knob with both hands, stepped down into the garage, and removed the gas-tank cover from my dad's shiny black Buick, a boat of a car with the tank opening at a perfect height for my nose. I inhaled, filling my small lungs with the blissful fragrance of leaded gasoline, the good stuff. I never truly got a high from the vapors, but I definitely felt lightheaded and giddy, just enough of a rush for a two-year old. I loved the floating sensation it gave me, and more importantly, the feeling of having the power to control pleasure. It was my initial lesson in self-reliance. I had discovered my first way to escape from being uncomfortable.

I ventured beyond mere aromatherapies, climbing up on the

kitchen counter to perch precariously as I searched for a container with a skull and crossbones image, which my mother no doubt thought she'd hidden out of my reach. As quickly as possible I'd consume the cleaning solutions and anything else I could get my hands on that was poisonous. Not surprisingly, I required several trips to the hospital to have my stomach pumped. My parents said I was just looking for attention. Yeah. I was. Absolutely. I wanted their love and attention; and, barring that, I wanted out.

I began wandering through the neighborhood of post-World War II colonials, Cape Cods, and ranch-style homes, all snuggled together in a shady suburb. I spent as much time as possible with friends I made on my own, following them to their houses to be with their families where I felt welcomed into their quiet, calm, happy homes. My best friend was Nancy, and I just had to walk across a small yard to visit her ... and the normalcy that existed in her house. I was stunned to see her climb into her father's lap one afternoon, as he smiled and tickled her. *Wow. So some dads actually love their little girls.*

At home, I had a bedroom, a sister, a mother, a father, but no sense of comfort or of belonging. My father paid me little attention. I knew better than to approach him with any kind of request or even to tell him something. Sometimes Dad would stop and stare at me, a look of pure dislike scrunching his eyes into a frown and tugging his mouth into a scowl. That look kept me away from him. I felt like there must be a secret closet somewhere that held something awful, something that made him furious, a box of memories or answers, and that I was part of it somehow. But I never found this box—not yet, anyway.

Fortunately, my sister, although a child herself—my eight-year-old little mommy—loved me. Mom said she loved me, and doted on my appearance, but I didn't *feel* her love the way I did from my sister. For one thing, my mother was always so very busy.

In 1963, she started modeling for commercials—print and runway. She stood five-feet, seven-and-a-half inches tall, and her jet-black hair and striking big, blue, bedroom eyes reflected her Irish ancestry. She wore dresses that were pretty and stylish, and was perfectly put together from hairdo down to her polished toenails that peeked out of open-toed high heels. Janet, at the age of ten, began modeling with her, and they were often gone, leaving me alone with a father who frequently worked at home. Though Janet had soft brown hair and Dad's hazel eyes, she resembled Mom, and they were both beautiful. Even though I had blue eyes, my dark hair was nothing like Mom's … or Dad's, whose hair was red. I was the ugly duckling of the family, different by appearance and disposition. I tried to stay out of Dad's way—and when I couldn't manage that, unfortunately, our relationship too often turned into conflict.

At age three, I was jabbering away at dinner one night. Even then I held strong opinions on most everything and expressed them freely!

"That'll be enough out of you!" Dad yelled at me. "You leave the table and go to your room!"

I stood on my chair with my hands on my hips and declared, "I'm NOT finished!"

Mom turned so Dad couldn't see and winked at me. Janet stifled a giggle. Dad glared at me, hating me even more. He reached over and jabbed me in the elbow with the prongs of his fork. It hurt, and I became quiet immediately. That was the first warning I got of the physical hurt my dad could cause if he didn't approve of my way of being.

In kindergarten I made friends with my classmates, as well as the entire faculty, creating an alternate family. My teacher let me visit her at her house, giving me some of the adult attention I craved. I loved school and found a sense of belonging that didn't exist at home. When I couldn't concentrate on my lessons in the classroom, I frequently slipped out of class—as my teacher must have known—to visit the nurse or the janitor, always seeking substitute parents.

At the end of my kindergarten year, our lives took a shocking turn. My dad's boss was also his longtime friend. Jim Bayley was silver haired and spoke with a Southern accent. Mom had been his secretary long before my birth, and the two couples—Jim and his wife, my mom and dad—had become close. Our families spent a good deal of time together, but my memories of these outings are dim, as they are of the players involved.

In the summer of 1966, that silver-haired man sent us all away. Dad was transferred to Tennessee, uprooting us to a place where we knew no one. A loyal friend and employee, Dad didn't protest and agreed to take over as sales manager of the southern division of the advertising company. The two families would no longer be seeing each other regularly.

Mom's usual preoccupation and unhappiness intensified. I assumed it stemmed from leaving the proximity of her siblings and parents. My mother came from a family of seven, and her parents and all four of her siblings still lived in Rochester. When not visiting each other, they talked on the phone daily. I especially cherished her mother, my Grandma O'Neill, who always had praise just for me. Grandma O'Neill loved me completely and unconditionally—a foreign experience for me at the time! She had the Serenity Prayer framed and hanging on her bedroom wall, the same one I hang now next to my desk. She taught me about God, and we frequently prayed together. Devout in her ways, she always tucked her brown scapular—two leather squares that she believed would keep her from dying in a state of mortal sin—into her bra. I didn't understand all that, but I thought I understood why Mom was so upset at our move. I, too, truly hated the idea of moving so far away from Grandma O'Neill. I also hated the thought of leaving my friends and school—my other family. I felt helpless.

My parents' ability to get along had always snapped regularly, exploding over issues large and small. Despite their ongoing battles, everything else in their lives was enviable: healthy kids, close extended families, friends, a nice house, a nice neighborhood, good jobs, nice cars. Now they were going to attempt to coexist in a faraway city where we knew no one.

The state line between Virginia and Tennessee ran right through the middle of the twin cities of Bristol. A sign hung above State Street, demarcating Virginia to the north and Tennessee to the south. I often asked Dad to stop the car under the sign so I could with six-year-old delight later tell my grandparents that I'd stood in two states at the same time.

Jim Bayley drove down with his wife for a company picnic at a horse farm in Virginia to introduce Dad to the new employees. There were several horses that were raised for harness racing, and kids were given rides in sulkies—two-wheeled horse carts. This I remember vaguely. However, I'm not sure that if someone had asked me to point out my dad's boss, I would have been able to. Certain memories lie buried because there is no reason to activate them—until that time comes, and I remember this silver-haired man speaking to me in his kindly Southern voice and lifting me onto his station wagon's tailgate, his crystal-blue eyes appraising me. Could my young soul really have known what my mind could not fathom?

Compared with the guardedness of Rochester's conservative townsfolk, the friendly openness of the people in Bristol surprised me, and I acquired a Southern accent immediately. I liked the way summer gave way to a crisp fall followed by a mild winter with little snow, and I didn't miss the frigid Januaries in upstate New York.

I made a group of friends at St. Anne's Catholic School, which my sister and I attended, and where I soon cultivated another family outside of my home. We attended Mass in the chapel every day in an old stone church, and I loved the peaceful mornings, finding protection and comfort there.

I memorized the Mass, and my teacher, Sister Mary, became my friend. A young woman still in her twenties, she invited me for lunch and to spend the night sometimes at the convent. I adored her, and she loved me. When I was with her, I felt like my true self, strong and worthy. We baked cookies together, and she let me dress up in her habit and jump on the beds. *Oh, so that was what a mother's love for a child was supposed to be like*, I remember thinking.

My father traveled all week, thank heaven. We had a peaceful home life during those days. The weekends, however, brought the return of unbearable fighting and Dad's withering scowls directed at me. That invisible closet, with the box of hidden memories, had somehow traveled with us to this new life. I know that God sent Sister Mary to me. Like Grandma O'Neill, she helped me to pray.

"Sister Mary," I said to her one day outside the convent when others were out of earshot. "Um … uh … at home …"

"Yes, sweetheart?" Her skin looked peachy in the sunlight, her blue eyes gazed upon me, and she smelled of strong soap.

I wanted to unburden myself, but the words I needed to say suddenly choked me. Truth is huge, and it scared me. *Honor thy father and thy mother …* that was God's commandment. Was I about to break it?

"You can tell me," she said. "It's okay."

I looked up at Sister and half-whispered, "I feel like I don't belong in my family." Her face disappeared in a blur of tears. Usually, I kept tight control of my tears and would shed them for no one. There, in the aura of her patience and understanding, I sobbed.

She knelt to my level and put her arms around me. "You can always talk to God. Your heavenly father is your friend and always listens."

Oh, how she comforted me and opened me to God's comfort. I hugged her as tight as I could, and didn't want to let go. Without her, without school and my other family, the battles that raged around me would have made my life utterly bleak.

The summer after we arrived in Tennessee, we moved to the Virginia side of town, to a nicer house that was closer to school. Good parenting, to my parents, meant giving your kids the skills to fit in with all classes, by being well-read, mannered, and poised. They insisted I take flute and piano lessons, even though I hated them. What I loved was to sing, but these lessons felt like an attempt to force-fit me into a family mold so that I could meet their expectations. On the other hand, Dad also pushed golf. At the country club, he signed his six-year-old daughter into a class that taught me to tee off and putt, something I find beneficial and enjoyable to this day.

"If you play golf," Dad said, "you'll never have to learn to type. You'll be able to hire someone else to do it for you." This would prove to be one of Dad's better bits of advice.

Mom's stomach began to grow, and she announced there would be a baby brother or sister by Christmas. During her pregnancy, my mother took up sewing, motivated by a need for budget tightening. She conjured up one custom-made, lined ensemble after another. Mom made us matching red-wool outfits for Christmas. We posed for the family portrait, and there we were, in bright color, for all the world to see: smiling faces—including Dad's—emanating togetherness, just like a normal family. I matched Mom and Janet and actually looked like I fit in. I was hoping the new family feeling was because of the tiny new person about to join us. I could hardly wait.

I had just turned seven when Tom, Junior, was born. My father seemed happy for the first time. He loved having a son and namesake. He seemed to calm down a little, and his agitation subsided. He and Mom started doing more things together, like going for morning jogs and playing golf on weekends. I should point out that even though Dad ranted and raved at her, he was crazy about my mother. She was a drop-dead gorgeous woman, smart and classy, and carried herself with grace and an elegant style.

Mom let me take care of my new brother, and I found a sense of purpose in the family. I also earned more responsibility. With Dad traveling Monday through Friday, my mother was basically a single parent of three, and we had to help clean the house and do laundry. She appreciated that I could take over for her feeding, bathing, and babysitting Tommy. Things were better, but I still needed and loved my friends at school, especially Sister Mary.

My mother missed her family and both parents wanted to show off Tommy, so we returned to Rochester in the summer, a reunion that would become a yearly tradition. My father's parents, Grandpa Fred and Grandma Pink (her real name was Mildred, but she went by Pink as a nickname from her favorite color), had retired to their summer cottage on Lake Ontario and added a second story, providing plenty of room for a visit from a family of five. When Grandpa Fred was a successful businessman, they'd lived in a large home in the suburbs of Rochester, and this had been their lake cottage; now they lived on the lake year 'round. My dad had two older sisters, but as the only son, much was expected of him. Dad felt he never quite measured up to his father's standards.

Grandpa Fred loved me though, and I felt safe with him. That, in turn, gave me a sense of freedom that allowed me to explore the lake in all its beauty. I loved the lapping surf and the wind in my hair, the blue vastness, the water birds, summer rain storms followed by calm and rainbows, the colors of dawns and dusks reflected on the water—all affected me deeply, both spiritually and emotionally. Strangely, I felt infinitely small and yet held my head higher, feeling the dignity of self-worth before God.

Mom and Dad didn't fight during those vacations, and I blended in with my thirteen cousins, as we fished, boated, and swam. I loved to swim until something happened to instill a fear of the water, from which I have never recovered.

Dad and I were alone at the lake walking out into the deeper water with the soft sand beneath our feet. As the water quickly rose to my chin level, I became afraid, and tried to grab hold of my dad. In a flash he was laughing and pushed my head beneath the water, holding it for what felt like an eternity to me. I opened my eyes in horror to see only the blackness everywhere. When he finally pulled me up out of the water, I began choking and crying.

"Oh, now Ellen, don't be a baby!" he said, laughing.

I remained silent, and never told anyone what had happened. I didn't want to admit how much I knew he hated me. I was certain he had hoped to drown me that day.

Sometimes, during those visits, I would catch my aunts staring at me, their heads together. They gushed and carried on over Janet and Tommy, but aunts and older cousins often stopped talking when I entered a room. Were they secretly discussing how I was very different?

After a week on the lake, we would head back into the city to visit Mom's side of the family, which included fourteen cousins. We gathered at the homes of different aunts and uncles—I especially liked Mom's youngest sister, Aunt Joby. She looked quite a bit like my mother, and was young and very cool. She and her family lived in a fancy house, and she always drove a new Cadillac. When I visited her home, I spent most of my time with her oldest daughter, Leanne, who was a year younger than I. We played and shared about our friends and school life, and no one whispered behind my back.

Those summers restored my spirit, and I felt happy enough to endure the routine of the next school year where I focused on my replacement family of classmates, staff, and Sister Mary. I stayed out of the house when my dad returned on weekends.

At the end of my third-grade year, Dad announced that his silver-haired boss was going to transfer him to Pennsylvania.
No one wanted this.
"Janet," I said, "I don't want to leave my friends! And the school! And Sister Mary! How can I leave her?"
"I hate it too," she said.
We whined to Mom, who looked like she'd been crying. She took Tommy to his room. Dad was more or less watching TV, a nearly empty bottle and a glass beside him.
Janet was congenitally sweet. Bad times then rolled off of her like rain off a roof, and she never held onto resentment or anger. She usually just looked forward to a brighter tomorrow. This move would upset her world though, and she couldn't imagine anything positive about it.
She summoned her nerve, and smiling, suggested, "Dad! You're friends with Mr. Bayley. Tell him that he can't do this to your family. ..."
"You shut the hell up!" He jumped up and slapped my sister.
Janet fell over and struggled to get up. Dad grabbed her shoulder, and jerked her to her feet. "You just be grateful I have this job!" He shoved her again and shouted, "NOW GO TO YOUR ROOM!"
I kept absolutely quiet, withdrawing into the shadows. I tried to comfort Janet in her room, but we both felt awful. This went beyond the spankings he meted out regularly—especially to me. Dad's violent anger was turning onto his children more, and this wouldn't be the last time.

3

➤ MY FAULT

After the three years of living in relative stability in Bristol, we moved to a townhouse in Pennsylvania. Unlike Tennessee, at this school I couldn't find my niche and had no friends. My mother increased her cigarette intake from one to two packs a day. She would consume a nightly hot-fudge sundae with chocolate-almond and butter-pecan ice cream, cool whip, and hot fudge topped with nuts. The cigarettes must have kept her a lean one-hundred-and-fifteen pounds. I envied her. She took comfort in desserts when Dad was gone on business travel all week, but I developed a sweet tooth when he was home on weekends, and the clash of the Titans picked up where it left off.

I found a secret closet of my own. The townhouse had a walk-in storage closet with a light under the stairs. I pulled a doll crib in there, and when things got too insane, I ran to get two-year-old Tommy and carried him into the closet, pretending to be his mommy and keeping him safe from the big bad wolf. And who took care of me?

I turned to Janet. There was no one else. Bless her, she took me everywhere with her when I wasn't taking care of my brother. Our six-year age gap ceased to exist. When Janet tried cigarettes, I joined in, though I hated smoking. By the time I turned ten, I was hanging out with sixteen-year olds and beginning to act like them. I learned about sex by walking in on two teenagers in the act. Mom spent her time either on the phone or in her room. *What did she do in there all day?* I wondered.

Janet and I looked after Tommy, and I made fried-bologna sandwiches on hamburger rolls for myself at breakfast. I stopped at the store on my walk home from school each day to buy cookies with my allowance. In this way, I began my addictions in earnest, the one to food being the most pernicious.

If I had thought life with my parents' fighting all the time was too much to bear, it didn't compare to when my father turned on me with his toxic teasing.

"Hello, Ellen," he said to me one Saturday morning while I watched cartoons. "You sure are cute today."

I turned to him quickly, a little surprised, and replied, "Hi, Dad." I turned back to my TV show.

"You know that cute means fat," he informed me.

I didn't look at him or reply. I just sat there continuing to watch my show, as I struggled to hold back the tears.

He decided I needed a nickname. "Hey, Ellen, Ellen Melon!" he said in a sing-song voice, almost like a kid's taunt. "Ellen Melon! The big fat watermelon! That's your shape, Ellen Melon."

He didn't call Janet or Tommy names. Why did he single me out for such cruelty? He'd always treated me differently, but now his dislike took a turn that terrified me.

"Hey, Ellen Melon, who left you on the doorstep?" he would say jokingly—only sometimes it sounded horribly serious.

One day when we were all packed and ready for our move to another town in Pennsylvania, my father came to me after breakfast. "Ellen Melon," he said, "come on, get your things on. We have someplace we have to go."

As the drive stretched out longer than I thought normal, I began to get nervous. I actually wondered if he'd finally decided to rid himself of me. My dread of the unknown stretched the half-hour car ride into hours in my mind. As we pulled into a park-like setting, relief swept through me. The sign said, "Hershey's Chocolate Factory." I couldn't believe it! Dad was doing something especially for me. He showed me kindness that day, and I ate as much chocolate as I wanted.

Of course, it confused me that he took me to indulge in my favorite food after teasing me about my weight so much, but I wasn't going to question it. I loved him that day, but more than that, I wanted him to love me. I wanted him to love me every day—an unresolved longing that, fueled by his mixed messages, would grow increasingly painful.

I don't know why we moved to a different part of Pennsylvania a few hours away, but Janet and I enrolled in new schools, and we settled into a newly built house. My dad's boss called and Dad argued with him on the phone.

"But we just got here," Dad protested. Then, after more arguing, Dad said, "No! We're not moving to Holland and that's final!" He hung up.

I guess he finally stood up to the silver-haired man. Maybe this was some kind of new beginning.

Shortly after that the doorbell rang. I answered it. There stood Aunt Joby and my four cousins at the door. Normally a stunning beauty, Aunt Joby looked tired and drawn. She and my mother fell into serious conversation, which didn't include eight-year olds. From what my cousin Leanne told me, Aunt Joby had apparently run away from her husband because he was violent when he drank, which was often. He came from an affluent Rochester family with deep Italian roots. Aunt Joby could never really leave, not with her four children under ten, but they stayed for a week, and then returned home. No one in the family ever discussed Aunt

Joby's unexpected visit again, but it left quite an impression on me. I got the message: women don't get to leave cruel men, especially rich ones.

One way Mom expressed love for her children was by creating a house that was very homey. She allowed me to help pick out my own color schemes and new furniture for this house in an attempt to make me feel included. I was delighted with my pale-pink bedroom completed by a white-lace cover over my full-sized canopy bed. I didn't know this natural knack of mine she encouraged would become useful and utilized later in my life.

My baby brother was a toddler and loads of fun. I loved to play with him when I returned home after school. One of my favorite games involved putting him in the middle of Janet's double bed and jumping up and down around him like a trampoline. One day, he ricocheted off the bed, cutting his eye and needing stitches. My father went into a rage, eyes flaring wide open, veins standing out in his neck. He yanked his belt out of its loops and beat me, leaving red stripes for hours. I'd endured many spankings, but this whipping with a belt pushed me beyond fear.

In that moment, I felt a conscious shame for existing. And the harsh physical punishment continued from then on. It seemed like everything was my fault, everything. But what had I done?

In general, Dad was civil from dinner until bedtime, but then from the time he woke up in the morning, his misery consumed him until his next evening's happy hour. I didn't realize it at the time, but there was an increasingly direct correlation between his moods and his alcohol intake.

In retrospect, I can see that he went into a kind of daze during his episodes of rage. He lost control and took all his frustrations and disappointments out on his daughters, especially toward me, in red-faced, roaring violence. Sometimes, Janet tried to intervene in order to protect me, but then the wrath turned to her. Where was Mom? Out. Dad was never physically violent when she was in the house, and he certainly never lashed out at her. He was still as crazy about her as ever. He made it very clear: If we EVER did anything to upset our mother, he would kill us. Mom was not my protector though. A nice pink bedroom and dainty canopy didn't begin to compensate for the abuse and the soul-shriveling contempt from Dad.

In the past, I'd looked to substitute families outside my home as an escape from the fear and pain, but at this new school I attended, I had no friends at all. Loneliness and self-loathing pervaded my very essence. To cope, I just ate more.

News came the summer after my fifth-grade school term. Dad's boss, who seemed less of a friend now, the man with the silver hair—was set to retire and move south. We could now return to Rochester. This had to be a turn for the better, a glimmer of sunlight lining the storm clouds. *Grandma O'Neill, Grandpa Fred, here I come!* I could see all my cousins again throughout the year, not just during the summers. There would be lovely family holidays. Dad would have to shape up, wouldn't he? Janet was less thrilled about the move because she'd be attending her fifth high school in four years. I felt a little bit uneasy for being so happy—along with that vague guilt that everything bad was my fault. I knew logically that feeling guilty for everything didn't quite make sense. But I felt responsible for everything: Were all of the moves we were subjected to not purely directives of my father's business? Did my very existence lie at the root of these geographical and emotional upheavals, affecting all of the lives around me? Whatever my mother thought about all of our relocations, she discussed them with no one. And the impact on Dad of our nearly nomad-like wanderings almost drove him crazy, and definitely drove him to just drink more.

To make the transition easier, Dad bought the house right next door to the ranch-style home I'd been born into. My best friend Nancy and some of my other friends were still there. I went back to the life I had known previously, and I was happy ... for a few short months. Then my parents decided to build a larger home in the neighboring suburb. Janet and I would start yet another new school with another new set of classmates.

At least while the construction progressed, I didn't have to be around Dad over the dreaded weekends. Mom drove me to Grandma O'Neill's where Grandma and I cooked, baked, and shopped together. I remember making her a pearl bracelet strung on black elastic thread, which she put on immediately and wore proudly. Grandpa O'Neill had died the winter before, and I didn't want Grandma O'Neill to endure any loneliness; plus, I was thrilled to eat and sleep in freedom away from my father's accusing eyes, to live and breathe without restraint in a place where I felt loved.

Once in a while, I spent nights in the house on the lake with Grandpa Fred and Grandma Pink. This, too, was wonderful. Grandpa Fred told me often, "You can do anything, Ellen. Someday, you'll work for Eastman Kodak!" His successful career had started in lithographs, where he served as Vice-President of a company named Ditto Corporation that contracted with Kodak. After retiring, he opened his own small company in Rochester that personalized business products.

When I encountered some of my worst times in life, I imagined Grandpa Fred's hand on my shoulder. *You can do it, Ellen. You can make it.* I felt that he understood me, that he respected my gumption and skills. He really believed in me, something I had never felt from anyone else in my immediate family. I also felt a hidden agenda on his part, an alignment with me in opposition to his son, my dad.

That agenda had less to do with me as a person than with a family history of which I was in complete ignorance at the time. Mom was a teenage beauty—to get an idea, blend a young Elizabeth Taylor and Natalie Wood—who came from a big, poor, Irish family once evicted from their home. Mom carried herself as though she were royalty, with no one the wiser. The class and style she possessed money could not buy. Dad was the son of a wealthy businessman, and drove a snazzy car in high school. Dad attended the all-male Jesuit High School, and Mom the girls' Catholic Sacred Heart Academy on scholarship. Dad fell for Mom with all his heart. She not only needed a way out of poverty, she was also a Scarlet O'Hara, who vowed to heaven that her life would be different. She accepted Dad's advances, though she wasn't smitten the way Dad was. When Dad brought Mom home to meet his parents for the first time, Grandpa Fred hauled off and decked him right there in front of Mom. Grandpa Fred came to admire my Mom, but felt his son wasn't ambitious enough, that he lacked the responsibility it would take to support a wife and family.

Father and son had their own war, and I think Grandpa Fred by favoring me, was more or less saying to Dad, *See, now this girl has what it takes, unlike you, who made such a mess of things.* Truth be told, I liked the way Grandpa Fred was sometimes in-your-face to my dad about his fondness for me, and I didn't want to know what lay behind it. I needed him too much.

My mother's agenda with me was more confusing, more complex. On the one hand it seemed like she was on a mission to make me perfect—almost as if I had to help justify my existence. She fussed over my hair and dressed me in cute outfits that coordinated with shoes, hair bands, purses, even jewelry. From age six on, my sleepwear was like hers: pastel chiffon peignoirs with matching slippers. Her attention to me usually made both Dad and Janet resent me; and so, rather than bringing me closer to Mom, it made me nervous, and alienated me further from the rest of the family.

On the other hand, Mom's agenda ran in the opposite direction, as if she resented me for existing and creating all the drama of my dad's rages. Her resentment usually took the form of the silent treatment—which wasn't always a bad thing—or sarcasm. I felt these mood swings, whether I understood them or not. I was a focal point, a lynchpin in drama I couldn't control. It added to the queasy feeling I had of walking on quicksand, that when bad stuff happened, it really was all my fault.

What happened in late July of that year was not my fault at all, but blamelessness didn't matter. The phone rang while my parents were out choosing materials for the house, and I was babysitting Tommy. Mom and my sister hadn't resumed modeling when we moved back to Rochester, so Janet spent her time either working at a retail store or out with her friends. I answered the phone.

"Ellen, oh Ellen," Aunt Joby cried hysterically. "Is your mother there? Where's your mother?"

"She's not here, Aunt Joby." I tried to calm her. "What's wrong? What's happened?"

She could barely respond at first, but then she managed a grief-twisted clarity. "Grandma O'Neill's been in a car accident. She's dead!"

4

➤ Jigsaw Puzzle

Aunt Joby's words horrified me, sending fingers of ice creeping down my spine, until my whole body shivered. I listened in shock as she explained what had happened. While backing out of the driveway at my aunt's house, Grandma O'Neill's heart had failed. She had collapsed over the steering wheel, causing the car to shift into drive and roll into a ravine.

In a heart-rending instant, I'd lost the only adult female who loved me deeply and truly. I was shattered.

That night, when my parents returned from Aunt Joby's, I saw the blank stare on my mother's face as she went up the stairs to her bedroom. I knew I would have to stay strong.

The house in our old neighborhood was a Cape-Cod style with four bedrooms. My parents and brother had their bedrooms upstairs, while Janet and I had our separate rooms off of the kitchen on the main level. I had no reason to go upstairs, so after a week, it felt like Mom didn't even exist. She would only see Dad when he took food up to her. She finally emerged to attend Grandma's funeral, a day I will remember forever.

After the funeral Mass, Mom handed me the pearl bracelet that I had made and given to my grandmother, and I finally broke down. I realized it must have been taken from her wrist before the viewing on the previous night. From the minute I had given that bracelet to her, she'd worn it as faithfully as she'd worn her brown scapular. My heart was heavy and ached with loss. How I wished I could have said goodbye and hugged her one last time.

If Mom coped with her grief by hiding herself away, I stayed busy doing the things that needed to be done. I fixed meals for sweet-natured little Tommy, who also stayed in his room most of the time. Janet was seventeen and into her own thing, so the completion of the house we were building and the planning of our upcoming move fell on my father's shoulders—and on me. Strangely, my mother's absence created an opportunity for me to find a new place in the family. Not yet twelve, I offered opinions that Dad seemed to respect. I selected bricks for the front entry. I'd enjoyed watching the cabinetry go from blueprint to completion and selected all the hardware for them. I chose the light fixtures. I paid the bills and organized the move, including hiring the movers. I felt very grown up, as if this were the real me, and I liked the feeling. My father was nicer to me and relied on my help with the household and with Tommy, now a first grader. We'd begun an unspoken partnership; I found that if I could really help Dad, he'd give me a hug once in a while.

Our new house, a four-bedroom colonial, was much larger and nicer than any of our other houses. My favorite space was the large family room with a fireplace off of the kitchen, carpeted with a harvest-gold-flecked shag. I loved to fall asleep there on Sundays with sports playing on the television. We mostly ate in the eat-in kitchen, but there were also formal living and dining rooms. Those rooms plus the full basement provided many more places to hide when Dad flew into his rages—which were starting again since Mom started making appearances downstairs. His happy hour now began at four.

After seemingly interminable weeks of mourning, Mom resumed her familiar role, so Dad no longer had much use for me. His anger toward me returned, even though I hadn't done anything wrong. Mom began a position in sales with Xerox Corporation, which totally consumed her. Once Mom took something on, she gave it her all. Their relationship improved, and they resumed jogging together in the mornings and golfing on weekends. They often met for lunch and Friday afternoons ... we were supposed to be gone from the house when Mom came home early. Dad actually played Starland Vocal Band's song, "Afternoon Delight," on the cassette player, speakers up full volume.

In September, I began seventh grade. Despite meeting two friends, Virginia and Mary, I was largely an outcast at my new private Catholic school. It didn't help that I stood four feet, eleven inches, the shortest girl in the class and still wearing a training bra. But I was growing. Kids made fun of my body and the terrible acne that accompanied my growth spurt. Did reassurance come from my family?

"Well, well, if it isn't Crater Face," said Dad, pleased he'd come up with yet another nickname.

Crater Face. How could I look so different from everyone else? My mother still possessed the beauty of a model. My redheaded dad—almost strawberry blond—stood five-feet, ten-inches tall with freckles and a stocky build. Despite darker coloring and lean height, Tommy would grow to resemble him in other ways. Janet's chestnut hair had grown long, and her hazel eyes and flawless skin that held a tan, allowed her to escape any awkward teenage pimples. Tall and slender, she was gorgeous, and everyone remarked on it. I felt short and chubby next to her. A truly accurate family portrait in our new home would be more like a jigsaw puzzle with a space where one piece was missing, and that was where my piece ought to have fit but didn't.

My parents practically overlooked my birthday that year. Janet and Tommy had occasional birthday parties, but not only did I not have them, the date often passed by very casually, without much effort to celebrate. I felt so discounted and unimportant compared to the others, but pretended not to notice. That year Janet spent her entire first paycheck from her job on the latest round transistor radio I had wanted. She made up for anything else that may have been lacking that year by going out of her way to make me feel special.

October did bring promise of the upcoming holidays. Mom created a Christmas with wonderful traditions I continue today: decorating, baking, preparing wonderful meals, and giving thoughtful gifts. Mom started my Madame Alexander doll collection one year, and added to it every Christmas; and I would look forward to meeting my new beautiful addition. Dad gave Mom, Janet, and me gold charm bracelets, followed by a new charm every year, each symbolic of mile-markers in our lives. "Little boxes" was what he said all girls deserved. These were fond memories that I clung to, making life bearable inside a fabricated Norman Rockwell picture.

By the first week in December, I'd grown to five feet, three inches and wore a full-figured C-cup bra. I was babysitting one day and found blood in my underwear. Janet had told me about menstruation and what to expect, so I was somewhat excited about this sign that I was growing up. I returned home from my job to find my father putting up the Christmas tree in the family room next to a warming fire in the grate.

"Hey, Dad," I said in a proud tone, "I just got my first period."

He stopped what he was doing and stared at me.

My childhood memories tend to focus on the upheaval and unwarranted abuse, but, while infrequent, Dad did hug me from time to time. That came to an abrupt end after my impromptu announcement however, and I assumed my ensuing (and confusing!) hormonal shifts. Whatever the cause, he never hugged me again after that day and stopped all physical contact with me—except when he went into rages and shoved me.

Mom, on the other hand, continued her off-and-on doting routine on me as if I were one of those collector dolls—fixing my hair and making sure my clothes were matched and coordinated. This inspired my dad to call me *Crater Face* and *Ellen Melon*, and wonder who left me on the porch. His happy hour now started as early as three in the afternoon. Janet rolled her eyes at Mom's hovering over me and left the house. Six-year-old Tommy liked to isolate himself in the safety of his room and read, but even he went sullen when Mom fussed over me and stuck out his tongue at me a lot. Eventually, Mom threw up her hands at all the hostility around me and backed off in the other direction. I became invisible to her. My family was a puzzle all right.

After Christmas, attention swung away from me. I came home from school one day to find my father sobbing. He'd found birth-control pills in Janet's room. Janet, a senior at a Catholic, all-girls, private high school, dated a boy from the nearby Jesuit school. Dad did not approve of the boyfriend. Before the discovery of the pills, the dating situation had already caused increased arguments and fighting in the house. Sometimes, Janet stayed out all night. When Janet walked into the house after work, my dad went crazy. He threw things at her and chased her down when she tried to escape to her room. As he shoved her into the wall, I thought he might kill her. Tommy ran into his room to hide.

I tried to defend my sister—as she had done so often for me—receiving flat-handed but punishing blows in her stead. While Dad focused on me, Janet locked herself in her room and called her boyfriend. He pulled up in his car soon after. Janet exited the house carrying a suitcase and jumped inside the car, which then took off. I'd had a feeling for a long time that she wanted to get out of this house. Would we ever see her again? I felt hollow, and my stomach knotted with dread. What would become of me without Janet as a buffer between my father and me?

I heard Mom's car drive into the garage. This was not going to be good. Books, ashtrays, a lamp—all still lay where Dad had thrown them, some in pieces. Mom worked until nearly dinnertime every day and hadn't seen Dad's daily tempestuous displays.

"Where is everybody? What's going on?" Mom called.

Dinner was not warming in the oven. Since Dad had left management and returned to sales, he had more freedom to set his own schedule, while Mom developed her career. He came home earlier and earlier to drink, but he also loved to cook, so he was in charge of preparing the evening meals.

I peeked from the hallway as Dad stepped into the kitchen, drink firmly in hand. "Janet has taken off with that creep of a bastard she's sleeping with, is what's happened!"

The yelling started in earnest and I scurried back to my room. There would be no dinner that night. For several days, they barely spoke, and Dad moved into the guest room. When they started speaking again, Mom and Dad each blamed the other, back and forth endlessly, for Janet's leaving. No one heard from Janet for months until finally Dad learned that Janet had eloped with her boyfriend, and they lived with his parents. Janet did not come home. I got her phone number and tried every day to contact her. She didn't call back. Dad was furious, and Mom cried.

The family portrait puzzle now had a piece missing that couldn't be replaced. I grieved at the loss of my sister, my substitute mother, my protector. It broke my heart, and I ate to feel better. I gained weight, becoming more than ever a misfit in our family.

I decided to talk to the priest who was the head of my confirmation class at my junior-high school. What a relief to finally talk to an adult about the upset at the house. Unfortunately, when I got home from school a few days after the conversation with the priest, I found Dad waiting for me. He was absolutely livid. He pushed me backward, and I fell onto the carpet, twisting my ankle, and smacked the back of my head on a TV tray, which toppled over. He never hit me directly in the face or on my arms, but his shoves always did damage. I'd crash into a dining chair or coffee table, resulting in a few red places, an occasional bruise.

"We don't talk about our problems!" he yelled at me.

I knew better than to pretend I had no idea what he was talking about. That priest had betrayed my confidence. I couldn't believe it.

We don't talk about our problems? Why don't we talk about anything? Dad was afraid the truth would come out about how cruel he was to me, and I knew it. How could he secretly be so mean and in front of other people act so differently toward me? And that priest! I was furious. No person could be trusted. No one.

That left me with only God. I would do what Grandma O'Neill and Sister Mary had said I should do years earlier. I would take my troubles to God directly and no one else. This new self-reliance and time spent in prayer proved to be a turning point in my life.

To avoid my father after school, I babysat almost every day for a family in the neighborhood that had twin toddlers. I loved the freedom of earning money. When other families would call for me to sit, I hired my girlfriends, paying them half of the hourly wage I charged and keeping the rest as my profit. This became quite a business; as I made more and more money, I began to fantasize about living on my own, completely independent from my parents.

At the same time, Virginia and I prepared for our eighth-grade confirmation, the reaffirmation of baptism. I chose Aunt Joby as my sponsor. Because her real name was Joan, I chose Saint Joan of Arc as my confirmation name. Preparation for the holy sacrament brought both another welcome distraction and a deepening of my faith.

It steadied me in the next round of craziness within my family.

The phone started ringing at odd hours, and Dad always ran to the phone—unusual in itself.

"Wrong number," Dad yelled and slammed the phone down.

He said this many times—too many times.

"Let someone else take the call," Mom said in the logical tone of voice of a reasonable suggestion. "Why do you have to rush to answer?"

Dad shouted, "THIS DOESN'T CONCERN YOU!" He poured another drink and retired early, as usual after drinking.

As I undressed and put on my nightgown and peignoir, I thought about Dad's behavior. I had only just become a teenager, but it seemed suspicious to me. I put on my slippers and returned to the family room to talk to my mother. She sat reading in her favorite armchair and looked up, probably unhappy at the interruption.

"Mom, I don't know how to say this," I began, "but I think Dad is having an affair."

She answered abruptly, "Ellen, you're crazy. Mind your own business." Then she pointed at me. "You've become quite a problem in this house, making crazy accusations of women calling. And you lied to the priest about Dad getting angry and violent when I'm not home. What's your problem?"

Why would she think it was impossible that he yelled and raged at me? I must have been staring with my mouth open. I was again the problem. Anything bad was my fault.

Mom then said, "You should see a psychologist. I'm making an appointment tomorrow."

Yup. Not one adult in my life could be trusted or counted on. Not one.

I saw the psychologist. I can barely recall her face or anything about her, but I remember perfectly what happened with my visit. She asked questions, and I wasn't going to lie. I told her what I'd told the priest and what I'd told Mom. After an hour with the woman, she asked my parents to come in for a session with her alone. They refused.

I was only in junior high, but I knew that their pretenses wouldn't wash with the psychologist. She'd never buy it that they were simply being good parents living a dandy life whose only problem was their daughter Ellen, and Mom and Dad knew it, too. I was never forced to see a psychologist again.

I began my high-school years in a public school, still a chubby girl and not athletic at all, acne blooming in ugly red welts on my face. Dad made another loving comment: "You look like you should be five ten, but somebody stepped on you." My peers teased me unmercifully, except for Virginia, and a new friend, Ann (Mary had gone onto a co-ed Catholic high school, and I missed seeing her every day.). Ann had two younger brothers in a close Italian family, and I loved the environment at their house. Her father was a successful attorney, and her mother a traditional Italian homemaker who always had spaghetti sauce cooking on the stove. Virginia, on the other hand, came from a home life similar to mine. Virginia was the second of four girls, and her house resembled my family with all its screaming and fighting. Her alcoholic father sat in the same chair and drank beer all night. He was mean to Virginia, and I knew she had no respect for him by the way she talked back to him—which made me love her even more. Both Ann and Virginia soon attracted boyfriends, which took up all of their time. Because I always babysat after school and on weekends, I had no social life—not that I could invite anyone to my house with my father's drinking and all of the chaos. I told myself I didn't really want a boyfriend, but maybe that was my defense to cover my fear that no one would want me—my self-image was so poor. I began suffering from migraines, and when they came on, I slept and could do nothing else, which caused my school work to suffer. Each day felt like drudgery. I devoutly hated my life. Earning money and eating were my only pleasures.

Still, something inside me wanted to prove my worth to my parents. If I was a puzzle piece that didn't fit, I was going to keep hurling myself at the empty space until I did. We needed a better kitchen table, and the more I looked at the woodwork in our house, the more I thought: *I could do that.* I decided to sign up for a woodshop class, thinking I'd surprise Dad and Mom for their twentieth-wedding anniversary in February. Amazingly, they'd lasted that long together. I would surprise them with a new kitchen table. Surely, this would please my father.

Bear in mind that my dad insisted I dress like a lady. I showed up for woodshop in my three-piece polyester pantsuit and got busy. I designed a five-foot-long trestle table of pine, and worked hard to perfect it, learning in the process to use the task specific woodworking tools: table saw, table sander, band saw, lathe, and drill press. I stained the table to match our kitchen—a lovely golden wheat color—which looked so fabulous with the design I had chosen that it won an award in a state-level competition. Filled with pride and anticipation, I had it brought to the house. My parents would love the table and be amazed and impressed by my hard work.

"This finish is totally wrong," Dad said when he saw it. "It needs to be re-sanded and re-varnished. Don't show this to your mother. Take it to the basement."

I held back my tears. My father's anger toward me apparently ran so deep; he wanted to exterminate my very spirit. Later I refinished the already gorgeous table, and it was placed in the kitchen. The family ate meals on it, and for years it reminded me of how painful it was to bear my father's animosity. I have memories of the beatings, to be sure, but I can no longer feel the physical pain. If I play mental tapes of my dad saying, "Ellen Melon" or "Crater

Face" or "This finish is totally wrong," my heart burns, and my gut seethes. I, a grown, confident, and successful woman, revert to feeling like a fearful child.

My freshman year of high school was a low point in my life, but I was getting tougher. I would show them all. ... I just wasn't sure when that would be. Dad wasn't the only person who felt rage. A critical mass of my own anger rumbled like a volcano in my soul: unpredictable and explosive. Now I just needed to find a way to channel it. ...

5

➤ Unstoppable

I had an unusual resourcefulness that I believe must have come from Grandpa Fred. It's probably also accurate to say that all those years of pain and frustration packed a fight-back response into my muscles, strengthened my backbone, and charged my energy. I was only fifteen, but I secretly looked for apartments and cars in the newspaper. I had enough cash, but from the time I started paying bills at age twelve, I'd understood the power of credit and paid attention when Dad yelled about the value of a good rating.

One rare day, my father's drinking left him mellow. With a *carpe diem* spirit, I convinced him to sign a little piece of paper—making him a cosigner on my first credit card. *Heh-heh-heh.*

Before he had a chance to change his mind, I took the bus to look for a used car. The salt from the snowy roads in the Northeast had eaten away at its paint, but the white Volkswagen Beetle that was in my price range looked like a luxury sedan to me. Though my babysitting money could cover a big chunk of the price, I chose to finance the car on my shiny new credit card, and in that way establish my own credit.

Dad may not have conceded my skills at carpentry, but I knew I'd done a great job with the kitchen table and in learning how to use all the tools. With a new vision of what I could accomplish, I signed up for an auto-body-shop course at a vocational school, and in my fancy pantsuit, set about restoring the Beetle's body to a corrosion-free smooth surface. As the only girl there, I felt a little awkward, but it was nothing new for me to be the odd one out. No one else would help me with this car, so I needed to learn how to take care of it. I went on to take a mechanics' course, too. I paid to have another student paint it like new, and my now blue Beetle was ready in time for my sixteenth birthday. I passed the driver's test in my dad's car, which had an automatic transmission. My Volkswagen had a semi-automatic shift on the floor, and I still didn't know how to operate it.

"Figure it out yourself," Dad said, angry at the level of personal resourcefulness I'd shown to this point regarding the car. "Good luck." He drove off to return to work.

Later, much later, I would become grateful for his callousness, because it fueled my tenacity and self-sufficiency, but back then? Gratitude did not cross my sixteen-year-old mind.

I'd met a group of boys in woodshop and body-shop classes. When they invited me to go off-road dirt biking, I accepted. I bought my first pair of jeans, which I had to hide from my dad, as I knew he would disapprove. The Kawasaki 250 motorcycle was bigger than I was. My feet barely touched the ground, but once I got going on it, I loved the feeling of power it gave me, and I also felt comfortable competing with the boys. With my own money, I went out and bought a motocross outfit and a lavender helmet. Going fast and doing the "guy thing" thrilled me. That man's world that scared off so many women? Not a big deal. There would be room for Ellen in it.

And I could pull off womanpower as well. Funny how abusive parents value outward appearances. Priests and teachers must have thought I was last on their list of possibly abused minors because I looked so cared for. Dad had always insisted that I dress like a lady, and Mom bought me the latest fashionably coordinated outfits. Consequently, I stood out from the other students in their jeans, and didn't relate well to my peers. My acne had lessened, and I looked older, dressed older, and felt older. They started calling me "that Ellen lady," which didn't bother me one bit. I was stunned at the helplessness of some of the female students—silly, boy-crazy little girls—something I vowed I'd never be. But my sister? ...

One day I came home from school to find my dad on the phone, talking to Janet. She'd been gone for two years.

"Janet! Honey, it's okay, it's okay," Dad said. "We'll come get you. ..."

Dad arranged to go pick her up, but she'd managed to acquire a lot of stuff. I called my friend, one of my off-roading buddies, and he came over with his truck and two friends. We caravanned out to a remote suburb where Janet lived in an apartment with her husband. He was working at the new pizza parlor they had opened together, thinking she was at home not feeling well. As we were inside furiously packing, we all looked toward the front door. A key clicked in the lock. I gasped along with Janet, thinking he had come home early.

A woman with big hair and big boobs entered instead. "Oh …" she said when she saw us staring at her. "I … thought you were at work. …" She left quickly.

Janet teared up and then wiped her face. "She lives in the apartment next door."

"And she just happens to have a key," I said. I was pretty sure I knew why.

Dad brought Janet home, and we cleaned out her belongings before her husband got back from work.

The next day after school, I knocked on the door to Janet's old room. There was no response, but I heard a rustling sound as though someone turned over in bed.

"Janet?"

I heard her sigh, then, "It's open."

I walked into a dark room with the curtains closed. Janet's eyes were puffy and her hair matted.

"What happened?" *Why didn't you ever call? How could you leave me like you did?*

"I caught him lying." She sat up in bed. "He'd finish up at the pizza place and then slept with that whore of a neighbor before coming home."

"I hate cheaters," I said. "And I hate your husband!"

Janet's marriage had broken up after two short years, leaving her depressed and jobless. She slept all day. Janet hadn't been silly and boy-crazy, but she'd made the mistake of thinking a boy could rescue her from the chaos of our home. She really only wanted to be taken care of.

To lift her spirits and encourage her to get a job—and possibly because my dad felt guilty for driving Janet out of the house, which, in turn, pushed her into the disastrous marriage—Dad bought her a gold AMC Gremlin hatchback. I didn't take it well that I'd had to pay for my car, but Dad simply gave Janet the hatchback. Yet I hoped it would help her get her life back on track.

My father drank even more, starting at noon every day. Janet, Tommy, and I walked on eggshells at all times to avoid setting off the human roller coaster Dad had become: normal-seeming in one moment, violent and angry the next. We couldn't determine exactly when the tide would turn, but we did know one thing: his life seemed to be falling apart.

My parents had become embroiled in some kind of unending legal battle that I gathered was my dad's fault. I stayed out of it but overheard phone calls where Dad yelled a lot. My mother had to attend several court dates with him and she screamed in protest. I heard words like *"paternity,"* but I'd stopped thinking of my parents' lives as coherent and meaningful in any way, and didn't connect one single dot. It was just more insanity, rage, and chaos. All I wanted to do was get out of the house.

Dad apparently wanted that too. "Since you earn your own money," he said, "you can pay all your own expenses. Entertainment, clothes, shoes, shampoo, toothpaste, makeup, whatever you use on your crater face—if you need something, you buy it yourself."

There we were at yet another someday-I'll-thank-him moment. That was when I found my slogan: *If it's meant to be, it's up to me.* I found a second job at a local drugstore.

As always, my dad had to take his frustrations out on somebody, and unfortunately, with me gone much of the time working, Janet bore the brunt.

Toward the end of my junior year, I met an older girl who worked at a restaurant and made much more money in tips from cocktail waitressing than I did at the drugstore. She said there was an opening coming up and that I should apply so we could work together. I figured out a way to forge my birth certificate in case they asked for proof of age. I looked eighteen, after all—the legal drinking age in the state of New York. It was the summer before my senior year, and that fall I'd only have one class a day, having completed all of my requirements in three years. From then on, I worked two restaurant jobs, a lunchtime shift three days a week and cocktail shift four nights. I kept my job working part-time at the drugstore and continued to babysit whenever I could, all the while watching my bank account grow. Earning money gave me a sense of empowerment that I never wanted to be without. I was a competent young woman with alternatives preparing for my own future.

Just before summer vacation, I came home and entered through the kitchen, which we all did to keep the formal areas presentable. My father was drunk. His whisky stank up the place like poison.

"Everything's your fault," he yelled at me. "Things would be better for the family without YOU!"

I saw the dazed look in his eyes as his anger grew, and I knew what lay in store for me. I should have run out of the house, but I stood frozen. He came at me there in the kitchen and grabbed me by the arm. I broke free and ran to my room. He chased me up the stairs, yelling and screaming. I kept moving, barely one step ahead of him. Fearful of what he might do, I closed and locked my door in his face. This only fueled his fury, and he broke the lock. I gasped in horror as he forced his way into my room. He'd never done anything like this. What was he capable of? His rage had boiled over to the point that I feared for my life.

Terror combined with my own anger, and I lifted a small wooden chest of drawers off the floor, the magazines and bric-a-brac cascading down. He kept coming at me. With all my strength, I flung it at him. All in the same instant, mahogany inlaid drawers slid open, the contents flying as the chest sailed on its collision course with my father's face. I heard the smack, and then the chest crashed to the floor, breaking one of the legs. Dad stood in slack-jawed shock, staring at me. Blood ran from the bridge of his nose and down to his chin onto his shirt. Not even he could stop me now.

6

➤ Shifting Gears

The man I'd called *Dad* for sixteen years turned and quietly left my room.

I was shaking. There were tears in my eyes and my cheeks were hot, but my feelings roiled around inside me, turning molten. I needed to think, to figure out as best I could what I had done to deserve such incredible treatment, but there was no time. What if Dad came back after me again?

Staying wasn't an option. I had to get out. I started throwing my things into my Beetle. With my last armload, Dad blocked my path in the kitchen.

"If you walk out that door, you're never coming back. It's one-way. It does not revolve."

"What about Janet?" I wanted to shout. "You allowed her to come back—what's the difference between us, your two daughters?"

But I didn't. Instead, I simply stepped around him, letting the door slam. I hopped into my blue Bug, backed out of the drive, and didn't even glance at the rearview mirror. No prodigal-daughter return for me, not ever. Even though I was still under age, I was gone for good, and my parents wouldn't try to get me to come back. I couldn't even tell Mom why I left because she'd never believe me; she couldn't allow anything to mess up her perfect picture. I couldn't tell anyone else either. It might have come out like this: *You see, I'm such a misfit that my own father couldn't stand the sight of me anymore.* I still felt so much shame. I hadn't learned to get completely out of the *it's-all-my-fault* gear just yet. Teach myself to drive a stick shift? No problem. Teach myself to shift to a higher emotional gear? I was working on it.

It finally sank in that I was now out of my cage and free to fly away anywhere I wanted. I felt a rush of excitement. I also felt relieved to know that I had an inner strength, and there was something determined inside me that would never be defeated.

Good to know.

I was ready for this day. I had my own savings, my own car, and two jobs. I thought briefly about my good fortune, if one can call it that. I knew I wasn't the only unwanted or abused child out there, but how many felt trapped and unable to escape? How many fled into a doomed marriage like Janet? Even though I was scared, I knew that would not be my story, thank God.

I drove to the apartment of a coworker in the city. She had a two-bedroom place that she shared with a guy friend, and I had been there a few times since we had met. They welcomed me to stay on their couch until I found my own place. I paid one-third of the monthly rent for the week I lived with them, and I truly appreciated their taking me in.

After looking at several possibilities, I found the perfect studio apartment on the top floor of a mansion that had been converted into rental units—so much charm and character—with refinished original hardwood floors and beautiful crown molding on the high ceilings. Located off of Park Avenue near downtown Rochester, it had easy access to a cultural area with several terrific cafés, shops, and art galleries. The sun finally began to shine on my life. It had required that I nudge the clouds a little, but I felt a sense of control over my own destiny. I adored my new home. I danced; I sang in the shower. What a total relief to have my own, safe place where no one could ridicule or blame or beat me anymore.

Summer flew by. Virginia, eighteen at this time, and I would go out once in a while, or I would visit Ann at her parents' house. I contacted Mom to let her know where I was. She was merely polite. I only saw a few of my high-school friends, as I worked so much; instead I started hanging out with an older crowd of people from the restaurant. I felt like I fit in comfortably in this new, grown-up world. I began to drink after work with my friends and stay up late at parties.

I returned to school in September, but I only took one class first period every day. I worked and paid rent and car insurance. That October, I turned seventeen and was a fully emancipated minor. I had established credit in my own name and could prove I was self-supporting.

Per usual, my parents didn't even acknowledge my birthday. It wasn't the first time, but I still hoped against hope that they would wish me well. I tried not to let it bother me too much and went out to celebrate with Virginia. My fake I.D. got me into the bars, but the following morning, I awoke to a screaming headache and could not recall what had happened. Even more alarming, I awoke to find myself in my bedroom at my parents' house. Incredible. How had I arrived there? Luckily, the sun had barely risen, so I slipped out unnoticed, hoping they wouldn't even know of my unannounced visit.

As I hurried away from the front door, I could not believe my eyes. The entire windshield of my car was cracked. Had Virginia driven me home? Straining to see through the fragmented lines in the glass, I immediately drove the car to Virginia's parents' house to find out what had occurred. Apparently, Virginia had driven us both home from the bar. Not knowing how to drive the Bug's semi-automatic stick shift, she slammed her foot on the brake thinking it was a clutch, sending me forward, my head striking the windshield. I wanted to shift gears in my new life, but this was horrendous.

"Because you laughed so hard, and I didn't see any blood, I decided you were okay," Virginia said.

"Right."

Wow. Apparently, I must have driven the car in that condition from her house to my parents' house by myself. I pretended to remember the whole night, secretly shaken over the fact that I recalled none of it. I vowed not to drink that way again.

But then I attracted my first boyfriend, another major shift. I began dating him at the start of the school year. He was cute with his blond hair and blue eyes. He stood about five feet, ten inches with a medium build, and Virginia thought I was lucky. He was a good kisser, yet I felt no stirrings of physical attraction. Ever since my dad's revulsion when I began menstruating, and seeing how he fell apart over my sister's use of birth-control pills, sexuality was something I couldn't even think about. Furthermore, my body was about as attractive as a watermelon's, wasn't it? And I still had skin issues.

Somehow, my new boyfriend wanted me despite my poor self-image and pressured me for months. One night we had been drinking, and things went farther than I planned, but he was my boyfriend, so it seemed okay. I lost my virginity to him in his father's Buick. It hurt, and I didn't remember much of it; but afterward, he came to expect sex regularly—which didn't interest me but I pretended it did so he would want to be with me.

I liked having my new boyfriend around, but in truth I was concentrating on more-important concerns, such as saving money and applying to colleges. I didn't have any guidance, so I only applied to state schools that offered grants for emancipated minors. I had no idea in what I wanted to major and no idea what I wanted to do with my life other than find a place where I would fit in. My world revolved around working and seeing Virginia and my boyfriend when I could.

He took me to my senior prom, and I was so nervous about looking chubby in my dress, along with my newly broken-out face, that I drank too much … again. I just couldn't stop myself from going over my limit. I hardly remembered the entire night, and I broke up with him after that before he beat me to it. I was just glad to get high school behind me. My family remained in the background of my life—special occasions and church every now and then. It was as if we were distant, slightly hostile relatives. And that was fine.

Virginia left for Syracuse University in the fall, and I was off to State University of New York (SUNY). I had visited several colleges and chosen this one, three hours north of Rochester, near Canada. It was challenging for me to move into the mandatory housing of college dorms after having lived on my own. I would only last one semester and then find a house to rent off campus. I sold my Volkswagen Beetle and bought my sister's gold AMC Gremlin hatchback from her; it had more storage than the VW Bug. It bothered me that I had to pay Janet for her car, which Dad had purchased for her, but I needed it, and she set the price. She was seriously dating again.

I was on a mission: to release the independent woman inside me who was yearning to be free. Unfortunately, college didn't look like it would be the means by which I would secure my future. As in high school, I didn't feel any sense of belonging. The courses bored me, and I had no focus whatsoever with regard to my education. The only thing I had was my faith. I joined a Catholic parish and became a Eucharistic minister to administer communion at Mass. I needed that spiritual connection to remind me that I wasn't entirely alone.

I quickly applied for a job in a restaurant named Morgan's in Potsdam, managing a fraternity bar. My future boss asked me about my experience as a cocktail waitress. She then hired me, showed me the books, the ordering system, what it took to open and close the bar, and gave me *carte blanche* overall. This was amazing. I was a businesswoman. My first managerial decision was to be open only Wednesday through Saturday nights, which were the prime college partying nights. Staying closed two nights saved on overhead, and success came quickly and easily.

The clientele was mostly boys my age and older, yet they seemed like little brothers to me, raucous, immature, goofy, horny. In the way that I was still "that Ellen lady," I think I came across as strictly business, and they didn't make passes at me, or if they did, I paid no attention. By now I had traded in the Gremlin that had mechanical problems for a yellow VW bug. The frat boys used to find my car outside and physically lift it out of its parking place and carry it someplace around the block. On snowy nights, I had to go looking for my car. They found this to be hilarious. I was not amused, finding it all rather childish.

I hired and trained two beautiful blonde identical twin sisters to bartend with me. Coincidentally, they were from another suburb of Rochester, and I drove them home on vacation breaks. One of the two became a good friend, Shelly. The three of us had a great following at the bar, and the tips alone could pay my rent. I enjoyed being in charge of ordering, payroll, and the entire operation. I felt needed and necessary. I loved this job. Managing the bar, along with the money I earned, fulfilled me in a way that college did not, and I earned a minimum of a thousand dollars a week. College just seemed like a silly idea, and with the voice of insecurity ringing in my ears, I froze up on tests, or came down with migraines before exams, but I persevered.

A friend of my boss in his early thirties frequently came to the bar to see me. He parked his black Porsche in the front, sat at the bar, and flirted with me. He owned his own insurance agency in town and another in the next town. He was nice looking, but I had no interest and couldn't be tempted into dating him. Why would I want to risk my relationship with my boss and the great position I had? I'd already decided never to rely on a man to take care of me. I knew I had what it took to survive on my own, and I wanted even more freedom, not less. I wanted the earning power that would keep me from dependence on anyone else—and more than that, I could still hear Grandpa Fred in my mind telling me I could really be something.

Despite my earnings, I still struggled with tuition, rent, and expenses. I needed books and summoned my courage to call Dad and ask if he would help out a little.

"Get a loan," he said and hung up.

So there I was. If I ever started thinking things could be different, all I had to do was ask for a tiny favor he'd have done without a blink for Janet or Tommy. I think I finally figured out something about my dad's animosity toward me. With me out of the way at home, he must have thought he had a shot at getting Mom to love him with even a fraction of the depth of feeling he felt for her. Never mind that he'd grown heavy and she was on her way to becoming the top realtor in Rochester who would soon be earning far more than he, that she admired success and a healthy physique, and that she hated his weakness for alcohol.

A bright spot shined during my freshman year. The computer-science department at my college posted applications for volunteers at the 1980 Winter Olympics in Lake Placid in February. I had the good fortune to land a fun job interacting with all kinds of interesting people. I risked letting the twins take over at the bar, juggled classes, and, once there, took great care not to drink that week in order to maintain my composure. I met the Vice President of the United States and his wife, along with the President of the Winter Olympics. I watched the Miracle on Ice, as the United States' hockey team took home the gold medal. What a fantastic experience it all was, and one that gave me a taste of the lifestyle I sought, as it showed me I had a talent for schmoozing, which would serve me well in the years ahead. (And because life is really odd, I would be fixed up on a blind date with one of those hockey players later in my forties—not that it went anywhere.)

After the Olympics were over, I returned to my bartending job and the temptations of alcohol. I only had a few drunken episodes that year and tried very hard not to overdo it. The problem was, I could never tell what would happen if I drank, whether it was one drink or six, and that worried me. I refused to end up like my dad, and I knew I needed to keep my head on straight to rise to fulfill the ever-more-promising vision I had of my future.

That April, however, I returned to Rochester for my sister's wedding. I was the maid of honor in a pretty terra-cotta dress with a sheer cape, while the other three bridesmaids wore peach. My brother was the ring-bearer. Because Janet couldn't marry a second time in the Catholic Church, the wedding was Episcopalian with a posh reception at a country club. My parents seemed thrilled that Janet was marrying into a prominent family. I always loved the chance to hug Grandpa Fred and Grandma Pink, while idolizing fashionable, gorgeous Aunt Joby. Mom and Dad were cordial to me. Life was perfect as far as they were concerned: I was out of their hair and Janet was now a source of pride. At one point my father pointed to one of Janet's friends who was still unmarried at twenty-five.

"Hopeless, if a girl isn't married by her age," he said, eyeing me, which I took as a signal that I'd better get on the ball and try to come close to Janet's successful arrival into a world that reflected the expectations of our parents.

The strain of getting through an occasion with my family drove me to the open bar, and the event was a blur beyond a certain point. I consoled myself that everyone else was pretty well toasted, and strengthened my resolve yet again not to overdo it in the future.

Yet, to my great shame, I still had episodes where I lost control—especially in my sophomore year. During Christmas vacation, the bar closed for the holidays, and I returned to Rochester to visit friends from high school. Janet and her husband let me stay with them. Things were fine until Shelly called me.

"Hey, there's a group renting a Winnebago and driving to New York City to watch the ball drop on New Year's Eve! A friend of mine there is having a party! Come with us!" she said.

Sounded fun. On the eve of our departure, we all met over drinks to finalize the logistics. We discussed finances and who would drive the Winnebago. I didn't see the harm in having just one drink. It had been several months since I'd had any alcohol at all, so I thought one teeny drink couldn't hurt. …

The next thing I knew, I woke up in a completely unfamiliar room. At first, I just stayed under the covers, trying to place my surroundings, and I could not. I recognized absolutely nothing. One of the guys from the group lay in the bed next to me—naked. I discovered that I, too, was unclothed and spotted my apparel draped and flung all over an unfamiliar room. Nausea and humiliation filled me as I jumped out of the bed and ran to the bathroom to vomit. I contemplated the probable activities of the night and felt awful, inside and out.

When this strange guy awoke, he seemed very happy. He was tall and lean, and apparently a senior at the University of Rochester. He gathered his things as he dressed and rambled on about what time everyone was meeting that afternoon, and that he needed to run errands in order to be ready in time. I finally realized I had spent the night at his apartment. My spirits worsened. After cleaning myself and dressing, he pulled me into his arms and kissed me romantically.

"Last night was fantastic." Kiss, kiss. "I'm so excited we'll be together again tonight." He walked me to my car and kissed me again. "See you at the Winnebago in a few …"

I was too embarrassed to admit I didn't know where I was, let alone how I'd gotten there. I couldn't believe I found myself in such a situation. Somehow, after driving around for a bit, I came across familiar landmarks and made it back to my sister's. I'd already chipped in my share of the money for the Winnebago and the gas, so I couldn't back out at this late date. Feeling numb, I called Shelly.

"Woo-hoo! You sure had a big night last night!" she gushed into the phone. "And get ready for another one!"

"Right … jeez, I'm so … uh … hung over. …"

"I'll bet. But, hey, you snagged a great guy!" Shelly said. "You two looked so cute together."

Mortified, nauseated, all I could do was go along with Shelly's happy spin on the evening. I was much too ashamed to admit that I had blacked out all night. The Winnebago excursion would only be an overnight trip, and there would be eight others with us, so I'd be okay. I showered, packed a bag, ate some saltine crackers, drank a flat soda, and left to meet the group. When I looked inside the Winnebago, I saw four sleeping areas, plus the two front seats. Everyone planned on pairing as couples. Because I absolutely would not be drinking, I offered to do the driving. The others were thrilled about that, all anxious to start their "party before the party" on the road. I drove the entire way, and when we got there, I was exhausted. I slept alone in the RV, as the others went out to party.

My friends laughed about my hangover, but all I felt was disgust. I wondered if my friends had those feelings or blacked out when they drank as I had. I avoided the guy from the night before as much as possible to dispel any impression that we were an item. I had no intentions of being together with anyone. We drove back to Rochester to return the motor home, and then each of us headed to our respective cars. I walked fast hoping to avoid conversation with the stranger I had slept with.

"Ellen, wait up!" It was him. "Can we talk a minute?" He looked hurt. "Why are you being so distant? We had a great night together. I don't get it."

"I'm sorry; I had too much to drink. It was a one-night thing."

He said nothing but bolted to his car and drove off, burning rubber.

Never again, Ellen, I told myself. I simply could not drink so much. Nobody had a clue how upset I was. Others thought I was easily social with friends, always confident and comfortable. The reality was that I was a loner and felt separate from others most of the time. Even among my friends I felt isolated and different. Church and work were the only experiences where I felt in control. In any situation that involved feelings and interpersonal relationships, up went the walls, keeping some part of me inaccessible … and safe. I think that subconsciously, I couldn't risk someone finding out that my dad might be right, that at my core, I was still a misfit who ruined everything.

I'd been on my own for more than a year and a half. In many ways I was thriving, and knew I would succeed in life, but even though you can take the girl away from the shaming home life, you can't always take the shame out of the girl. I still hadn't shifted gears.

7

➤ I Want to Be Like the Guys

While I was back in Rochester that summer after college, Janet and her husband let me use their future nursery until I figured out what I wanted to do. Staying under the same roof with my parents still felt like too much of an emotional danger zone, though I saw them at family gatherings—where they were distantly polite. Janet's husband's family held memberships in several private country clubs, and she invited me to spend the afternoon with her at the pool of the Yacht Club on Lake Ontario, where a few of her husband's relatives and ancestors could boast of having served as Commodores. Women were never allowed to be members there, only guests, which made me a guest of a guest.

Janet was pregnant with her first child, as was her girlfriend who joined us. My sister's friend had come to her second marriage in a series of events similar to Janet's; after getting married in her late teens, she got divorced, and remarried in her early twenties to a successful man with whom she started a family. Like Janet, she was also a very pretty woman. In contrast to Janet's five feet, seven inches, she was petite with dark hair pulled back in a ponytail. She had striking blue eyes.

As I sat with the two pregnant wives, talking about pedicures and shopping and what they'd had to hide from their husbands who fussed about expenses, two men approached a patio area adjacent to the pool where members and guests could enjoy lunch outdoors on beautiful days like this one. They were dressed in custom-tailored suits, judging by the fit around their broad shoulders and trim torsos, one carrying *The Wall Street Journal* and the other, *The New York Times*. Both stood fully erect, one with dark hair and a medium build, and the other tall and lean with graying hair and blue eyes. Janet and her girlfriend gave polite waves, and they waved back.

"Janet," I whispered, "who are those guys?"

"They're members here, but they're married."

"I don't want to date them," I said, "but I'd love to meet them."

I couldn't stop myself from watching them as they ordered food and interacted with other members and guests, engaging in conversation about investing. That was the conversation I wished had included me. As they departed, I noticed the valets pull up in their vehicles, a Mercedes 450SL and a Porsche Carrera.

That was a moment of intense clarity. I knew I had no desire to hang on the shirttails of a husband and live out my life, hiding secret purchases from him or being a guest at the country club instead of a member. I wanted to be like these men instead. I wanted the lifestyle and control a husband enjoyed. Of course I had no idea then that much later in life, those two terrific gentlemen would become clients of mine, and we would travel in the same circles.

I'd secured a small apartment in the rear of a home converted into three apartments that was located in the area in which I had lived during my senior year of high school. It had a small entry porch, a living room, small eat-in kitchen, bedroom, and bathroom. The modest furnishings suited me, and I could pay the reasonable rent. I don't know if it was because of my regular prayers or if I'm a bit psychic or what, but I felt strongly that something would occur to guide me—and it did the next weekend after my day at the yacht club.

Janet wanted me to meet some of her friends, and invited me to a cocktail party held at yet another private club downtown. I was pleased she wanted to include me, just like when we were growing up. I chatted with several interesting people, and engaged in conversation with one woman in particular. She was petite, standing about five-feet tall with short hair and light eyes. Married without children, she worked as a financial planner for one of the large investment firms in downtown Rochester. We discussed her career and my struggle to determine what I wanted to do with my life.

"Would you like to come visit my office and observe what I do for a living?" she asked with a knowing smile.

"I'd like that very much." Very much indeed.

That visit turned into further discussions and another meeting, where she taught me how to cold call potential clients to increase her business. Now I understand that, for some people, cold calling ranks right up there with public speaking in terms of unpleasant situations one fears worse than death. But I felt no such trepidation—I saw cold calls as the opportunity to begin achieving my dreams. I'd never held high expectations from people, so I never worried about pleasing anyone to gain their approval. A rejection didn't bother me in the least. An unfriendly *no* meant I was getting that much closer to a future *yes*.

I agreed to work for a flat fee for every call I made that turned into an appointment—another incentive to succeed. I went in to her office after dinnertime three nights a week for a few months to make calls for her. I did so well, the manager hired me to head a recruiting seminar. I earned more than I had when running the fraternity bar in Potsdam, and I decided not to return to college in the fall.

The office was expanding and needed to hire qualified professionals who wanted a career in investment management. After being sent to New York City for a two-week training program, I put together scripts to test the cold-calling skills of applicants from other fields of work with the goal of targeting the best possible candidates to become stockbrokers.

I'd enrolled in evening classes to continue working toward my college degree in business, but upon completion of the cold-calling seminar, the manager of the firm said he needed to meet with me. My work was about to change in a way that made my college courses seem like junior-high material compared to what I did on a daily basis. The top broker in the firm had returned from the south Florida office where he worked during the winters. He had a staff of five, and desired someone to groom as a junior partner so he could spend more time at golf, where he competed as a scratch player. The manager wanted to recommend me for the position. I met with the broker the next week, and he hired me. I had faith in myself, but still, I could hardly believe this. It was the sort of job landed by Harvard MBAs or Wharton graduates. Had I embarked upon the goal that I had set for myself alongside the yacht-club pool?

I arrived at the office before eight in the morning, called a dozen-and-a-half clients throughout the day to go over the value of their investments, and attended frequent dinner meetings for future planning that lasted until nine or ten at night. On the phone, I reported the stock quotes for their very large holdings. This was the early 1980s, and advanced technology meant the telephone—attached by wires. Computers had just begun to be used to track client accounts and information. Ticker tapes showing real-time stock quotes were not commonplace outside of investment houses, and investors needed to speak to their advisors to obtain the information on their accounts. This meant daily discussions with clients holding portfolios of vast proportions.

Getting paid to have fascinating conversations … had I died and gone to heaven? My male clients not only discussed stock prices, they confided in me about their businesses, their partners, their family members. My new boss valued my immediate rapport with these clients, and gave me even more responsibility. Though he picked the investments, I executed the plan. I began financial managing in earnest, building futures through private placements, estate planning, and working directly with their personal attorneys and accountants. My involvement soon advanced to weekend social functions, which carried me personally, as well as professionally, to a whole new level.

I went out and bought a gorgeous new blue Chevrolet Monte Carlo.

My boss wanted me to accompany a friend of his to a wedding they were attending where several of our clients would be present. I had been on the phone for months with these men but had yet to meet any of them. My date was twenty-three years older than I, the same age as my boss. That, coupled with the extreme wealth of these people, made me a little uncomfortable. As the event approached, I decided not to drink that evening, knowing at the same time that social tension often prompted me to act in a different direction than my best intentions.

The wedding and reception would take place at a home on one of the freshwater Finger Lakes, Canandaigua. I knew that only the very affluent had second homes along the fifteen-mile length of this body of water, and that the land values were astronomical, but I'd never spent any time there.

I drove my new car to meet my boss and his wife, and their friend. We all met at his beautiful cobblestone farmhouse that had been restored to perfection and was listed in the historical registry. We rode together in a stunning chocolate brown 1957 Mercedes sedan convertible. Their friend seemed pleasant, but too old for me. The young second wife of my new employer was closer to my age, so we chatted easily on the thirty-mile drive. To my amazement, we passed home after home that didn't look anything like summer cottages along the lakeshores. Each home had perfectly manicured landscaping and varied architectural styles. As we drove along West Lake Road, they each commented on properties that belonged to their clients and friends. I was fascinated.

We arrived at the imposing red colonial home situated on several acres with the lake as the backdrop. It had been in the groom's family for generations. Behind the house and overlooking the lake were a gazebo for the ceremony, and a small village of tents under which were housed dining tables, a dance floor, gorgeous flowers, and a band playing jazz music. During dinner and dancing, I needn't have felt any concern at all about mingling with the super wealthy. I felt natural and at ease meeting so many new people. I stood tall and confidently engaged with people from all walks of life. I never did take a drink that night. Too much was at stake.

The men I had been speaking with daily for months were hugely successful high-profile people: politicians, founders of publicly traded companies, CEOs, and even professional sports team owners. I found the conversations in person even more engaging and stimulating than those we'd held over the phone. Of course, their fascinating careers, families, and overall lives were of importance to me, but it was realizing the connection that filled my soul. I felt a sense of purpose and belonging I had never known until then. The clients with whom I spoke needed me, and most of all, they trusted me.

The magnitude of the career opportunity I'd embarked on hit me. I made two decisions while riding back to my car that night. First, I would acquire another car—my own Mercedes Benz—very soon. Second, I, too, would own a home on Lake Canandaigua someday.

One evening, I arrived late for a dinner with my parents, my sister, her husband, and the new in-laws.

"We've been waiting a half-hour!" Dad said. "Where've you been?"

"I'm really sorry," I said to him and to Janet and her new family. "I had to pick up some old Jones guy from the airport. Then I had to drive him out to meet with one of our investment groups considering building a links' course on Lake Ontario."

Dad looked at me oddly. "Jones guy?"

"Yeah. He's supposed to draw it up for them."

Dad and Janet's father-in-law stared at me.

Dad asked, "You wouldn't be talking about Robert Trent Jones, Senior, by any chance?"

"Yes! That's who it was. You know him?"

The dads roared their astonishment.

"He's only the premier architect of golf courses in the world!" Dad practically yelled.

Janet's father-in-law said, "They joke that there are so many that the sun never sets on a Robert Trent Jones' golf course!"

Had I actually managed to impress my dad without trying? Needless to say, my tardiness was excused.

That summer, my work kept me so busy in Rochester, including time on the golf course and at Lake Canandaigua with clients, that I didn't see much of my family until the christening of Janet's new baby girl Carolyn. Janet asked me to be her godmother, and I was thrilled. Not visiting my parents didn't bother me; however, I did regret the loss of my relationship with Tommy. I had spent so many years taking care of him and playing with him, but as a twelve-year-old boy, he now had little in common with me. Even though Dad's rages had placed him under tremendous stress, Dad had never been abusive to Tommy, so far as I knew. I hoped his relationship with my parents had grown more positive since I'd left, and I prayed he received the attention he deserved. My fulfillment came through my work relationships, and I felt as though I belonged in that setting more than with my family. I was relieved to know that this way worked better for everyone, or so I thought.

I'd understood my new employment meant winters in Florida, and my boss reminded me by saying, "Of course, you will need to get a place in Florida."

Of course? Well, why not? This seemed like an adventure, and I assumed my family wouldn't present any obstacles. Grandpa Fred returned from Hawaii with Grandma Pink, and I drove out to the lake house for a visit one Sunday. His surprising frailty concerned me. He'd been a robust man, having played football in his youth, and he'd kept his shape throughout his life. I suppressed my shock as I warmly hugged him and kissed his cheek.

We walked into the living room, where I told him about my decision not to continue with college, and about my job and how I'd work in south Florida from November through May. He gave me a thoughtful look and led me to the sitting area that faced Lake Ontario through bay windows. The sound of the surf brought back memories of many a night in the guest room above, falling asleep to the sound of waves gently slapping the concrete sea wall.

There was nothing rustic about the lake house. Grandpa sat on one of the tufted emerald-green loveseats, and I sat on a tapestry chair with a needlepoint footstool on one of the many petit-point wool area rugs softening the glossy hardwood floors. The massive brick fireplace had been gentrified with a coat of white paint. Grandpa patted the cushion beside him on the sofa.

"Come sit beside your grandpa, sweetheart," he said.

I felt a chill at the sadness that fell over his face. This could not be good news. I sat close beside him.

"Ellen, darling, I have a very bad cancer." He looked out at the clear sky over the lake. "The doctors say I only have six months to live."

I went directly from shock into tears and then sobbing. When I could talk again, I said, "Grandpa, I can't imagine life without you." I lay my head on his shoulder, tears dripping onto his shirtsleeve.

He patted my arm and smiled. "Now, now. You're just crying because before you know it, I'll be up in heaven knowing everything you are up to!"

I loved the way he could turn grief into humor. There would never be anyone in my life like this man again. I couldn't match his humor, but I said, "You're the only one who ever believed in me, the only one I could trust who ever really loved me. You never told me I couldn't accomplish things because of being a girl or that I should just look for a husband." Somehow, I managed to smile at him through my sniffles.

He hugged me and then said, "El, you can do anything. I know you were born for greatness. Never forget: Kodak ... in outside sales. I can see you there." He winked. "The best revenge is a successful life."

I found that a strange thing for him to say. It seemed to reflect that mysterious agenda that I both did and did not understand. On the one hand, I was pretty sure he was aware that sixteen-year olds don't just bolt away from parents who love and support them. He'd probably known that his son was an alcoholic and had treated me so badly that I'd fled in terror. On the other hand, nobody talked openly then, so it's hard to say for sure.

I managed to stifle my emotions throughout lunch with him and Grandma Pink, but I cried on the entire trip home. I feared for him, for the pain he would endure, and I feared for me, despite my recent accomplishments. I always felt like he had my back, no matter what. I don't know that I fully realized what a deeply profound comfort he was until that Sunday. And he would soon be gone.

I needed a drink. I wanted to call Virginia to go meet her and get sloshed to numb the pain, but thought better of it. I had to stay focused for my pending move to Florida, though nothing could keep me from returning for Christmas to see Grandpa Fred.

8

➤ Dancing on a Throw Rug

By October, I was tracking companies, and had learned how to pick good investments myself, even choosing a few stocks to invest in for our clients. I was shocked that my first month's commission check for September was $15,000 over and above my salary. The incentive program was based on a percentage of the increased production I brought. My boss said we needed to be committed to excellence in all areas, and gave me a membership to the University Club gym as part of my compensation package. He also added parking and gas allowance for my car, and all travel expenses.

I started working out daily, and was soon trim and feeling good about myself. Before I knew it, I was on my way to find a place to live in Florida for the winter. The condo I rented was across the street from the beach with the office two blocks away. While the office itself lacked the mahogany-paneled elegance of the Rochester office, the ocean and weather made up for it.

Funny thing about dreams: the universe can be a bit capricious in granting us what we ask. By the time I got my new French blue Mercedes Benz, it seemed less spectacular than the restored antique models our clients and my boss drove. Now those were classy cars. Of course, the new car pleased me as I drove around Palm Beach, soaking in the blue of sea and sky in an elegant automobile. I felt lucky and grateful, but I didn't feel the elation I'd expected. Based on what I'd envisioned only a year ago, I'd exceeded my expectations of how fast I would rise in the business world. My previous dreams now seemed inadequate. Somewhere inside, I knew this was just the start of continually wanting more. I should have been wondering when I would ever have enough. Would I ever be enough?

I met a whole new group of clients that had me attend events at Society of the Four Arts and frequent all the private clubs in Palm Beach, a beach club in Delray, and the Ocean Reef Club in Key Largo, where I became a member right along with some of our clients.

One, a racer himself, introduced me to racecar driving at Moroso Speedway in Palm Beach. I was exposed to golf at legendary East Coast golf courses like Augusta National, Congressional in Bethesda, Pinehurst, and Kiawah Island. I saw both Mara-a-Lago, owned by Donald Trump, and the Biltmore Estate in North Carolina, both being restored by a client who was a famous architectural preservationist—with whom I still maintain contact. With such dizzying excitement, dancing along with the rich and famous, my itch to continue the path of success became compelling. I had fire in the belly, the drive that Grandpa Fred had so longed to see in his son.

When a huge commission check came in, I purchased a new luxury car for my father. With bonuses, I paid for my parents' trips to visit me in Florida, especially for birthdays. To be honest, I wasn't trying to buy their love and respect—I was basically flaunting my success. Were they impressed? Not particularly. Dad had always had things handed to him, so he just accepted it as his due. My true motives were that I was still trying desperately to fit in and be accepted by a family that didn't want me.

The children and wife of my boss hadn't come down from New York yet, but I didn't think too much of it.

"Ellen," my boss said, "my family won't be joining me for a

while, so I'm putting you in charge of overseeing construction on the new addition." He was talking about his home.

I already ran the office with its five employees, but the extra work seemed exciting. I had an eye for finishes and design, and I loved working with contractors when the end result would be an architecturally magnificent home. And it led me to a friendship with Vicki, the loan officer at the bank who helped me get the construction loan on the house. Vicki and I would go out to the clubs together.

"Ellen," my boss said later, "I'll need you to manage my personal finances. Here's the checkbook."

I suppose I could have wondered if I was becoming more of a personal assistant than a financial planner; but again, I enjoyed managing money and seeing all those quirks you learn about a person by following their money trail.

"Ellen, I need you to oversee my cars ..." came next.

The fleet of sensational antique cars. Well, that was a big *can do*.

Except for Grandpa Fred's declining health, my life was pretty fabulous, I thought.

That Christmas, I headed to the West Palm Beach airport for the flight to Rochester. At my departure gate, a handsome guy approached me. He looked to be about six-feet tall with dark hair and blue eyes. I looked away quickly.

He asked, "Can I help you with that?" His gaze shifted to my overstuffed carry-on luggage.

How brash, I thought. "No!" I sharply replied. "I am perfectly capable by myself."

I paid him no further attention and boarded the plane. He changed his seat in order to sit next to me. I learned he was from Maryland practicing law in Palm Beach. Luckily it was only a two-hour flight to D.C., where I was making a connecting flight, but he'd reached his destination. After our interesting conversation, I decided to give him my number, wondering if he'd ever call.

I left sunny, pleasant Florida and stepped into the arctic freezer that was Rochester in winter, especially right on Lake Ontario where I stayed with Grandpa Fred and Grandma Pink. The sky and water were stone gray, the lake rimmed in frosty white. Inside, Grandma had decked the halls, and the big white fireplace roared. Grandpa was much thinner and very weak. Everyone came for a last Christmas with him: aunts and uncles, cousins, parents, Tommy, brother-in-law and Janet, along with my adorable baby goddaughter Carolyn. At the end of my stay, I knew I couldn't stand to make this my goodbye. There was a bachelors' cotillion at the end of January, and I'd return for that, forestalling the inevitable.

The new year of 1984 began with the boss out of the office, golfing so much that I was virtually running everything. The handsome lawyer from the plane called, and we met for a lovely dinner. I jokingly invited him to the black-tie event in Rochester I was attending in January, and he agreed.

My generous gifts to my parents had earned a certain approval; and my mother insisted we stay at their house. On the evening of the event, we dined at a wonderful restaurant and went on to the ball with my parents. Mom definitely approved of the handsome attorney I had brought along as a date. In fact, she proceeded to dance the night away with him, behaving as though she were hitting on him. She still looked gorgeous, and him—that cad— seemed to fully enjoy her attention. My ability to personally trust men had always been low, but I was still appalled at their behavior. Dad solved things with his usual approach: staggering amounts of alcohol.

My main reason for the trip was to see Grandpa Fred. The next morning, I dressed in warm layers for the visit, heart heavy with the finality of his approaching death. I headed to the kitchen for coffee. The four of us made for an interesting group—my parents, the cad, and me.

Possibly sensing my irritation over the previous evening, and perhaps recognizing the potential residue of awkwardness with my flirtatious mom, and my dad nursing a hangover, my Florida date asked, "Mind if I join you?"

"Fine," I said, the single syllable only slightly less frosty than the air outside.

I didn't tell him that my grandfather's hospice care had begun or that he lay in a hospital bed in what had been the dining room. This guy could jump in Lake Ontario for all I cared. If he stood too close, I'd probably have given him a push.

It was a tender visit with Grandpa Fred. The room smelled like sickness, but I talked about our walks along the lake when I was a child, the storms and rainbows, the fish caught and fried. He smiled weakly, eyes red-rimmed, but didn't say much.

"Never forget ..." he finally rasped, "the best revenge is a successful life."

I smiled and kissed him.

"Promise me ..." He stopped and closed his eyes, breathing with great effort. When he opened his eyes again, he said, "Promise me you'll apply to Eastman Kodak."

Kodak, at a time like this? I almost laughed, but then I fought off tears. "I will, Grandpa. I promise."

"Remember," he managed a grin, "I'll be watching."

"I love you, Grandpa." I hugged his frail shoulders, my cheek next to his gaunt face. Razor stubble from uneven shaving prickled. I caught a scent of what I would come to know as death. "Goodbye. ..."

The flight back to Florida with this guy was awkward, but eventually we talked through what had happened.

"I admit I had too much to drink and acted foolishly," he said.

"Well, you made up for it by being such a good sport going to visit my dying grandfather."

We eventually laughed off the bachelors' cotillion, departing as, and remaining friends.

Within days of being back in my twelve-hour-a-day routine at work, the call came that Grandpa Fred had passed. I dreaded the funeral. It would take place in a strange church with my father's clan. Would they be as cordial without Grandpa to protect me? Grandma Pink was always kind, of course, and I called her.

"You don't need to turn around and fly back up for this, Ellen," she said. "Your grandpa knows how much you love and miss him."

I focused only on work, morning, noon, and night.

Simply to honor my promise to Grandpa, though, I decided to send a résumé to the sales department at Kodak right away. I was not at all eager to leave my job and not really expecting anything. Kodak typically didn't hire anyone without at least a bachelor's degree, so I knew my chances were slim to none, but ... Grandpa Fred was watching.

If there was one thing he taught me that was even more important than believing in myself, it was that I had to live my word. The saying, *a man is only as good as his word*, was sacred to him, and I respected him for that and chose to live by it. I would honor my promise.

Still, I was happy to be back at work and had no intention of switching jobs.

"When is your family coming down?" I asked my boss over lunch one day.

Because I handled all of his personal and professional operations, we had formed a strong bond, lunching together daily to go over things.

"Oh, we decided the kids were too little to be running around the house during construction. I think it's better if I wait until the work is finished before having them join me."

This conveniently left him free to participate in several golf tournaments, which I assumed had also influenced his decision. A few weeks later, the construction was completed, and on a sunny day in early March, we were to do the final walk through with the construction manager.

Thrilled with the results, he commented, "You've completed this job to perfection, Ellen."

"I hope your wife loves it, too. When are they coming?" I asked.

"There's been a change of plans. Hey, I have a surprise for you to show my appreciation."

We went back inside, and the dining-room table had been set for two. A chef and server stood in the kitchen. My boss poured us each a glass of wine for a toast. It felt a little awkward; however, the meal was fantastic, and the evening flowed. The two of us never were at a loss for words. When the staff left, I felt even more uncomfortable, even though I'd never dressed in any way that could be considered provocative, and I always looked professional. I'd certainly never flirted, yet his eager glances told me there was something here beyond a business-like camaraderie.

I rose, saying, "I need to get home."

He quickly stood and rushed to me, engulfing me in his arms and kissed me. I pulled away and froze.

"Ellen, listen," he said, "I actually separated from my wife a few months ago. I wanted you to take over the renovations so they'd be to your liking."

My head began to spin. I'd unwisely had one too many glasses of wine. The shock of what I had just been told made me reel. I loved my job, and didn't want to risk losing it. Certainly I'd grown fond of him, yet I'd never looked at him in that light. He was a handsome man with silver hair, blue eyes, and even though he was forty-five, he had the physique of a man in his thirties.

But ... BUT, he had four grown children from his first wife, and the two toddlers with the second. He was also one of the most prominent, successful men in my hometown, not to mention twenty-three years older than me! What was he thinking? I felt light-headed as he embraced me again.

"Ellen," he said, "It would be so great if we could be full partners, and we'd make beautiful babies."

"This is all too much for me. I can't even consider this." I took a deep breath. "I need to leave." I felt sick.

He obliged by seeing me to my car.

I barely slept. My mind was racing over how to handle myself at work the next day. There was no one to talk to about it, so I whispered to Grandpa Fred, and I prayed. God knows he must have been rolling in his grave over this one. When my boss showed up at the office at his usual time, about two hours after my arrival, the tension in the air virtually crackled. At lunchtime, I asked him to join me, and he agreed, but he was very quiet.

"I'm so flattered by your affection, but it would be disastrous for the clients if we were to mix our personal life with business. It's definitely not in their best interest."

"I know." He combed his hair with his fingers. "I thought about all that, but …" He shook his head.

"I love the relationship we've developed with each other," I said, "along with the relationship with our clients, and most especially how much they trust me. A romantic involvement with you would discredit that."

"Right. …" He seemed remarkably agreeable during lunch, and we went back to work as usual.

Over the following days, though, he became increasingly remote. I went to pay some of his personal bills, and opened the drawer of my desk where I kept his checkbook. It was gone.

A bit disconcerted, I called him.

"I'm taking over my personal affairs again," he said coolly over the phone, "now that the house is finished. I've removed your Power of Attorney."

The next morning his wife and children arrived. *Well, well, well …*

That afternoon the manager from the northern office called me. "I must ask you to take this call in private," he said formally.

My stomach churned as I walked through space now devoid of oxygen. My dance was coming to an end. The rug would be yanked from under me mid-whirl. I picked up the phone in another office.

"I'm alone," I said, determined to keep any tremor from my voice.

"Ellen, the firm has to make cutbacks, so we're letting you go. There will be no severance pay."

9
➤ A Gathering Storm

Outwardly, I kept my cool, and left for lunch to think. Of course, I couldn't eat anything. I personally represented a major revenue increase for the firm, so telling me they were letting me go because of cutbacks was like saying, *We decided we need to make less money in the future, and since you bring in a disproportionately high figure, you're the logical person to cut.*

My rejected boss had instigated this.

I shifted into survival mode, setting my emotions aside. I knew I could prove my case in court, and so the beginnings of a plan helped me keep myself together. I called my handsome new lawyer friend—thank goodness I made it a practice of always staying on good terms with people wherever possible—and ran it by him.

"This guy is a hundred percent in the wrong, Ellen," he said. "What you have in mind is the right way to go. I'll be happy to assist in any way I can."

I thanked him and returned to work, where I barged into our office. "I'd like to speak with you outside," I said with all the cold power I could muster.

In the courtyard, he looked wary and drew a breath to speak, but I beat him to it.

"Unless you pay me six full months of commissions as severance, I'll file a sexual harassment suit against you and against the firm."

"Now, Ellen, calm down. This is not …"

"I'm well within my rights," I said calmly, "and you know it. You have until the time the market closes tomorrow to agree to my terms, or my lawyer starts litigation."

I was headstrong when it came to my survival. I went inside to gather my personal belongings. He did not follow me, and my stomach was in knots, yet I still remained composed, praying and holding my head high. It was humiliating to have the staff that worked under me witness this injustice. Worse than taking a tumble and losing my high lifestyle, I felt unwanted and unloved and ashamed—feelings I'd thought I'd left behind when I left my family. Suddenly I had become the misfit that didn't belong, and once again felt like I was the only problem. I was about to leave when my now ex-boss returned and closed my office door. He handed me one of two identical documents, agreements stating I wouldn't share the details of my release of employment, and he would furnish a stellar recommendation along with a cashier's check in return. I looked at the check. The amount I demanded was substantially increased. Threatening to sue the firm must have had an impact. I took a deep breath, and his expression softened as we faced each other.

I nodded, and he called in a staff member who was a notary. She witnessed the signing and then stamped the agreement.

"Ellen," he said, "I'm sorry about all this … all of it."

I could see his sincerity. I left without a word.

I suppose we all have our demons, but what would have happened if I hadn't turned fierce? There was no doubt. I had no financial cushion. I'd have been absolutely shafted. Because of Grandpa Fred, I knew that a few rare men existed who could be trusted, but it seemed to me that, yet again, my battle armor had proven quite necessary. And again, because life is strange, I would learn years later that after his complete financial ruin and divorce from his second wife, my ex-boss would later attempt to start his own Christian investment fund. A form of redemption, I wondered? I would hear from him again only once on a sad occasion when he had no place to stay. I gave him money to check into a hotel in Palm Beach.

That afternoon, I phoned my parents—not that I thought the gifts I'd lavished on them entitled me to any form of emotional support—just to connect with family during a crisis.

"Your mother's with a client," Dad said. "And I gotta go meet a guy."

Of course. Why had I bothered? I contacted my friend Vicki from the bank to meet for dinner. I don't remember what I said about losing my job, but it worried her enough that she called my sister Janet in Rochester without telling me.

That night, Vicki and I proceeded to get drunk together at a nearby bar. Luckily, it was within walking distance, and Vicki stayed at my place that night. The next morning Vicki left for work, and I had a splitting headache. I didn't have a clue what I would do next.

I wandered over to the beach to pray, meditate, and think.

When I returned to get some lunch, I still didn't have any bright ideas, but there was a taxi in front of my condo. The woman getting out was my wonderful sister Janet. She balanced little Carolyn on her hip as she paid the driver. I was overjoyed. I wouldn't have bothered Janet, so thank God for Vicki's call. I rushed over for hugs, brought her and the baby inside, and immediately got on the phone to arrange for a crib and highchair to be delivered. We spent time at the beach, went shopping, and enjoyed long talks while Carolyn napped. I was profoundly grateful not to have to be alone. With the loss of Grandpa Fred, my sister was the only person left in my family who loved and supported me. The visit strengthened me and kept me from drinking. By the end of a too-short week, Janet needed to get back home, and I had to face the future.

As if prompted by the invisible hand of Grandpa Fred, a letter came in the mail the following day, its return address indicating none other than Eastman Kodak. The letter stated they were interested in me as a candidate for their sales/management training program, and were willing to cover all my expenses to get me to Rochester for a series of interviews.

Grandpa must have had clout with the angels! I phoned the Human Resources Department and was back in my hometown in two days. While not thrilled with the idea of that particular job, I thought this might have happened for a reason, so I'd give it a shot. I was also glad that this job prospect provided me with an immediate purpose, which would further help prevent me from drinking to escape how uncomfortable this all had been. The interviews were grueling, but I was offered a position at the end of the day; the salary was half what I'd been earning, yet it was quite substantial. Fortunately, the training phase wouldn't begin for another three weeks. I accepted the position, and flew back to Florida. It was late spring.

Vicki was happy for me, but "your former clients"—who were also her customers at the bank—"have been clamoring to hear about you," she said. "They want to know what happened and how to reach you."

I was pleased to hear this. There was a sense of redemption hearing my absence was noted. I so missed the daily conversations that kept me current on their lives, contemplations, families, and investments. My abrupt departure hadn't allowed time for explanations or closure.

"Here's what to tell them, if you wouldn't mind," I said. "I'd be grateful if you'd say that I was offered a better position with Kodak that could lead to management, and I decided to take it."

"No problem. What about contact information?"

"Definitely. Give my cell-phone number to any of them who

want it." I had just acquired the new Motorola cell-phone device, which was heavy and looked like a brick.

"So," Vicki said, "you've got three weeks to kick back. Any plans?"

Yes. I'd just booked a week's cruise around the Caribbean.

The balcony of my cruise-ship cabin placed me directly above the infinite turquoise sea. My intentions were to reflect and rest in these balmy latitudes; however, on the first day, I met an Italian. Ah, me. He was older than I, suave and gracious in his advances, and also alone. We became lovers for the week, and I let go of my inhibitions in a way I never had with my high-school boyfriend. I felt better about myself being fit and knowing there would be no strings, which meant no emotional risk for me. He was an experienced lover, and the week proved more therapeutic than it would have with meditation as the major highlight. I still didn't feel any great sexual attraction, but I guess I just craved intimate human contact.

Refreshed and reenergized at the end of the week, I was ready to get on with things. I was able to sublet my Delray condo and stored some of my clothing at Vicki's. I flew to Rochester to begin the job Grandpa Fred had always been sure would become my career.

For the first three months in Rochester, trainees were paired in company-owned townhomes to build team skills, and given a rental car along with an expense account. At the end of the ninety-day training, we'd either get the ax, or we'd be assigned our territories anywhere in the United States, and then handed a one-way ticket for immediate departure.

The training lasted through summertime, which was glorious in Rochester. I had loved the lilac festival that took place during that time each year, along with the art festivals. However, the training was so stressful, I didn't have time for any of those delights. My inner inadequacy got the best of me, so I found time to drink—too many times—and I blacked out more than once, and even wet my bed. I felt horrible about myself. I hadn't been to the gym in months and had lost muscle tone, becoming thin. Interesting the way the psyche works—even though I was down to a size two, all I saw was Ellen Melon in the mirror.

When the final day of training arrived, I was certain mine would be a pink slip. Instead, it was a one-way ticket to New York City. I was dumbfounded that I hadn't been let go after putting forth minimal effort. I hadn't yet realized how "together" my outside appearance seemed, even while I was feeling so awful on the inside. Maybe I should have taken up acting.

Soooooo, the Big Apple it would be.

The company provided six weeks' housing at a fancy hotel in Midtown near the office, but no relocation assistance. I knew very little of Manhattan, and didn't have any idea about how to get around. I convinced human resources that it was cheaper to put me up in the hotel Monday through Thursday and pay for a flight to Upstate on the weekends. So, I flew back on Friday night each week and partied with the lake group from the Bachelors' Club, staying with friends.

Eventually, I found a small studio on East Eighty-third, but I made no friends at Kodak, neither with my clients nor with my neighbors. I roamed the streets for hours every evening. Despite the swarms of people in Manhattan, it felt like the loneliest place on earth to me. Being in New York City was, if anything, worse than the training experience. I was such an emotional wreck, I couldn't take advantage of being in the city.

The job was boring compared to the excitement I'd experienced with financial planning. Large copier duplicators are sold purely on features and benefits, and it could take up to nine months for a company's decision to purchase a six-figure machine. There was nothing to look forward to every day in comparison to the hourly bustle of the stock market.

I spent one weekend with my sister and little Carolyn. Janet was pregnant again with her second child, and while she had seemed generally happy with her life, it appeared stifling to me. She and my brother-in-law had started having problems, which no one knew about, except me. After the devastation that accompanied the dissolution of her terrible first marriage, she couldn't face anything like that again. Even though pregnant, she turned daily to drinking and smoking cigarettes to ease the tension and fear of another divorce.

In early October, on the weekend of my twenty-third birthday, my parents asked if I could come and stay with Tommy from Thursday night until Sunday so they could go to Toronto. By this time, I'd have been amazed if they had actually remembered the date of my birth. Again, I said nothing. I was simply excited about the opportunity to spend time with Tommy. I arrived at the house late Thursday, after my parents had gone. Tommy was home after eating dinner at a friend's house. He'd just started tenth grade and was a stellar student at the private Jesuit boys' school. In my parents' eyes, Tommy could do no wrong. Brilliant and well-behaved, he never caused any waves in the family.

He was in his room when I got there, so I ducked my head in to say goodnight, catching a smile from him as he read in bed. In the morning, I made him pancakes, and he caught the bus to school. I got ready to go to the Kodak office headquarters. Just as I was about to walk out the door, the phone rang. It was the principal at Tommy's school.

"This is an emergency, and I need to speak with Tommy's parents immediately," he said.

"They're in Toronto, …"

"Then you need to reach them, and you'd better come quickly. We had to call an ambulance. Your brother may have overdosed on drugs."

10

➤ A Crisis and a Proposal—of Sorts

Heart pounding with panic, I drove too fast, but I arrived at the hospital just as Tommy was being taken into the emergency room. I tried phoning the hotel where my parents were staying in Toronto, but there was no answer, so I left a message. Next, I called the family pediatrician, who said he'd be right there. Janet was in no state to handle another crisis, so I waited alone, feeling a weird suspension of time and space, of everything coming to a standstill. After a nerve-wracking hour, I saw the emergency-room doctor step out. He asked to speak to me.

"We pumped his stomach and took a blood test to see what's in his system. That'll take several hours for the results, but, luckily, he should be okay."

"Thank God." Relief rushed through me as if a floodgate had opened. "Can I take him home?"

"Not yet. We need him to stay overnight for observation and a psychiatric examination." He looked at me directly. "We're concerned that this was a suicide attempt."

I thought I understood Tommy only too well. The thought of him attempting suicide made me sick and filled me with sorrow.

The doctor escorted me to my brother, who was just waking up and looked disturbingly pale.

I began to sob and hugged him. "I'm so happy you didn't die. ..."

Tommy spoke softly. "I'm sorry Ellen. ..."

I nodded, dripping tears. "Tommy, please don't ..." *Don't want to die.* I didn't know what to say. I held the hand that didn't have an IV in it.

"I did this with Mom and Dad away," he said, waiting for me to look into his eyes, "because I knew you'd be here."

I hadn't seen that coming. "What do you mean?"

"I need help, El."

"Okay ..."

"There's this place in Minnesota I already looked into ..." The pediatrician walked in, and Tommy said to both of us, "I know I'm addicted ... alcohol, pot ..."

The pediatrician held the blood work results. "Based on these, I agree." He said he'd go make some calls and research the treatment facility for teenagers in Minnesota and elsewhere, and then left.

Tommy fell asleep, and I went to the cafeteria to get coffee. It was already afternoon, and I hadn't reached my parents yet. By early evening, I finally got them in their hotel room.

"Dad, it's Ellen. I've been trying to reach you all day."

"We're just getting ready to go out to dinner," he said. "Is it important?"

"Yes, Dad. Tommy's in the hospital. He's okay, but he OD'd on drugs."

Dad remained calm, as I explained in detail what happened. "We'll be there in three hours."

I left a note for Tommy, who was still in a deep sleep, and returned to my parents' house to change and eat something.

My father would be a wreck after a three-hour drive worried about Tommy, and he'd come in yelling. I poured some whisky into a plastic jug and put it in my purse, in order to keep him pacified. My conscientiousness might actually come to Dad's rescue for once. Surely, he'd appreciate *that.* By the time I got back to the hospital, a nurse was checking Tommy's vitals. His pediatrician left a note that he wanted to be there when our parents arrived, so I called him with their probable arrival time.

Tommy was alert, watching me. When the nurse left, he said, "I'm scared to see Mom and Dad. ..."

"It's going to be all right," I said, hoping it was true. "I'll be right beside you."

The pediatrician walked in just before my parents, and Mom was sobbing. Dad's glare and agitation told me he was very angry, exactly what Tommy didn't need. So I took him aside into the hall and offered the container of whisky.

"You have to get a grip," I said.

Without a word, he nodded and took a big slug. It reminded me of his demeanor when Mom had lost Grandma O'Neill and went to bed depressed, leaving him to finish the house and arrange the move. He'd deferred to me then, and I'd felt needed in the family.

We walked back in together as the doctor started to explain what had occurred and to make recommendations. "It's vital that Tommy goes immediately to the adolescent rehabilitation center in Minnesota for a minimum of thirty days. They have an opening, and I've reserved it for him."

My parents nodded meekly.

Tommy told them what had been going on with his substance abuse, as I held his hand. In that moment he looked like the baby boy I took care of when I was a little girl, and it felt good that he trusted me.

He would be discharged in the morning, and put on a direct flight, where a staff member of the facility would meet him at the airport in Minnesota. It all seemed surreal.

I'd gone back to New York City for three weeks, working at the job I disliked more with each day, when Dad called.

"Ellen, we've all been asked to come out to Minnesota for a family week to support Tommy. Janet says she is too busy, but we'd like you to come."

I knew there was no way Janet was going for this. That would mean she may have to face her own issues.

I agreed and went to my boss, explaining I had a family emergency. He released me, and I felt relieved to be taking a week off.

I landed just ahead of my parents in Minnesota and picked up the rental car. Once they arrived, Dad's breath smelled of the drinks he'd obviously ordered on the plane, so after we all gathered our luggage, I drove for half an hour to the hotel next door to the treatment center. Mom chattered non-stop, obviously nervous. None of us had any idea of what to expect.

The director of the program was waiting to greet us and led us into a family waiting room where Tommy was sitting. I was glad to see how healthy and positive he looked. Something was obviously different about him though. He seemed more mature, yet stood at a remote distance, as if to embrace a newfound independence. We all ate dinner together there, and afterward the director gave us a regimented schedule for the following day.

"And now, I'd like to meet with you three alone," he said to us.

"Excuse me," Tommy said formally. "See you tomorrow." He left us alone with the director.

The director passed out papers. "I have some contracts for you to sign."

We each signed an agreement that we would remain free of alcohol and any other mood-altering substances for the week. Good thing Janet didn't join us; there was no way she could go without a drink for a week. We all agreed, and went back to the hotel to rest up for whatever was ahead.

My father was miserable to be around, as he was actually in withdrawal from alcohol. We sat through lectures on the disease of addiction, a barrage of information that made us all squirm. We participated in family-therapy groups where Mom and Dad reenacted incidents from the past that were upsetting to Tommy. We individually sat through one-on-one therapy with a counselor. We observed group therapies with other families, and attended recovery meetings every night. It became clear that this was a family illness, and everyone needed help to heal.

With Tommy as the focal point, there were no teasing or hurtful comments directed toward me from my father all week. I understood now why Tommy had faded into his own world—first through reading and then through alcohol and drugs—until he almost disappeared entirely. My gentle brother didn't feel safe in the family either.

Every night, Dad attended the nightly meetings for alcoholics, while Mom and I went to meetings that were targeted for family members and friends of addicted people. I identified almost too much with what I heard about the signs of alcoholism. By week's end, Dad admitted he was an alcoholic, and my mother had admitted she was a co-dependent. Tommy seemed stable and committed to staying clean, and I had a strong sense he'd be staying there longer than his thirty days. I wasn't sure where I fit in, other than knowing I needed to be in my own support group. I was anxious to get back to my own life and make some changes.

On the return flight to New York, I decided to give two-weeks' resignation notice to Kodak—an essential step if I was to avoid the stress that might push me into an alcohol addiction myself. I called Vicki to fill her in on everything that had happened, and she suggested I return to Florida. That sounded wonderful to me. She welcomed me to stay with her until I found work, and with that, I soon booked my one-way flight back to West Palm Beach.

Vicki picked me up at the airport, and we went out to dinner before getting my car out of storage. She'd started a new job at a different bank, and when we were back at her place, she showed me photos of a recent company party. There was one particular guy who appealed to me in a group picture. He was tall, dark, and handsome, probably about five years older than I.

I pointed to him. "Who's that guy?"

"Jim? He's an officer at the bank. Your type, huh?"

"Is he single?"

"As far as I know. I heard his father died a few months ago from cancer. Maybe he could use some TLC."

I was intrigued and thought about him over the next few days while I relaxed at the beach, shopped, or hung out with Vicki when she wasn't at work. One afternoon I went to her office to use the fax machine to tidy up the loose ends with Human Resources at Kodak. In the parking lot, as I returned to my car, I noticed a guy checking me out. I smiled as he drew near. Amazingly, this was the guy I'd seen in Vicki's picture. He said "hello" as he passed by, and I smiled in return. What a coincidence. Later, at dinner, I told Vicki about it.

"I spoke to him earlier today, and I mentioned I had someone he might enjoy meeting. He seemed very interested and said he wasn't dating anyone."

"No kidding!" This seemed like destiny at work.

"I said I could bring you to join the group of my fellow employees who meet for Friday-night cocktails after work. He said, 'Great.'"

I was excited and couldn't wait to see this Jim's expression once he figured out that he was being set up with the same woman he'd already checked out in the parking lot.

That Friday-night cocktail hour with Vicki and her co-workers proved to be the start of something. Jim's family was from Grand Rapids, Michigan, and he had spent all of his summers on Lake Charlevoix, and winters in Florida. Jim liked me right away, but I wasn't sure about him. He chased me like a mad dog with his endless calls, until I agreed to a second date. It started out with dinner and drinks. And then more drinks.

I blacked out ...

And got physically sick.

Apparently we slept together.

Next morning, he cheerfully declared, "I'm going to marry you and father your children someday."

11

➤ Unglued and Alone

I couldn't see myself as a mother, but that was the least of my worries. I'd blacked out and unconsciously allowed sex for the second time in my life. I took a long walk on the beach that afternoon, trying to quell my rising panic. I thought about my college days and that awful night with the senior from Rochester right before New Year's Eve. Rather than feeling revolted and terrified of my own mind as I'd felt then, I placed the experience with this handsome and respectable-seeming man in a different context. I gave myself a moral obligation to keep seeing him, framing our sexuality with the dignity of a relationship of which sex was a natural part. And I would stop drinking entirely.

I soon discovered that Jim smoked, both cigarettes and pot, on a daily basis, which made him increasingly unattractive to me. It was nice to have a steady relationship though, even if it was already turning volatile over our different lifestyles.

Vicki loved to drink socially and never seemed to have a problem with alcohol, so I couldn't go out clubbing with her anymore. I needed to move out of her apartment in any case, so I focused on my career and earning an income. Some of my former clients tried to reach me, and I loved hearing from them.

One client had a problem and a request. "Ellen, you remember my father?"

"Yes, I do. How's he doing?"

"He turned ninety and he's failing, Ellen."

"I'm sorry to hear that."

"We have several reasons to be sorry. He lives in Palm Beach on a large estate on Everglades Island with several guest quarters. He decided to change his will at the last minute, omitting us—his family—and leaving everything to his domestic staff."

"Oh, no, this is terrible. Your family belongs there when the time comes."

"Yes. And I don't want any ugliness with lawyers. Listen, I know you two hit it off, and I was hoping that you'd pay him a visit and work your magic. See if you can get him to change his mind."

I possessed no wand, but I agreed to try. As it turned out, the old man and I had a marvelous chat. He'd been the first naval aviator for FDR, and had wonderful stories to tell. Hearing I was newly returned, he offered me one of his guesthouses, and I agreed. The time we spent talking and hearing his stories made me reminisce about Grandpa Fred, and I learned much from this man. A few days turned into three months on beautiful Everglades Island. Being in close proximity afforded me the time to get him to turn his financial matters back to where they belonged, and everyone was happy.

During that time, I attended delightful functions in Palm Beach, seeing former clients and associates. It was interesting, and I was much happier than in New York City. Jim sometimes took me out on a date, but it was increasingly difficult to tolerate his pot smoking. I joined a support group for Adult Children of Alcoholics that met weekly at the church of Bethesda by the Sea and made some new friends. When I cooled things with Jim, he finally agreed to quit smoking cigarettes if I'd keep seeing him. I hung in there a bit longer.

After I completed the task of getting my client's father to see the light with his estate, an investment firm hired me on a temporary basis, though I hoped the position would become permanent. I found my own apartment on Hypoluxo Island near South Palm Beach and settled in for the summer.

By Labor Day, I hadn't had a drink in nine months. Jim's father had died the year before we had met, but he wanted me to meet his remaining family, staunch Episcopalians all.

The evening of our dinner, Jim wore a Brooks Brothers jacket and khaki trousers, which was typical. We were seated in the dining room of a private country club in Gulfstream, Florida, with his mother, brother, and sister-in-law, facing a view of the golf course, the very land Jim's father had once owned in the 1940s. Everyone ordered a cocktail.

"Just water for me, please," I said.

Jane, Jim's mother, had a perfect hairdo and wore pearls. "Oh, nonsense," she said. "Of course you're having a drink, dear. They make wonderful martinis here. It would be a crime not to have one." She winked at her son. "Or two."

"Actually, I prefer not to drink," I said.

Jane turned to me, blood draining from her face as she stared. She turned silent.

The waiter watched me as if about to say, *whenever you're ready, princess.* Jim said nothing.

"It's just not an appropriate family gathering without a few cocktails," Jane said firmly.

His mother was relentless, so I complied with a glass of wine.

"Wine is for dinner," Jane said, her tone disapproving.

Their drinks arrived along with my wine, and they all toasted and imbibed happily. I took one sip, and had a moment of clarity. I looked at Jim and his family, and knew that I no longer wanted or needed to anesthetize myself in order to fit in with others. I realized in that instant I could not afford to drink at all. I put my wine down and never touched it again that night. The festivities went downhill from there: Jane dubbed me the official killjoy of that evening, and I experienced the familiar feeling of not fitting in or feeling wanted.

The next day, I decided to join a twelve-step group—as an alcoholic.

When Jim came over, I told him about my new group and said, "I want to work on myself. I need to. So, I think we should stop seeing each other, …"

The look on his face stopped me.

"… at least while I'm going through this process."

"Ellen, I still want to be with you," he said. "I already proved I can quit smoking for you. I wasn't ready to quit … the other stuff all at once, but I promise I'll try."

I found this touching and didn't end things completely, but it took him three months to join a twelve-step program for his own addiction. At least he'd begun his journey to get clean.

With alcohol banished from my life, the lure of food hit me smack in the face by December when Jane, Jim's mother, had sent him a Christmas box of French chocolate-lace cookies from Neiman Marcus. We enjoyed a few, and then Jim, at six feet, four inches, put them away in the space above the kitchen cabinets. He wasn't trying to hide them—or was he? I assumed he just liked clean counters and that slot was handy for a guy his height. I woke up at 3:00 A.M., troubled about our relationship and a million other things. In the dark kitchen, I climbed up onto the counter—in much the same way as I'd done when I was a toddler looking for containers with a skull and crossbones image. I didn't want to climb back up again later, so I started stuffing my face with the delectable cookies right there.

"Ellen?" The lights went on.

I froze.

"What are you doing?"

I knew I looked ridiculous and sneaky as well as pathetic. It was all I could do to hold back the tears. "I think I have a little sugar problem, Jim," I said, putting the cookies back where they'd been.

He laughed. "No, no. Bring them down. Let's eat the whole box!"

I sat on the counter, and we laughed together and gobbled away. Was it possible that Jim understood me? Could I finally fit in with someone, a man at that?

Within three months of beginning my program and without numbing my feelings, I was an emotional wreck. I was sober and attended meetings regularly, but the past had fully arisen before my face, and was in the process of overwhelming me. Without alcohol to turn to when I needed to mask all my insecurities, I had no tools to deal with the emotions that were emerging from deep within me. I had no coping mechanisms for living. I had exhausted myself, faking it as though I had everything under control, looking like a cool contender to the outside world; while inside, I felt as though I was coming unglued and would fragment into a broken heap at the slightest challenge.

I was seeing a counselor who suggested I go to a thirty-day treatment center, and I agreed. Sun Coast Hospital in Clearwater, Florida, didn't have any beds available until December twenty-sixth, but I booked one and left the temporary job at the investment firm where I'd been working. I flew north to visit my family in Rochester for Christmas, planning to fly to the treatment center on the west coast of Florida the following day.

Some things are simply meant to be. Dad had remained sober for more than a year, as had Tommy, who was home after his extended stay at an after-care sober living in Minnesota. Mom had attended co-dependency support groups that whole time. When I arrived the day before Christmas, anxious to tell them I could only stay for a few days and why, it was I who was in for a surprise. A professional interventionist was waiting for me when I walked in. Her challenge: to attempt to get me into co-dependency treatment—at the exact place I'd already booked for myself. Clearly, Sun Coast Hospital in Clearwater, Florida, was my destiny. And I looked forward to it. That was probably the best Christmas I'd ever had with my immediate family. Then again, it was only three days. …

Unable to be in contact with the outside world, I was forced to go within and do some serious soul searching at Sun Coast. I discovered undercurrents of anger and isolation—they boggled the part of me that coped and appeared to be in control. I couldn't get a full grasp on it, but I was told that by diligently attending support-group meetings and with further twelve-step work, these feelings would subside in time. The counselors might prove overly optimistic on that account, as I was nowhere near grasping what truly lay behind all my inner turmoil, but the month did focus me and gave me an emotional jumpstart.

When I returned to my apartment on Hypoluxo Island, a message was waiting for me from an investment firm based in Boston. The manager had heard of me, and wanted to discuss a potential employment opportunity. I returned the call immediately.

"I'm interested in opening the office in Boca Raton. I'll need a partner who can take over the office while I'm away."

This sounded almost too perfect, and I wanted the job—but not enough to sell my soul to get it. I was not interested in hiding my truths any longer, so I said, "This offer sounds very interesting, but I must confess to you that I just checked out of a treatment center featuring twelve-step programs."

He chuckled. "That's great! When can you come in?" he asked.

In that moment, I knew we'd get along well.

I found a new condo in Delray near the beach. I loved the new opportunity ahead of me, and I could start the year with a clean slate, which included my love life—as my recovery program recommended. I called Jim.

"You got the job?" he said.

"I did. ..."

"Well, congratulations. ... I guess I know what's coming next. ..."

His own commitment to staying sober had wavered and caused many a disagreement. I couldn't allow anything like that to slow my progress. "Right," I said. "We need to say goodbye Jim."

He said he understood, and left me alone after that.

Alone.

I was so alone, a good girl, working hard, and going to meetings all by herself that I turned to my refrigerator and pantry for comfort.

12

➤ Fitting in My Own Skin

My new employer was married to a woman he adored and they lived in New York City and Boca Raton. He was madly in love with her—thank God. They were both expert Marlin fishermen, and he wanted to be out of the office several months a year for events like the International Marlin Fishing Tournament held every winter.

Working at this firm taught me everything I hadn't learned yet about the investment business. I learned the entire back-office operations, SEC regulations, and how to execute transactions directly with traders on the stock-exchange floor. Our clients were at the same level of wealth I already had experienced working with in Rochester and Palm Beach, but the office consisted of men with names like: Friedman, Bedick, Deutcher, and Levine; I was to be the token female and gentile; unaware that this, in and of itself, would provide an education unlike any learned in a classroom.

During my first few weeks of work, my boss called me into his office. "Close the door, please," he said, and motioned to a chair.

I sat down, but on the edge. He remained standing.

"Ellen, you have unique promise," he began. "However, there is not enough room in this entire office for that chip on your shoulder. I need you to go home every night, look in the mirror, and say: 'I was wrong, and you were right, and I am sorry.'"

This really irked me, but I could take it because of my work in recovery. I knew that beyond the set ways of my new office mates, I had hidden hostility that sneaked out as perhaps an overly assertive need to stand up for myself. Additionally, I respected this man. He was brilliant, having attended UPenn and Georgetown Law School. He was a man of integrity, well-liked, and respected. Even though I'd only been there a short time, I already trusted that he had my best interests at heart. I knew he cared about me and believed in me, similar to the way Grandpa Fred had. I swallowed my pique and took a deep breath.

"Right, boss," I said. "'I was wrong, and you were right, and I am sorry.' Got it."

I tried even more diligently to work my twelve-step program. Staying sober in recovery required a sponsor, and as I found a woman I respected, my progress intensified. The over-eating subsided as time passed, and I became naturally comfortable in my own skin. I made a group of girlfriends to spend time with and felt like I had found a place where I finally belonged. It was phenomenal to me to be able to sit in a room for an hour with a group of strangers and feel more at home than I ever did with my own family. I learned about the power of "the herd" for healing. It seemed to be working for me.

Since leaving treatment early that year, I had pulled back even farther from my family. My brother was still in Minnesota, and we had no contact. Janet and her husband were busy with their family and life in Rochester—besides, she had absolutely no interest in the newfound family recovery that had transpired with the rest of us, and delighted instead in her bottle of wine nightly and her smoking addiction.

Just as Tommy had turned the family on its ear with his overdose, my mother made a move next that would prove even more disruptive. After a year of living with Dad without Tommy and without alcohol, she decided to fly down and attend the same treatment center I had for co-dependency a few months after I went. Upon being discharged, she decided to divorce my father after thirty-seven years of marriage.

This threw him into a tailspin, and he suffered an emotional breakdown that combined with years of poor earning power and debt. He filed for bankruptcy and also checked in to the same facility in Clearwater shortly thereafter. I participated when each of my parents was there by attending family weeks. In an intensive process, I healed what I thought were all the old wounds with my parents. So much of my eating, drinking, and feelings of inadequacy originated in response to my childhood confusion over family dysfunction. This was my opportunity to have a clean slate with both of my parents, I thought. The new footing was mostly with Dad. Amazingly, he moved to Delray to be near me, right down the street, hoping to shore up his self-esteem, recovery, and finances.

My new boss had been remarkably understanding in giving me time off for these weeks of intervention and crisis management. Over time, he became much more than an employer to me. He genuinely cared for me, and I knew it. He didn't have his own children, and treated me like family. My area of operations expanded, and I took on extraordinary projects like overseeing the building of a Bertram Yacht, along with managing his mother's finances.

One client was on the advance team for President Reagan, and his best friend was the president's executive assistant. This afforded me a private tour of the White House into areas to which the public had no access. The tour was amazing, but by the time I saw the third jar of jellybeans, I wanted to snitch a handful.

"Who's the jellybean fanatic?" I blurted.

My client shot me a stern look as his friend replied, "That would be our president."

I'm sure I turned a bit pink. When I saw that there was a cot in the hall near the back door to the Japanese Rose Garden where

President Reagan would nap every day, I chose to refrain from further inquiries. I was instructed specifically not to mention that cot to anyone. History would reveal that this was perhaps an indication of the early onset of his Alzheimer's disease. I saw the personal trophy room, and even sat at the desk in the Oval Office. Later that day, the president and vice president landed by helicopter, and I was introduced to President Reagan, the First Lady, the Vice-President, and his wife. I was feeling confident and honored to be there.

I'd been working at my new job for a little less than a year and finding balance in my recovery. I was eating healthy meals again and staying in shape. And then it was my birthday. I was at work, wondering what I could do to feel special—because my family still seemed unaware that there was something unique and important about October seventh.

A magnificent bouquet of red roses along with my favorite perfume was delivered to the office. I gasped in delight. Had Dad experienced a moment of grace and remembered? Was he trying to build a bridge to a more authentic relationship? I grabbed the enclosed card, which read:

> *I've missed you. You know we belong together. I want to see you.*
> *Happy Birthday,*
> *Jim*

I'd had no contact with Jim for a year, and he'd remembered my birthday. I was truly surprised. Jim knew I was touchy about that day, and he'd made big points with me by remembering. When he called, I was glad to hear his voice. He took me to dinner, and we began dating again. His certainty about a future with me was something I'd never experienced, and it felt solid. Having been on my own since I was sixteen and disconnected from family, I felt like being with Jim was a safe haven. I didn't have strong romantic chemistry with him, but I'd never really felt that way about anyone—even my Italian lover. Was there something special about it? I honestly didn't have any idea.

I totally admired him for having stayed clean and sober almost a year. Although it was at my expense at times, I liked it that he was close to his mother, and his story touched me. He was the youngest of three boys, but when Jim was twenty-one, his eldest brother, Jerry, had been camping in the woods, gotten lost, and was found dead. The later loss of Jim's father to cancer left Jim unable to cope emotionally. The losses devastated the family, and Jim felt special concern for his mother. Bill, his older brother by fourteen years, had his own family to take care of, so his mother looked to Jim for support.

Jim and I were together almost constantly, and despite many small fights, life seemed to be going pretty well for both of us. Fighting—that's what couples did, right? It felt normal. We decided to formalize the arrangement and became engaged, but Jim made it clear that ours would be a traditional marriage with me in the role of homemaker, involved in community service, and to support his success. My career would have to come to a halt, but at that point, I wanted a change.

The matter of a ring gave rise to an occasion that I should have seen as a huge red flag. Jim's father had left him an engagement ring for when he decided to marry. Because Jane didn't like me, she refused to give it to him, and he didn't take a stand. I was terribly hurt, but I guess I didn't get too upset because the unhealthy triangulation was all too familiar to me from my own family dynamics. I convinced myself that the future looked like the rosy dawn of a new era.

For my boss, it was the dark twilight of an era. He lost his father suddenly, and then his beloved wife was diagnosed with Parkinson's, followed by cancer—which was soon arrested—but the Parkinson's weighed heavily on her husband, and he turned to Xanax and other prescription drugs. On many days he didn't show up at the office, and I started making excuses for him, running his sales meetings, and even covering up his lapses in my reports to the Boston office where his good friend was CEO. This man and his wife were wonderful people, and we became close because I now had to be in touch with him on a daily basis. The CEO had hired his good friend, my boss, against the better judgment of the firm's board, but had backed his own choice, and also wanted to keep face. I was on board to support that, and also to support my boss, even in a situation that was spiraling downwards.

The CEO eventually flew down to check on things, figured out what was happening, and decided to close the office. These two men had known one another thirty years, so my boss took the closing of the office personally and eventually shunned his friend. The last six months prior to the doors finally closing were very hard on him. The brokers and other people in his social life were not aware of the intense strain, but I was. The office was his baby, its failure the final straw in terms of his losses.

I'd worked for this man for three years by the time the business shut down. I stayed and helped with the transition of the clients to another firm, but by this time I was well into planning a new life with Jim. My boss and mentor never got over that, feeling as if I was disloyal and had abandoned him personally. I felt horrible about it, but there was little I could do.

In hindsight, I wish I could have said to him, *I was probably wrong, and you were probably right, and I am sorry.* I was finally feeling comfortable within my own skin, and I wanted to build my life around that. However, I was terribly mistaken in associating this new feeling with Jim and the security of a relationship.

And because life is sometimes sad and shocking, his story would end in stark tragedy. The love of his life would die in 2005, and within a year of her death, he would shoot himself in the heart to join her.

I could not have imagined this horror in the late summer of 1987. I wanted to be a bride, wanted to be a wife, and wanted my own family to be a part of. In addition, I was talking extensively to Dad every day. When I told him of my engagement, he congratulated me and then moved back to Rochester where his roots were, which was the best thing that could have happened for him.

My fiancé started fighting with me again, but at that point, our bouts still weren't as bad as what I'd grown up with. One frequent cause of our disagreements was the fact that whenever his mother phoned, he dropped me to be at her side.

Even when I protested and felt my body being shoved across the room onto the bed, my denial system took over: everyone fights sometimes, I told myself—but I told no one else about his behavior. I was tired, and I wanted to be married. I wanted to belong to someone, and Jim understood me like no one had before. He was my best friend, and I wanted security. I ached for it.

The weekend of the wedding arrived, with friends from all over the country converging on Rochester, and we housed everyone at a swanky boutique hotel. On October second, 1987, we hosted a sit-down rehearsal dinner for fifty, featuring rack of lamb. A Western Union telegram arrived from the CEO of my firm. He had never met Jim, but he often asked me about my new fiancé during our many phone conversations. He had listened to my answers, and I think he read between the lines. The telegram read:

Ellen, Congratulations, but DON'T DO IT! It's the wrong partnership! Stay with the firm instead. Love, Mr. CEO and wife

I laughed, and I was touched, though I couldn't show it to Jim. The sentiment wasn't exactly auspicious.

Mom called my hotel on the morning of October third, 1987, the wedding day, but it was not to have a tender mother-daughter exchange of confidences or dreams of the future. This was in regard to another matter. My parents' divorce had just finalized, and they'd agreed not to bring dates, though Dad had started seeing a terrific woman, and Mom had begun dating a successful man who was known to have a terrible reputation with women. She was awestruck, and blind.

"Ellen," Mom's voice sounded brisk on the phone. "I changed my mind, and I'm bringing someone anyway. Please understand. See you at the wedding."

Horrified, I called my father immediately, sobbing.

Dad calmly said, "Ellen, do you really think your mother woke up this morning planning to cause you harm or ruin your day? If she knew better, she'd do better."

He was so calm and supportive, exactly as a dad should be. I was amazed. And so, on with the show. The color theme was black and white, and I watched my stunning bridesmaids line up: Shelly from my bartending days in Potsdam, my friend Mary from junior high, cousin Leanne, and Holly, a friend from recovery in Florida. Janet was my matron of honor, escorted by Jim's brother Bill along with his other friends. My goddaughter Carolyn was the flower girl. My best friend, Virginia, sadly couldn't make it. Or was that an omen?

Standing at the rear of the beautiful old Catholic Church my parents had been married in, Dad and I stood side by side as we watched the procession down the aisle, little Carolyn following with her basket of rose petals. Dad peered over his shoulder at the black Rolls Royce waiting to transport me and my soon-to-be husband, and then looked directly into my eyes.

"El," he said, "we can just as easily go that way and hop into the car and get out of here."

I never found that odd. I knew my parents had concerns over this union. What was odd was my response.

"Easy for you to say; this weekend isn't on your nickel!"

There it was, my pragmatic thinking without emotion or reason. I just wanted the picture to be right in my life for once.

We strode down the aisle, solemnly moving toward Jim in his Brooks Brothers tux and Brooks Brothers shoes, quite the perfect picture indeed.

High tea at a beautiful mansion ensued, followed by a sit-down dinner at the Yacht Club where we danced to the band until two in the morning.

I planned a brunch on Sunday for guests before they departed for the airport, and then we'd be off to our honeymoon.

Within a month I found out there was another woman.

13

➤ Hurricane

Jim's journal lay open on our shared desk. He wrote with a fountain pen, and, oddly, the one sentence, *I have been interested in another woman for quite some time,* was darker than the rest of the print. I went straight into denial and pretended it didn't matter. I chose him, and this was my vision of what would lead to a fulfilling life, and it would work, by God, come hell or hurricane.

Someone I trusted recommended an astrologer. This was not something I normally would have considered, but I knew some very famous people that had consulted one, so I reasoned that it couldn't hurt. I needed some guidance, and figured I was woman enough to sort out the truth of what I was being told. Trudi Rossi had been an opera singer and was shorter than I, quite petite. She wore her black hair in a taut chignon, and looked as Italian as her name. I'd come prepared with my exact hour and date of birth, and with her long fingernails pointing at the numbers and symbols on her circular charts, she worked her divinations and then looked up.

"Have you forgiven your mother yet?"

I frowned. I hadn't been *that* angry with my mom over bringing a date to the wedding. Was this some bogus nonsense?

She looked at her chart again. "Oh, you're not at that cycle yet. Sorry."

I was thoroughly perplexed. She went on to tell me that I would have three pregnancies, but only two children. This woman was starting to scare me. She also said, "Your marriage will entail moving north, but I must urge you not to make this move. It will prove disastrous. Your sister will be diagnosed with a debilitating disease, and get through it. You will be very successful, but a late bloomer in love. …"

Trudi was very kind, I thought, but surely wrong. I didn't want these things to be true. And if I didn't want them to be true, then I could make them untrue, right?

We bought a three-bedroom townhome in Boca Raton where I joined the Junior League and the Historical Society. I entertained Jim's boss and wife from the bank, and he tripled his position and income within a year, becoming responsible for the entire East Coast of his division.

We spent holidays with his mother, brother, and his wife, and I didn't fit in at all. His mother was horrible to me, and he never said a word about it. Sometimes he would "overreact" the way my father had, and shove me. I pretended it didn't happen. By the end of the first year the couples I tried to socialize with didn't want to be around us, confiding that his behavior toward me was degrading and his comments too off-color. I told myself it would get better.

After an ill-timed business trip with Jim, I suffered a miscarriage, which I had to admit was consistent with Trudi Rossi's first prediction. When I became pregnant again, I was especially overjoyed because I trusted that Trudi was also accurate in foretelling that I'd have two children, which meant that I'd carry this baby to term. The doctor agreed but informed me I had a rare blood type: RH negative. I wondered how that could be because no one in our family had a blood type that would account for it. Must be some recessive gene somewhere, I thought.

That summer, we spent two weeks of Jim's vacation time at his mother's summer cottage in Charlevoix, Michigan—along with Jane, still wearing her pearls. I was three months into my pregnancy. At dinner one evening, Jane passed me the salad. The sight and smell of the ranch dressing made me nauseous.

"No, thank you," I said, assuming she'd understand. "Certain things make me feel sick."

She glared at me, slammed the salad plate down, got up, and stormed upstairs to her room, slamming her door behind her. Before I could ask Jim what had happened, I was off the floor and against the wall. His strong arms pinned me by my neck.

"I'm s-sorry!" I managed to croak.

I was the one who apologized. I never knew when a rage would descend on him, never saw them coming. He was rarely upset in any way that would signal his sudden fury. It was as though his emotions went from neutral to maniacal without warning.

Two weeks before my due date, Jim hadn't had another one of his episodes in months, and I was grateful. However, he took off hunting with his friend to Mexico without leaving a contact number and without a cell phone, not even the location of where he'd be staying. He never called to check on me while he was gone. Given the nature of my relationship with my father, I still saw Jim's obvious emotional disconnect as being normal behavior for a male. I secretly thought this was all I deserved. Fortunately, Jim made it back in time for my delivery.

Our daughter was born February twelfth, weighing only five pounds, three ounces. The moment I held her, I knew why God had made me, and my purpose. I, who used to think I never wanted children, didn't know the depth of love I was capable of feeling for another person until that moment. I named her Jane Fletcher after Jim's mother, who'd always wanted a girl and seemed ecstatic to finally have one in the family. Jim echoed her joy. His only strangeness occurred over my appearance. Jim weighed two hundred, seventy-five pounds, but I was a petite five feet, four inches and had only gained seventeen pounds during my pregnancy.

"Start wearing the strongest girdle you can find," he said. "You don't want your hips to spread from delivering, do you?"

Whatever. If it kept him from freaking out, I did it. I shouldn't have been surprised. He had been very vocal over the fact he had always wanted to marry a five-foot tall blonde. No girdle would ever make that happen!

We bought a house, and I decorated it as I pleased because he had no interest in participating. Because I'd given her a namesake, his mother was kinder to me on our summer visit to Charlevoix the following summer—where I insisted on a separate cottage.

When little Jane was six months old, she refused to breast-feed. That was how I learned I was pregnant again. The pediatrician said the taste of the milk had probably changed and suggested a home pregnancy test, which I took. I placed the results on the bedside table for Jim to see when he woke up.

"Thank goodness," he said. "I didn't want another child. Not now anyway!"

"Look again, Jim," I replied.

His behavior worsened after that, yelling and becoming violent over tiny incidents. We went in for counseling, and I had set the boundary that if he raised a hand to me again, he'd have to leave. If I'd learned anything growing up, it was how to walk on eggshells, so I dusted off my old skills and gave them some new practice. He began to travel frequently for work, which made life easier, and I had a group of pregnant girlfriends for mutual support, some of whom were in recovery with me. Unfortunately he was home one weekend when I was about seven months pregnant and raging so loudly, the baby did a complete flip into breech position, burrowing his or her little head under my rib cage as if for protection. The doctor said I was too small to be able to turn the baby manually, and I would need a C-section.

I was eight months pregnant when Jane was crying from teething. Jim had just returned late one evening from a three-day trip. He wanted to go soothe her, and I explained she'd probably get all excited to see him and then not go back to sleep.

"How about waiting until morning and get her when she wakes up?" I suggested.

He said, "Sure."

As I was holding Jane on my hip by her crib, careful of my eight-month baby bump, I felt my body being pulled around as fourteen-month-old Jane yelled, "Daddy! Don't!"

He had his fist drawn, about to punch me.

I slept in Jane's room on the day bed that night, and when I woke, demanded he pack a bag. I was reliving my childhood.

I phoned my mother that day, telling her about having to have a C-section, but that Jim and I were separating.

"Mom, I need your help," I said. "Can you come down and watch Jane while I'm in the hospital?"

She sighed. "Ellen, I already raised three kids, and I'm not doing it again. You made your own bed, you know. If you need help, hire someone."

I shouldn't have been surprised, but what was I going to do? I was too ashamed to ask my friends. I couldn't possibly leave Jane with a stranger for three days. Resigned, I called Jim and gave him another chance.

Usually he was remorseful, and came bearing flowers after these "episodes." This time, he shocked me by declaring he had quit his job to be a better husband and father. I still couldn't quite let go of the dream of a happy family staying intact, and I wanted to be optimistic, but I was terrified of his presence full time and the possibility that we wouldn't have enough money.

Fifteen months after little Jane arrived, our son, Britton O'Neill, was born as a scheduled C-section on June twenty-eighth, weighing six pounds, ten ounces. Recovering from the surgery was a challenge compared to natural childbirth with Jane. The doctor said he found a rare genetic defect in my uterus, called *bicornate*, which basically meant that my babies could only grow in one of two divided parts of the womb. They could only grow as large as the space would allow. It explained their low birth weight, but not how I ended up with it.

Brit was reasonably healthy, and Trudi Rossi had proven to be correct again.

"You have to be ready next week to fly to Charlevoix!" Jim said to me in the hospital.

I couldn't believe it, but we were on a plane six days later in time for Jim to participate in the annual Fourth-of-July golf tournament. It never occurred to me that it was odd to travel a week after a C-section delivery, but I wanted to carry on as if everything was fine.

During that summer he decided to look for a job in his hometown of Grand Rapids. This made no sense to me because, while he had spent part of his childhood there, he had no family remaining, or friends to speak of. I begged that he consider Rochester, where I would have family support and lifetime friends, but he was adamant. So, we hired movers, and as I watched them drive off, fully loaded with our belongings, I remembered Trudy Rossi's urging me not to go. All I could do at that point was hope she'd be proven wrong.

By September we had leased a home in Grand Rapids, found a tenant for our house in Florida, and were getting settled in Michigan. I transferred to the Junior League there, met other mothers, and began entertaining. Photos of us from that time would create the illusion of an ideal life.

Was Jim happy now? No. Usually his outbursts would occur late at night, and I told myself the babies couldn't hear, yet my stress level caused little Jane at eighteen months to want to resume nursing before her nap and bedtime. I knew she needed the security and reassurance with the changes, the yelling, and a new baby brother on my breast. I felt intuitively that it was right to meet her needs, but I was the skinniest I had ever been.

The problem was living in a leased home, I told myself. I hoped that if we owned a home, Jim might settle in and mellow out. I found one that I could renovate nicely. After the embarrassment of having our mortgage turned down, I called upon the influence of Jim's brother Bill, who arranged our financing through his bank. Thank goodness he was an officer with some pull. How could a mortgage banker be turned down? This ought to have been a red flag for me, but like the others, I tried to push it under the rug with the rest of my denial.

We moved into the home in early January, but Jim's "episodes" resumed. My deep faith and my desire to provide a home with a father for my children kept me going somehow.

I had to have surgery relating to my caesarean, and the doctor was adamant that I rest afterward. A month later during one of his fits, Jim shoved me, and I hit a wall, which caused bleeding. I had to go to the hospital for a second surgery. I was livid. I knew my physical safety was at stake, and I didn't want to raise children in the chaos I had experienced.

So, that was it for me. I'd exhausted my bag of tricks, my patience, and my physical endurance. The cherished dream of living my life in a loving family finally ended.

"Jim, I need a little vacation at the Beach Club in Delray," I said one March morning before he left for work. "Of course, I'll take the children," I said. I had no intention of returning, except to move.

I had some funds of my own and arranged to stay at the penthouse apartment at the beach club, which was owned by a former client. I then paid off the tenant to break the lease on my home in Boca Raton I'd so lovingly decorated. That way the children and I could go back to familiar surroundings. After some weeks of rest and sun, I called Grand Rapids and arranged for our move by phone and then flew back to Michigan. Jim assumed we had simply returned, and I said nothing to the contrary. I went through the motions at the country club on Easter Sunday with the babies in matching outfits for the Easter-egg hunt. While Jim was at work the next day, I supervised splitting our possessions, and the movers loaded mine into the huge truck. The auto-transport company loaded my car to bring to Florida, and I took the children to the airport for our permanent return.

We relaxed at the beach for the day after spending the night at the Beach Club while waiting for the movers who were due later that day. The sun disappeared into suddenly overcast skies, so we checked out of the hotel and looked forward to returning to our home. I took the children to the supermarket, finding the shelves strangely bare. I hadn't contacted anyone about my return, nor seen the news of the impending hurricane. With meager supplies, I hurried home with my babies and reached the mover.

"I'm in northern Florida," he said, "and staying put. Hurricane Andrew is about to hit."

The reality of our situation also hit. The beach club had already been evacuated, as had my neighborhood. All homes east of Interstate I95 were under mandatory evacuation, and that applied to our house. At Kmart, I was able to find sleeping bags, water, pillows, a flashlight, and a few other essentials. My little ones and I huddled on the floor of our empty house, listening to a hurricane tear through outside. Miraculously, the babies slept, but through the window, I saw a large tree fall. *God help us,* I whispered as it just missed the house. Debris flew everywhere outside.

To me, it was symbolic of the shape my life was in. Andrew was at least outside. I'd take that over the hurricane I felt inside. Holding my two-year-old daughter and my ten-month-old son, I prayed, vowing to God and to myself that they would have a better life than I had. I would be the one person they could rely on NO MATTER WHAT for the rest of their lives.

14

➤ Reckonings

I wasn't ready to leave Jane and Brit with a sitter to go back to work, and Jim's family trust provided some financial support. I kept a routine with the children, but I began to doubt what life would be like as a single mother. What would happen to us without Jim? Could I raise these children alone? What if I started drinking again—turning to my old friend *and becoming like my father, God forbid*—rather than contemplate the unknown? I needed my twelve-step meetings. Fortunately, I found some part-time childcare that allowed me to continue the ongoing work of recovery and beyond that, to participate in some community involvement, which I greatly enjoyed.

Jim eventually sold the Michigan house, followed me to Florida, and rented a home a mile away. I would learn much later that the reason he'd originally quit his banking job to move to Michigan had nothing to do with career or family and everything to do with the open page I'd found in his journal a month after our wedding. He was following a woman he'd met in the banking business.

He attempted to visit the children, yet there was constant breakdown. He'd lose his patience and call for me to come get them on several occasions. I assumed that because he was a man, two children alone were just too overwhelming for him.

One Saturday, I took the children over to his house for a visit. Three-year-old Brit and Jane, four, sat buckled in car seats in the back of my station wagon. Jim came out to the car to help us. As I tugged Brit lose from his seat, I sensed that Jim's energy was off. He began to yell at me for no apparent reason, and I was very frightened that his rage was about to erupt.

Jane screamed, "Get me out!" as she clawed at her seatbelt.

Frantically, I clutched Brit in my arms, heading toward her side of the car where I pulled Jane out toward me.

Shouting what a terrible person I was—in much stronger language, Jim came at us. I ran, holding both children, toward his house, hoping to reach the kitchen phone to call 911. Somehow, I made it, but he came up behind me and ripped the phone from the wall. He then pushed me down with Brit still in my arms and pinned us to the floor.

Somehow little Jane found her way to the front door and ran to the neighbors for help. The next thing I remember was talking to the police and giving them a statement. They escorted me along with the children back to our house. I later filed a restraining order, which included my concerns that Jim had a gun collection. Deep down, I feared we would become one of those awful stories, where the deranged husband who can't have his wife and family takes them all out and then himself as well.

I was referred to a counselor, Dr. Sarah Sicliano-Hartt, and began to see her weekly. She was a Godsend right from the outset. Emotionally, I felt like I had an imaginary fire extinguisher in hand, waiting for any likely outbreak of wildfire. Would things ever become peaceful and safe? Sarah specialized in family therapy and child education, and assured me she had taken others through and to the other side of similar situations. I knew there was work ahead but felt relieved and hopeful.

If Jim couldn't get the attention of my heart, he'd find a way to use legal means to get his family back, which he desperately wanted. He attended anger-management classes faithfully and then agreed to only be with the children in public places or have supervised visits with the children. About that same time, Bill, the rock in Jim's family and his remaining living brother, was diagnosed with colon cancer, throwing the family into turmoil.

I felt sorry for Jim and for his mother, and I was impressed that he hung in there with the behavior classes. I opened up to the possibility of trying to work things out yet again, seeing the goodness I knew lived beneath his surface of pain. I lifted the restraining order. I was a committed woman, and didn't want my children to have divorced parents. Yet if that wasn't possible, I'd do whatever it took to have my children raised by both parents, even if it meant not being in the same household. If *insanity* means doing the same thing over and over and expecting different results, then I was the certifiable one.

One night while visiting us, Jim erupted for no apparent reason and began shattering dishware in my home. The children watched wide-eyed and ran to hide behind me.

Jane said, "Mommy, there's someone else inside of Daddy's body!"

My little Jane, still only three at the time, proved to be incredibly astute in her assessment. I was so accustomed to these episodes, I didn't see that Jim's entire coloring changed as he raged.

I had foolishly dared to hope again, and this time I felt like my heart would break apart. How was it I could easily accept the fact that alcohol was no longer an option in my life yet I couldn't do the same with my marriage? I didn't want to admit defeat. I tried to focus my energy on the children, their education, and my involvement in the Junior League of Boca Raton, and perhaps most critically on my recovery—where everything else good would stem from. I dared not even think about being in the same room with a bottle of vodka. One of my friends took me aside and recommended that I get a massage to help relieve my stress.

This masseuse came highly recommended, and I felt comfortable the moment I met him. I lay face down on a massage table, an antique bed from the 1920s on one side, the sunlight streaming in through French doors on the other, but I was barely aware of my surroundings. It was early summer of 1993, and I had already been in and out of hell in my three decades of life, yet I hoped the massage therapy and regression might help keep me centered while my family splintered. The deep voice of the New Age therapist carried me away to another time, as he guided me through slow, rhythmic breathing and massaged my back muscles, pressing me out of myself and away from the recent disasters that had prompted me to hire the man.

"Inhale air down through your whole being and into the earth," he said. "Good … and exhale. Your breath rises into the infinite sky. Again. Good. … And again."

My eyelids drooped, and I entered into a trance-like state. Vivid conversations and faces played in my mind, as though they were taking place in that very room until a snug blanket of darkness somehow nudged the sunlight away.

I heard my dad's voice as if he were underwater. He asked, "Why can't I connect to this pregnancy like I did with the first? Is this baby mine?"

"What are you talking about? Are you crazy?" This was my mother's voice, also dim and sounding as if muted by water. Some part of me wanted to linger there, but the dream-like scenario faded and the room grew light again.

"Inhaling deeply, down to the center of the planet. … Annnnnd exhaling out into the cosmos. …" the therapist droned.

I saw the face of a man. He was talking to me as he lifted my six-year-old self onto the tailgate of a Country Squire station wagon. He had widespread crystal-blue eyes in a square-shaped face, a low forehead, and silver-gray hair. His voice was gentle, Southern, and

I sensed a comforting closeness between us. This man was kind. Around us, our two families were picnicking on a horse farm near Bristol, Virginia.

I gasped, startled out of my trance. Was all this a dream ... or a memory? I was pretty sure I knew the answer, but only one person would be able to tell me. I got up, paid the therapist, and sent him on his way. I checked on my napping children, beautiful, innocent, loved ... safe. I kissed them in their sleep, then hurried to my bedroom and closed the door. My hands began to shake as I dialed the number in Upstate New York.

"Hello?" said the familiar voice.

"Dad?" I could barely get the word out.

"Ellen? What's wrong?" We now spoke daily, so he knew when something was amiss.

As I recounted that first groggy-sounding argument between him and Mom, my father began to sob. When he could speak again, he said, "You can't possibly remember that conversation, Ellen. We were alone in our bedroom when I said those words. Your mother was seven months pregnant with you at the time."

Dear God. This was insane. How could it possibly be true?

It would, at least, account for the strangely muffled quality of the words I'd heard. Though I didn't tell him that. It was just too weird.

In a shaky voice he explained why he remembered the exchange exactly as I had recounted. He spoke of his guilt and shame over the fact that he'd never felt connected to me in the way he had with my siblings, Janet and Tommy. Failure to connect was only part of the problem, but this was not the time to delve into all he should feel bad about. Only one horrendous issue at a time.

"Dad, is it possible someone else could have fathered me?" I described the face, hair, and voice of the man in my vision and the Southern accent I'd heard in his voice.

Dad choked, and I heard the phone drop.

When he came on again, he said my description confirmed the fears he'd held since he learned of my conception. This in turn established what I'd always suspected in a thousand questions and dark thoughts and in my nightmares: that I did not belong in my family. Now I was, in fact, what the world branded as illegitimate. Illegitimate. Message from society to child: you shouldn't exist.

I booked a flight to Rochester, where I was born, and which happened to have one of the most advanced genetic-testing facilities in the United States.

Later that evening, I called Janet, my older sister, to tell her I was coming back for DNA testing with Dad.

"Oh, yeah," she said nonchalantly. "I remember now. Mom mentioned something once about not being quite sure whose you were."

Oh, yeah …? The foundation of my identity was a forehead-slapping *Oh, yeah, I forgot to tell ya … oops* moment? I held my breath, stunned and confused. Why would my mother share her uncertainty about my biological father with Janet and not with me?

I'd hoped for some kind of help and control over my dissolving family. Instead, after the results of that test came in, the disintegration mushroomed, and everything I knew about myself was false, even my maiden name. *Ellen who?* Genetic traits and talents I'd imagined as coming from my dad's side of the family—gone, evaporated, impossibility. His people were not my people. What was left of me? Did I have a future? Who was I? I felt overwhelmed, flooded, as if a dark river had just carried me away and left me adrift with no one but the moon to ask for answers.

I hired a woman I knew to stay with the children while I flew north for a few days. Strong Memorial Hospital had an established genetic lab, but before I knew the results—which would take a week—there was someone I had to see.

In a rental car, I drove to my mother's townhouse in Rochester. I'd called to say I would be there for a few days, and she was happy I was coming. I waited to tell her face-to-face the purpose of my visit.

She offered me a cup of coffee after our customary greeting of a hug and kiss, and we stood in her kitchen together while it brewed.

"Mom, I need to talk to you about why I am here."

"I already know. Your sister called and told me," she replied.

Why wasn't I surprised? There was so much triangulation in my family, so much inappropriate sharing. I got right to the point.

"Did you always know I was really the daughter of Mr. Bayley?"

"Ellen, I used the rhythm method of birth control then and wasn't sure."

"For God's sake, Mom, there are only thirty-some hours in a month a woman can conceive! You must have been very busy!"

I felt the sting of her hand across my face as she slapped me. She burst into tears.

We sat for hours as I listened to her talk about her four-year relationship with my biological father. She hadn't started the affair when she'd been his secretary. It was after she left the company, and he'd remained Dad's boss. He and his wife had never had children of their own and had been married since their late twenties. The two couples formed a friendship, so much so, that they were at the hospital the day I was born.

"Jim Bayley was the first one to hold you," she said.

He was twenty-one years older than Mom, and she had been madly in love with him, and he with her. She explained how, despite being a Catholic, she had allowed all of her principles and values to go by the wayside, and ultimately couldn't live with the guilt of her secret affair. She went on to explain about her increased drinking over it, and how she coped by trying to forget about it.

"We were both big drinkers then," she said.

Mr. Bayley had wanted her to leave Dad, as he would his wife, so they could marry. He had wanted to raise my sister and me as well. Mom visited her priest to seek guidance, and when he told her she needed to stop seeing Jim Bayley, she ceased all contact. That was when Mr. Bayley began transferring Dad all over the East Coast in order not to have to see Mom or me. Apparently, he really loved her, and was heartbroken over her decision to stay with Dad. The only time she ever saw him again was when he showed up at both of her parents' funerals. He only transferred Dad back to Rochester after he and his wife retired to Florida.

"You do look like him, and you have many of his characteristics," Mom said. "Of course, you were clearly different from Dad, Janet, and Tommy—inside and out."

I felt like she'd reached in and plucked things by the root out of my gut and my heart. We were both in tears, and I couldn't talk.

"Ellen," Mom added, "I'm so sorry for all this pain I caused you."

My skin crawled. I nodded and wiped my tears. This was surreal, an episode of the *Twilight Zone*.

"I felt stuck, like it was a lose-lose situation. Whether I divorced Dad or stayed in the affair or kept you a secret—no matter what I did …" She broke down and wept again.

I sipped my coffee and watched her. I couldn't forgive this woman, even though I knew I needed to. Finally, I said, "It's going to take some therapy to come to terms with this, Mom."

She nodded. "I understand. I need it, too. I hope you can forgive me someday."

I looked into her still lovely blue eyes. There were layers and layers of my life to re-examine, so much to think about, not least of which was how inappropriate she'd been in sharing all this with my sister before telling me. I knew she was incapable of seeing her part in how dysfunctional that was. I had to leave.

My visit with Dad was much lighter. We talked about what a relief it would be if this explained all the animosity we'd felt toward each other all of my life. We went out for a bite and went to a twelve-step meeting together afterward.

As expected, the test results that arrived a few weeks later after I was back in Florida indicated that there was a 99.9 percent chance that Dad was not my biological father. Although I was fairly certain that would be the outcome, it nevertheless sent me into a state of shock. My identity had changed, and I felt like an alien's blood ran through me.

With the delivery of a singular letter, I had gone suddenly from what I thought to be of French-Canadian origin to English. What was the medical history of my ancestors? Were there any genetic diseases that could have been passed on to me, or Jane and Brit? Did Jim Bayley know I was his daughter all along?

At night, when the kids were in bed, questions kept popping up. How different would I be if I'd grown up a part of a normal family with a loving biological father? Would I feel differently about men? About love? About belonging? Dad's words: your fault kept tormenting me. If I hadn't been born to that family, how different would Janet and Tommy be if their father had been good natured instead of raging and obsessed to the point of alcoholic addiction? What would my friends think? Should I keep this hidden?

I was illegitimate.

I stared at the moon.

Next morning, the world hadn't changed. I needed and looked forward to processing the whole experience with Sarah, my new therapist, but for now the daily routine commenced. Every now and then, I'd watch my children and wonder to what extent my mistakes would affect them. I knew one thing—I would never let a man like their father into my life again. Hell would freeze over before I'd let any man near my children and risk our being hurt again.

Sarah helped me hammer out my new information, but after several sessions over three months, she and I discussed the possibility of contacting my biological father.

"I think you should do it," she said.

15

➤ RIPPLES

It was late fall, and I was feeling less shell-shocked and more grateful for all that I had. I found my biological father's address and phone number online. He was living in Jacksonville, Florida, with his wife of more than forty years. He answered the phone on the third ring.

"Hello?" a Southern male voice said.

"Mr. Bayley?" I asked.

"Yes?"

"It's Ellen. ..." I used my mother's name. "Remember me?"

"Of course. How are you, Ellen?"

"I'm fine. Let me cut right to the chase, Mr. Bayley. Dad and I had DNA tests, and, genetically, he can't be my biological father." I grew increasingly nervous by the second.

There was a long pause, followed by, "I don't know what this has to do with me, Ellen."

"Mom told me about your affair. You're the only other man who could possibly be my father." I was trembling at that point. "Mr. Bayley, I don't want anything from you. It's just that I have two children of my own, and in a day I have gone from French-Canadian to English. I'm curious about any potential medical history I may need to know about for myself and my children."

Without acknowledging anything, he talked to me briefly and shared information about his mother and father who had lived into their nineties, his own good health, and said there were no medical history concerns he knew of.

"That's all I can do for you," he said and ended the call.

I gawked at the phone, knowing I shouldn't have expected anything, but my inner toddler had apparently wanted to hear something like, *ever since I held you on the day you were born and then lifted you onto the station wagon's tailgate when you were six, I've held on to a secret love for you, Ellen. I thank God for your existence even though we couldn't be together as I had so desperately wanted. …*

Logically, I told myself things like, well, *of course he couldn't tolerate you in his life now because of his wife.* But secretly I wanted any father to want me. I tried to insist to Sarah in my subsequent therapy session that it didn't truly matter, but she knew I needed a lot more processing. She suggested another therapist that specialized in anger therapy and regression work.

In the first visit, I went into a trance, and within the first thirty minutes of our session, the new therapist managed to tap into my feelings around the many betrayals and about Mr. Bayley.

I "came to" with a mess around me. "Wow …" I said.

I'd shredded the entire Fort Lauderdale Yellow Pages directory into a thousand pieces with my bare hands. Hurricane Ellen. Clients sometimes referred to me as a force of nature, but this surprised even me.

This was the first baby step on a long journey toward healing. Over the next year I would see this new therapist weekly, for anger and forgiveness issues, along with my sessions with Sarah that were oriented toward successfully raising Jane and Brit. I would figure this out, with or without Jim.

That Christmas, I invited Jim for brunch on Christmas Day, and then he was taking the children to see his mother for an early dinner.

At the table during brunch, Jane said, "Mommy, why is Daddy here?"

To which I replied, "Jane, it's Christmas, and he is still your Daddy."

Jane went on, "But, Mommy, he isn't your friend."

Profoundly true. We can pretend the elephant is not in the kitchen, but it often takes a child to point out the reality. Jim muttered something about trying to do better and excused himself to get more coffee. I gave Jane a hug.

The children left to see their grandmother.

My mother came to visit that February for Jane's birthday. Mom had been on her own, enjoying her single life in Upstate, along with a new job. She'd met a man, Pete, who seemed promising after Mom had been alone for several years. I tried not to expect too much of her and kept things as pleasant as possible while she was visiting. She loved Jane and Brit.

Though she didn't dye the gray hair that now salted her pepper, somehow, at fifty-eight, Mom had become even more beautiful and reminded me of my Grandmother O'Neill, both in looks and expressions. She still carried herself with an air of elegance, her figure still a perfectly proportioned size six, her height undiminished. She worked out regularly and played golf.

My mom tried her best, but there seemed to always be an underlying tension between us. I'd started to feel her love during small moments like when I took the time to fix foods the kids especially liked or read to them or played with them.

Mom said, "You are a wonderful mother, Ellen."

I smiled at her, feeling validated. "Thanks, Mom."

Moments later, she remarked, "Too bad you couldn't keep your marriage together for the children. …" *The way I did,* her sarcastic tone implied.

My spirit stubbed its toe, but I said nothing, though the dynamic repeated itself often. I was working on forgiveness, yet she didn't seem able to forgive herself. I think it came out as criticism of me, as if to say, *See you're not perfect either*. I had compassion for her.

I went to my therapies. I meditated. I prayed. Then I tried a Bible-study group I had heard about in Palm Beach from one of my former clients. And what happened next was the kind of magic that made me believe in the effectiveness of both lightening my spirit and the power of prayer.

My former client was at the study group when I attended my first class. He knew I was having a difficult time, and we went to breakfast afterward.

He was a famous award-winning jewelry designer who also collected and raced cars. He had homes in South Hampton, Europe, and Palm Beach. Armenian with dark hair and eyes, he was also very attractive with a distinct Mediterranean look and style. He carried himself with a presence that reflected his success.

He asked my preference and ordered for both of us. We sipped coffee and chatted about the Bible class and mutual acquaintances, but I could tell he had something in mind. Our food arrived.

"Ellen, I must go to Europe," he said. "My mother has fallen ill. ..."

"I'm so sorry to hear that," I said.

"Thank you. I'll be there indefinitely while she undergoes treatment. The problem is that I just started a total renovation on my home here in Palm Beach. I remember what a wonderful job you did for your boss a few years back, and I need someone I can trust."

My heart sped up. "Would you like me to oversee the construction?"

He nodded, smiling. "And look after my car collection."

I was so excited I could barely finish my food, but when I saw the property and the plans, I was mentally jumping up and down.

The home was a French Normandy style with a separate guesthouse, between Ocean Avenue and South County Road. It was in a marvelous location, and I could visualize the completion as we walked through the already-framed shell of the structure. It had been totally gutted and drywall was just being installed. I would be choosing all the finishing materials and color schemes with his approval via fax and emails. I'd be paid the percentage the project manager would have charged, which would supplement me nicely. This was creative work, which I loved. I needed something to do while the children were in pre-school.

When he gave me the inventory list of the automobiles, along with the security code for entry to the warehouse and combination to the safe for the keys, my heart went into overdrive. A job overseeing exotic cars—I'd have almost paid *him*. In several garages sat a Rolls Royce Shadow, a Rolls Royce Corniche convertible, a 1959 Mercedes 190SL, and several racing vehicles. I was beyond thrilled. My responsibility would be to make sure the engines were run periodically, to meet the mechanic for scheduled maintenance, and to take delivery on a custom Ferrari he had specially ordered to be built and shipped from Europe.

I loved the work. I also loved keeping busy, which allowed me to get my mind off the past, as well as ongoing divorce issues and a lack of income. That June, en route Upstate, I took the children to the home in South Hampton. It was wonderful for the three of us to be out of our routine environment. Upon returning, my Armenian jewelry designer was elated with the renovation of his home and with my performance in general.

And because life is full of strange coincidences, he later shared an amazing confidence with me. His mother had improved, but they had only been close in the last few years.

"She had kept a terrible secret from me, Ellen," he said. "The man who raised me was not my biological father."

Oh, yes, we had quite a discussion that day of all the many painful consequences of such secrets.

"By the time I learned of all this, my biological father had passed on," he said sadly. "I will never speak with him or know him."

"You're close with your mother now?" I asked.

"Yes, but it took me a long time to forgive her."

I understood all too well.

Working with him seemed to open some kind of weird synchronistic circuitry in terms of my career, as if angel wings had spread news of my project-management skills and my many connections. A former client phoned asking if I knew someone to accomplish a certain task. I hadn't heard from this person in years, but he somehow knew I could get the job done. I started a consulting business as a referral specialist.

Basically, I provided services such as payroll, employee leasing, computers, web design, and other services to clients who owned companies. I also knew the company heads of the service providers, and was able to bring them together. Whenever parties entered into a contract, each would pay me a percentage. I loved the work and the ability to set my own schedule to be with my children when they needed me. See what I mean about angels?

A marriage was about to take place in my family, and it wouldn't be mine. My feelings of being alone again hit hard. With my new income, I had options, however. The impending wedding would unite my mother and Pete at the end of June, so I took Jane and Brit north to a rented home on Lake Canandaigua for the summer.

Pete's wife of thirty-four years had died the year before, and I was glad he and Mom had found one another. Pete was a good man, sober for decades, and would take good care of her. It seemed as though the truth had set my mother free, and now she could have love in her life. I wondered if that might come true for me one day.

The small wedding included family, the only witnesses being me, my brother and sister, and our children. My goddaughter Carolyn was such a big girl at almost ten, and she seemed to love Jane and Brit. Janet's son was another Tommy. When we were all together, the afternoon went well, but there was still that family tension. My brother Tom felt like a stranger. My sister put out a distant vibe as she stepped outside for a smoke. I joined her outside overlooking the golf course.

Janet said, "I hate being cooped up with you and Mom."

I was shocked. This was so unlike my sweet sister. "My God, Janet! Why?"

"Mom puts you on such a pedestal," she said. "I always felt as though I couldn't measure up to it."

"That's rich," I said, "after all those years of me wanting to measure up to you, you now think you're supposed to measure up to me?"

She ground out her cigarette butt and shrugged. "I better get back inside."

We couldn't even have a long sisterly talk about all this because she knew I'd have to mention how much my therapy and recovery work had helped me. She most especially didn't want to hear about that. It was so odd how we stood on such different emotional terrain: my odd-man-out existence caused so much trouble for Janet and Tom, yet now that I had achieved some success in my life, that too was a problem. It was as though we were raised in entirely different families. In a way, we were.

It was a lovely day, and I was happy for my mother, but I wanted to flee from all of the family dysfunction and my feelings as quickly as possible.

As I drove the kids back to our rental on Lake Canandaigua, I just kept shaking my head. *How was it that people who love each other couldn't just get together and be happy? Why did we still carry around all our old wounds that seemed ready to bleed at the prickle of a tone of voice or an awkward silence?* Mom's affair thirty-one years ago was a pebble tossed in a pond, with ripples still crashing on the surrounding shores.

"Mommy, can we go swimming tomorrow?" Jane asked and Brit echoed her.

"Absolutely," I said.

16

✈ How Could You Do That?

As far as a love life was concerned, here's what my heart looked like: it had high thick walls around it, but maybe the gates were getting easier to open. The early spring of 1995 would test that on a ski trip to Vail.

I'd found an older woman to help us by staying with the children because I didn't want to take them out of school. Brit enjoyed Montessori and was reading full sentences and books at the age of four. Jane was in kindergarten at the Gulfstream School that Jim had attended as a winter student when he was a child. (The school offered a special seasonal student program for families that were "snowbirds.") I thought if we were a family enrolled in the "right schools," we'd have a place to fit.

I loved being Jane and Brit's mother. It filled my soul like nothing before ever had, and my two little ones were pure joy. Jim was still in anger management, and things seemed to be going well with his visits. He was involved with a new woman and left us in peace. I told my friends I was fine with that, but I was reeling from my identity crisis while the man who hurt my children and me was out having fun. I definitely needed a distraction, and my own adventure. One friend suggested I learn to ski in Colorado. I'd never been there and had only skied a few times in Upstate, but I could instantly see myself on exciting new slopes among fascinating new people. I made arrangements for the children, packed my bags, and took off by myself.

The view of the mountain range from the small commuter plane from Denver into Vail was breathtaking. I stayed at a beautiful resort, and right away attended a twelve-step meeting across the street. Being in recovery made it easy to go anywhere, connect to others in the area, and never feel alone. Afterward, I went into the hotel lobby and asked where to get a bite to eat. A man was waiting behind me for the concierge, and began chatting with me. Realizing I was alone and new to the area, he offered to take me to dinner at one of his favorite restaurants in town. I felt an energy from him that was very powerful. He was from Boston, in a business that was similar to mine, and while talking, we realized we knew some of the same people. I agreed to dinner if I could freshen up in my room first. There I made a quick phone call for a character reference on this man before I spent time with him. I was given the green light by my contact.

We had dinner that night, followed by breakfast and dinner the following four days. We talked about so many things, including how much I was struggling with my identity, and he seemed especially interested. By the end of the evening, I found him to be a good kisser. Our connection was instant and natural, and I felt as though I had known him a very long time. He was highly educated, having attended Harvard as an undergrad, followed by "The" Business School.

He told me all the details of the international expansion of his financial business, and I was with him when he purchased his condo in Vail. His hand shook as he wrote the check for what would, in a few years, prove to be pocket change in comparison to his success. The trip ended, but he phoned me daily until we had dinner in Florida on the following Saturday. The weekend after that, I flew to Boston, because the children seemed okay with our grandmotherly sitter.

He was brilliant, fun, and young-spirited, considering he was fifteen years my senior. He'd held a prominent position in Washington in finance with one administration, had run a well-known foundation, and had opened his own firm, which was on its way to international acclaim. He introduced me to his best friend, who had been the executive dean of one of Boston's prominent universities. His friend and wife invited us to their home in Cambridge, and when they began to discuss their upcoming World Economic Forum, which was being held in Paris in a few months, I realized how much I enjoyed and had missed the mental stimulation of the business world. Everything seemed wonderful about being with this man.

So why was my gut telling me not to get too involved? Was it because of all the heart damage Jim had done, and my father before him? Or was this some kind of psychic vibe telling me something was a bit off?

We saw each other a few times after that and would become good friends for years to come, attending an annual black-tie event in Vail every holiday with mutual friends. The connection I felt with this man was strong and familiar, but I wouldn't know the reason for my hesitation for seventeen more years.

After Boston, I returned to Florida and decided to take Jane and Brit back to Vail two weeks later during their school spring break. We rented a condo, took ski lessons, and had a fabulous time. This became a yearly spring tradition over the next several years. On long weekend breaks, we went to Ocean Reef, and hit Disney World—the start of a semi-annual pilgrimage to see Mickey.

That year, in Upstate, the country club to which Mom and Pete belonged was hosting the International Ryder Cup Golf Tournament. One of my former clients and his wife were throwing a massive gala the evening the tournament ended for which they had hired the local Rochester Philharmonic Orchestra. The women were required to wear red, white, or blue, and I had found a gorgeous full-length beaded navy-and-silver gown. The hostess and I became friends because we were both in the PTA at the Gulfstream School in Florida. She was also part of the support group network I belonged to, so we had an unspoken bond. When I described my gown, she asked where I had found it; she was looking for something unusual for herself. At the last minute, I was able to locate a beaded formal jacket for her that was red, white, and blue, with stars and stripes like the American flag. She would look smashing.

She and her husband had arranged a blind date for me that I had planned to meet the evening prior to break the ice. When we met at his house before going to dinner, he asked if I'd like to smoke a joint with him. Immediately, I knew this wouldn't work. I was approaching my tenth year of sobriety. I summoned my graciousness and made it through the evening, but I told him at the end that I wouldn't be going with him the following night to the gala. He tried to talk me into it, to no avail.

I called my friend, the hostess, the next day, and she understood completely. I was perfectly comfortable going solo and looked forward to the evening.

The massive acreage surrounding this couple's historic farmhouse provided a perfect location for the affair. Several hundred people strolled through five huge tents, all lavishly decorated, heated, and equipped with hardwood flooring. The orchestra was set up at the far end, which housed a dance floor. Gourmet food stations and open bars were scattered throughout. Reconnecting with old friends and clients was marvelous.

A handsome gentleman that I had never known asked me to dance. He was tall, slender with strawberry-blonde hair, and hazel eyes—my father's name and coloring too, ironically. We danced and spent much of the evening together. I'd heard of him and knew he'd sold his share of his company for tens of millions of dollars a few years back. I actually knew his former partner, meaning vetting him would be easy. As the evening went on, Tom shared that he was going through a divorce after a long-term marriage. His two boys were in high school, and they were close.

"I must admit I'm involved, sort of. She's an employee who is married with two little children," he said, his tone seemed to add that he hoped this detail wouldn't be a problem for me.

I began looking for an escape route.

"May I offer you a ride?" he asked at the end of the evening.

"No, thank you. I drove myself here."

He gave me his business card, and we said goodnight. While some single women may have been impressed with how he looked on paper, I couldn't wait to get away from him. Cheating was my hot button, and he had just hit it.

The next morning, he phoned. He must have gotten my number from the hostess of the party. He was very assertive and asked what my thoughts were on seeing him again. I told him I was unclear regarding my schedule with the children and would get back to him later in the week. He also had a home in Florida, so in his mind, getting together would be relatively seamless.

That afternoon, while at a favorite bookstore in town, I purchased *How Could You Do That? The Abdication of Character, Courage, and Conscience* by Laura Schlessinger, and promptly took it to the mailing store where I overnighted it to his office, addressing it with Tom's full name, his title of CEO, and "Personal" written on the package. I enclosed a note saying, "I told you I would get back to you with my thoughts. Best of luck, E."

Years later, that man would call to thank me. He came to my home in Boca Raton where we had a lovely dinner together, and met again in New York City for lunch. He was a nice man, but I knew that first evening, given my value system and the circumstances of my origins, he was a man to date only casually.

Guard, close the gates. Adventures of the heart are not welcome at this time, and possibly never.

Brit and Jane looked forward to being at the same school for Kindergarten and first grade. I was happy to be able to volunteer on the PTA and for holiday parties in one place since Brit had successfully completed Montessori school.

I was able to stop seeing my regression therapist, once the anger subsided, but continued seeing Sarah and my recovery meetings. I also used my time to stay in contact with former clients who hired me intermittently to complete a certain project, research a concept, or come up with ideas for them.

I had a special rate arrangement via former clients with management at the Waldorf Astoria, affording the opportunity to stay at a suite in the towers several times a year. So, I took Jane and Brit to New York City at Christmas to see the famously decorated windows at the department stores, admire the Christmas tree, skate at Rockefeller Center, watch the Rockettes perform at Radio City Music Hall, and enjoy Broadway shows. They adored the famous frozen hot chocolate at Serendipity on East Sixtieth Street and sipped proper tea at the Plaza. It was the start of a tradition as essential to Christmas as Santa and Rudolph.

Except when we were traveling, Jim tried to see the children weekly, but there always seemed to be an episode that upset the children. He was no longer with the woman he'd been dating and had changed jobs again. He also had a new place to live. I sensed that he was unsettled, but he was their father. Brit was finishing kindergarten, and Jim wanted to have both of them for an overnight at his new residence and then take them to church. He'd bring them to me at the beach club I belonged to afterward. I reluctantly complied because there was nothing specific I could point to as a reason to say no.

The next day, he brought the children to meet me as planned. Both Jane and Brit seemed glum. Brit asked to change into his trunks in the women's locker room. I knew then that something was wrong.

In his sweet voice, he said, "Mommy, you know I love my dad, right?"

I bent to his level. "Yes, of course I do, honey."

His little head fell along with his beautiful hazel eyes toward the tile floor as he spoke words that tore my heart in half. "Dad did something I think a grown-up could get arrested for, Mom."

He pulled up the sleeve of his oxford-cloth pinstripe shirt, revealing an entirely black and blue forearm and began to cry. "I was arguing with Jane. I tried to hit her … but Dad said he'd show me what it was like to get hit."

I held him and immediately assured him it was not his fault, that he didn't deserve it, and that telling me was the right thing to do.

"He held my wrist tight and 'bam' punched his fist on my arm real hard!" was how my five-year-old little Brit explained the incident.

I phoned a doctor, also a member of the club, who had a daughter that was friends with my children and invited them to join us at the club as soon as possible. When I told him on the phone what had happened, he said he'd be right over. He'd be able to examine Brit's arm inconspicuously. I wanted to go on with the fun afternoon as planned for Brit's sake.

Afterward, I explained to both children that we needed to go file a report, which they understood, and we did. Later, after the children were asleep, I phoned Jim. Calmly, I asked if he had anything he wanted to explain.

He simply said, "I'll agree to whatever you want to protect the children."

I contained the rage building inside me until after my attorney drafted a modified visitation order that stated Jim could only see the children with an adult supervisor of my choosing present. In addition, they would stay with me permanently, and in the event any future physical violence occurred from him, Jim would relinquish all parental rights and visitation of both children. It was tougher than any court would enforce; however, I needed to have assurance the children were protected, and he agreed by signing.

One day, just before the end of the school year, the Department of Family Services visited the school to follow up on the police report of abuse with Brit. I was mortified. Fortunately, we were going to be in Canandaigua for the summer months and out of that environment, where the children and I could heal. I told them I had a big surprise once we got there, which kept their little brains occupied. A few days after we were settled at the cottage, I drove them to see Niagara Falls, and they loved it. My own set of surprises awaited me that summer—a prince and another stab or two at romance.

We returned in the fall, hopeful for a fresh start in the new school year. I arranged for the children to have abuse counseling as planned. Brit still cried about things his father said and did. Even with supervised visitation, and although he desperately tried, Jim simply couldn't be a loving, supportive father. That was when I learned that Jim's brother Bill was dying. Bill had been traveling back and forth to Sloan Kettering as part of a specialized cancer-research study, extending his life by a few good years. Yet he succumbed that November, at the age of forty-nine. The effect on Jim was catastrophic.

I knew that years ago, Jim's other brother Jerry, and his father, as well, had died in November. It was a horrible time of year for him all around. He had experienced so much loss in his life. I understood the undercurrent of sadness, anger, and rage, but I couldn't let myself or my children swim in it—or we would all be drowned.

Strangely, Dad provided some badly needed help at that time. He'd just ended a ten-year relationship with a woman in Rochester. I asked him to visit us for an extended period, and he flew down. He still had friends from his sobriety groups while in Florida years earlier and he was happy to be coming south. Once he realized what had happened between Jim and his grandson, he offered to stay in Florida on a more-permanent basis to be supportive of us. Jane and Brit adored their "Papas" and were so happy about him being there. I knew it was his way of making living amends to me for what he hadn't been capable of giving during my childhood, so I was grateful.

He moved back down just before the holidays, and initially stayed with Jim at his three-bedroom town home. During that time, there was another physical incident with Jim toward Brit that thankfully didn't leave a bruise. Dad contacted me immediately.

"Jim's emotional state has declined," Dad said. "He needs a psychiatrist, Ellen."

Jim knew deep down he had troubles. How could he treat his little boy this way? Even in the work environment, he'd been unable to sustain a team capacity, resulting in his losing several jobs over the years. I went with Jim to a highly recommended psychiatrist, and after a series of tests, he was diagnosed with multiple conditions. He was informed he needed to be medicated in order to function in a civil manner with others. The thought of needing medication terrified him, and it seemed as though there was a reason he wasn't revealing. Neither of us felt like eating, but we bought coffee and sat in a park-like courtyard, and I probed.

The family had kept secrets, but threatened with the possibility of facing his own mental illness, Jim finally told me about his brother.

Jim's brother Jerry had been admitted twice to Yale Psychiatric Center, and after his last discharge, he went off into the woods. He wasn't lost geographically as the family had maintained, but he was emotionally.

"He sent my birthday present early that year, which was odd, Ellen," Jim said. "On my twenty-first birthday, my brother got drunk and hanged himself from a tree."

We were both tearful and silent. I was aghast. How could Jerry do that to his family? How could he do that?

17

➤ Betty Ford's Revelation

In many ways, I still loved the father of my children, and this was heart-wrenching for both of us. I couldn't imagine the fear Jim was experiencing over his sanity; however, I had to think of my children and our safety. He knew the modified visitation order was now in place since the most recent incident with Brit and he'd foregone visitation rights. I was worried, wondering what he may do next.

He took what, for him, was a courageous step. He agreed to go on medication and see the psychiatrist each week. After months of this, I felt hopeful, so much so that I would actually contemplate one more time if I could rebuild our shattered marriage and stay a family somehow. By hanging tough with my dad, I saw him finally come around. It had been a long and boulder-strewn road, but he was now a solid presence in my life. Maybe that could be true with Jim. Maybe this was a new beginning.

His psychiatrists, a husband-and-wife team, requested a session with me. I sat in their office, and, after an exchange of pleasantries, there was a straightforward one-liner.

"We know clearly the explanation for Jim's erratic behavior," the male psychiatrist said. "The question is, why have you stayed in the picture?"

Indeed. I couldn't articulate the shame that bound me. The extent of my false pride and ego hit me. I supposed that was what was behind my stubborn refusal to accept the idea that I—someone determined to do things better than my parents had and give my children a happy, normal home—had failed miserably with marriage. I shared in that session that I felt this was all my fault, too, just like in my childhood. If I could only do better, be better, or make it better, everything would be normal ... *wouldn't it*? I was still seeing my counselor Sarah every week, and, looking back, I'm surprised she didn't have me committed!

And yet ... Jim took his meds and showed steady improvement. He could be such a good friend when he was in his right mind. Surely this calmer Jim was his true self. Even visits with the kids seemed to be going well.

He wanted to be involved somehow with Brit and had decided to volunteer with his Cub Scouts. All of the activities were in a group setting, with the leader being an attorney and father of Brit's schoolmate. I knew and liked him and felt comfortable with Brit being in his safekeeping. I actually hoped this would give Jim a chance to be seen as a good father and normal guy.

Within a month, I received a call from the Cub Scout leader, followed by the principal at the school. The Cub Scout group had been on a field trip, and Jim lost his temper with Brit inappropriately. The consensus was that Jim could not return to the Scouts to volunteer, and he was not permitted on school grounds. His behavior was so unacceptable that he was considered a threat to the children. I felt so terrible for Brit and horribly ashamed that people knew our saga and about our failed family life.

More therapy sessions. More recovery meetings. Meditation. Prayer.

Dad helped, especially with Brit. We muddled through.

In early fall of 1998, Jim's mother became very ill. November was fast approaching, the hardest time of year for Jim, as he was reminded of the losses of all the men in his family. We were going to Canandaigua for two weeks, having rented a large historic colonial of a former client. Dad was coming with us, and all the cousins, aunts, and uncles were joining us Christmas day. I couldn't leave the father of my children alone with a failing mother and no other family. So we included Jim in our holiday plans. His mom encouraged him to go, because she would be staying in the hospital, and thanked me privately for looking after him. We would be safe with him on medication and with so many people around. Amazingly, for the first time in forever, all interactions were kind, loving, and peaceful. I wasn't walking on eggshells, nor reacting out of fear. My girlfriends Shelly, Virginia, and their husbands came for dinner one evening, and there was a constant stream of visitors at the lake. The crackling of the fire burning, and the snowy lakefront view through the charming lead-paned windows, turned life into a Hallmark setting. Perhaps things could work out after all.

At midnight on January second, 1999, we got a phone call that Jim's mom had gone into intensive care. I called the airlines, booked flights for five to Florida, and packed all our things while the children slept. I had everything set for a morning departure, but a storm in Chicago delayed our connecting flight, which made for a long day of travel. I was already exhausted from lack of sleep the night before, and even more so once we landed. Dad stayed at my house with the children, while Jim and I made it to the hospital late that night to find his mother being kept alive by a respirator. She had gone into congestive heart failure. The doctor assured us he would call if there was a drastic change, and we drove the twenty minutes back home. Jim stayed at my house that night, and I passed out as soon as my head hit the pillow.

The phone rang early the next morning next to my bed. It was the doctor, and my heart sank, dreading bad news, but he said Jim's mom had a remarkable comeback and was off the respirator. Dad had the children up and eating breakfast, and I went to wake Jim with the news. We each got ready and were back at the hospital in no time.

Jane sat upright in her private room, looking better than she had in months. She asked that I get her hairdresser to come immediately—which was so her—and said she wanted to see her attorney as well. I arranged both while she visited with Jim. When it was my turn to sit with my former mother-in-law, she told me to listen carefully.

"Dear, I need you to promise me something. Promise you will look after my Jimmy. He'll have no one after I am gone, and I'm afraid so much of what has happened is my fault."

Tears filled her eyes, but she went on, "I'm sorry you have had to endure so much difficulty from my son. I wasn't a very good mother. I hope you can forgive me. Please make certain that you do not repeat my mistakes and take the best care of those two babies. I also want Jim to leave soon, and not be here to see me go."

I climbed next to her on the bed and held her, saying, "Of course I forgive you, Mother, and I promise."

She then shared pieces of her own lonely childhood, having lost her mother at the age of six, and I felt a kinship that we had never had.

The hairdresser arrived shortly thereafter, and made her look beautiful, just as she had every morning at Jane's house, except on Sundays, for most of her life. The attorney followed, and Thomas came after the attorney left.

She passed an hour later, at age eighty-five, on January third, 1999.

Oddly, while she could well afford hired help in those months before the holidays, it was I who tended to her personally at the end. In those few hours, we'd grown close. I'd healed old grievances and felt love in my heart for her. There were still more layers to this story, but I would only learn about them in the mountains of Colorado from none other than Betty Ford.

There was a memorial service in Florida where I gave the eulogy, and her namesake, my Jane, read a passage. Although she had been in Florida since the 1940s, and the church was packed full, no one wanted to participate in her service. This astonished me. I wondered if she had pushed everyone away with her stern, cold manner. Maybe it wasn't just me.

Leaving Jane and Brit with Dad, I went with Jim to Grand Rapids for another service, and on to Charlevoix where we were able to arrange burial in the wintertime. Jim took it very hard. Watching the casket lowered into the ground—alongside the graves of his entire family of two brothers and now both parents—was heartbreaking.

Perhaps the very hardest part was how connected I still felt to Jim.

Within a day of landing back in Florida, Jim wanted to buy a nicer home for us. He would be coming into an inheritance and wanted to do this. A big, beautiful house in a prestigious location, one that I could customize—he knew my weakness, my best dreams. We found a place just under construction that I knew I could turn into something really special, a massive five-bedroom, five-bath Mediterranean courtyard-style home. I felt like I was in heaven, not knowing I was about to enter hell.

I had extensively remodeled the home I had owned since 1989, and put it up for sale. We then bought the new home jointly in both our names, though we were legally divorced. I was truly delusional. For a woman who had a career managing assets and estates, I knew better. I was on site while the children were in school all day and enjoyed the building process, using it as a distraction, as if it were an infusion of pure oxygen in an air-depleted closet.

Jim was with us most of the time, and things were going nicely. There was no intimacy between us, but the picture was looking good on the outside. I asked him what he thought of a color swatch or tile sample, but increasingly, he just shrugged his indifference. He seemed disconnected again. Then he gave me a beautiful, enormous, three-diamond platinum ring.

"Three stones," he said, "one for the past, one for the present, and one for the future."

I gushed, kissed him, slipped it on my finger, and envisioned a new life together in our gorgeous new house.

The very next day I asked him to look at cabinet samples for the kitchen, and he responded in a full-blown rage, calling me that ugly word beginning with a "c." He began breaking things in the house. I am not a woman who swears, and never dreamed he'd say the word he used that day. I would never be called that again, and as he left, we both knew that was finally it.

Within a week, Jim came to talk to me. "I'm leaving, Ellen," he said. "I'm going somewhere in the Midwest. I always dreamed of owning a farm."

I stared at him. "A farm."

He looked into my eyes and nodded.

I knew in my heart that he had the wherewithal to know he was doing the right thing to protect us, because he absolutely could not contain himself. The part of him I had loved didn't know any other way to stop hurting us other than staying away.

I watched him walk away. I was angry, hurt, scared, and heartbroken all at once. I felt like I had been hit by an eighteen-wheeler emotionally.

More therapy sessions. More recovery meetings. More meditation. I prayed like a penitent nun. For weeks, I would get into bed at the end of the day and quietly sob. I felt so responsible for having put us in this position. And I felt such excruciating loss. I was alone—again.

I needed to stay strong though to handle the affairs at hand. We needed to sell Jim's place and find Dad a condo of his own. Now that Jim was leaving the state of Florida, what were the legal implications regarding the new house?

One way or another, the house had to be finished. I stayed cheerful, allowing Jane and Brit to make selections for the rooms that would be theirs. I immersed myself in choosing hardware, paint colors, furnishings, and overall design. The reality didn't hit me until I went to close on the sale of my original home, that I could not afford the dream home by myself.

After some legal battling with attorneys, we'd be able to move in, but I knew we wouldn't stay there permanently. I wanted to give my children a lifestyle that I'd never had, and while this home was extraordinary, it was too lavish for this family of three.

The children were entering fourth and fifth grades. I was very active in each of their classrooms and enjoyed living in our beautiful home. Brit seemed much more relaxed and even more outgoing, but I never saw that gleam reappear that he used to have in his eyes. Sometimes our gaze would meet, and there was an unspoken understanding and knowingness between us; no matter the circumstances, our bond could not break. At the same time, I felt powerless over the hurt I knew stayed in his heart.

Dad was a Godsend in helping with Jane and Brit and also in cheering them in all of their sporting events and extracurricular activities. His full-time male support for my children was vital because they no longer had a father around. Dad came with us on our weekends to Ocean Reef, and he loved it. We took him to swim with dolphins, and when the opportunity arose for tandem parasailing above the ocean, he gamely went up with Brit while I rode with Jane. We were living joyfully in the present while creating wonderful memories.

The adventure continued into the winter. My girlfriend had purchased a condo in Beaver Creek, Colorado, and charged me next to nothing to use it, so we went skiing there several times a year. The mountains were calling to me. Dad had no desire to ski, so the following year, we took him with us for Father's Day in June because he'd never been to the Rocky Mountains. Vail was beautiful with wildflowers and greenery in the summertime. There were outdoor music events at the Ford Amphitheater; coincidentally enough, it was the "second home" of our Rochester Philharmonic each summer. Dad loved Vail, and, unexpectedly, after showing him the Betty Ford Gardens one day, we stumbled upon the Vail Mountain School and went inside.

As a sixth grader in the fall, Jane would be moving up to the new upper campus of her school in Florida and had some trepidation. The lower school was quaint and contained, while the upper school housed twelve-hundred students on a vast campus. Although it had been a few years since the State Department of Family Services had visited the school after the police report of abuse with Brit, things had never seemed the same and had worsened after the incident with the Cub Scout leader. I thought we were viewed differently, but maybe what I thought were stares of either pity or contempt was simply my shame at work, coloring my perception. Nevertheless, a fresh start in Vail sounded wonderful to me.

Both children liked the tour of the Vail Mountain School, as did I. I completed applications for each, but the classes were already full for the next year. We spent two fun-filled weeks in Colorado, and I took up mountain biking and hiking with new friends in recovery while Jane and Brit went to a summer camp.

We flew directly to Rochester afterward, and the lake was only a forty-five-minute drive from the airport. I rented the beautiful historic colonial farmhouse with one hundred and twenty feet of waterfront that we had rented the Christmas before. We water-skied, swam, barbecued, and hung out with friends at the lake. I began to look at houses for sale, thinking that if I were to sell the Florida property, I could have the home I'd always wanted on Canandaigua.

The Vail Mountain School admissions department called while we were there on the lake. They had last-minute openings due to a family needing to move.

"Mom?" Jane said. "If I were to try Vail for one school year, could we keep our house in Florida and go back if we didn't like Colorado?"

I thought I could figure out a way to work that out. "Sure."

Without hesitation, her fearless spirit replied, "Let's do it!"

The move was a whirlwind that challenged all my managerial skills, but with high spirits and sincere prayers, everything fell into place. Dad didn't want to move to Colorado, having become settled in Florida and preferring the mild winter; however, he agreed that a fresh start was a good move for the three of us. I relied on him for so many things with the children; I worried what it would be like without him there with us all the time. We said our sad goodbyes and left.

The community of Vail was unlike any I had experienced. The people there embraced us fully. Friends from my meetings helped me get settled, and I worked at the school Home Tour Fundraiser a week after arriving. Jane and Brit had classmates right on our street.

At the Vail Post Office, the town's true social hub because there was no mail delivery, I met a woman in line named Tori. She was from Chicago and had a son Brit's age and a daughter two years younger. She was the only other single woman—having left her husband as I had—and was raising her children by herself. We became great friends and a strong support for one another.

The mountains were soothing to me, as I felt myself relax into nature and the outdoors, adjusting to the reality that it was now only, "We Three." At least we were safe, and had each other, along with a supportive community. I finally felt as though I could exhale and look forward to autumn and the change of seasons.

One of my routines while preparing the children's breakfast was to have television on in the kitchen to hear the morning news. The children had been at school just two weeks when one morning the television showed surreal footage. The Twin Towers in New York City were struck in a coordinated terrorist attack, as was the Pentagon. I felt both horrified and relieved we were safe far up in the mountains. Everyone remembers that day. I remember noticing a female news anchor as she mouthed a man's name to her cameraman, asking to find him. That very man would enter our lives in a profound way some years later. I always found it interesting, though, that this moment stood out in my mind.

I realized that morning that the markets would fluctuate, and I may not have the luxury of keeping the big home in Florida. I wouldn't be able to execute the plan I had laid out financially. Deep down, I was very worried.

The recovery group was very small in the Vail Valley in comparison to what I had been accustomed to in Florida and Upstate, but I enjoyed the intimacy of it and made friends quickly. One particular day at a noon meeting at the Chapel at Beaver Creek, which I attended weekly, I had a stunning and pivotal experience—the kind the angels must have had a hand in.

I gawked at the Secret Service standing outside the room where the twelve-step meeting was to take place. At the close of the meeting, we all held hands in prayer. Afterward, the woman holding my hand to my left said, "Hello, my name is Betty Ford, what's yours?"

When I gave my full married name, her face lit up, and before she could ask, I said, "Yes, the same family from Grand Rapids."

I hadn't known Betty and President Ford had been close with my former in-laws. They belonged to the same country club where the men played bridge weekly and golfed, and the two wives were best friends—best drinking friends that is.

"I had to end the friendship with Jane once I decided to get sober," she said sadly.

She told me the story about how the father-in-law I never met had owned car dealerships and had surprised the Fords with a new car, which was waiting for them in Washington when they decided to run for Congress. She spoke about the wonderful man Jim's father had been and as a friend to her husband.

"Now tell me every detail you can about Jane," the former First Lady said.

I talked about my former mother-in-law for quite a while.

"I knew your ex-husband," she said, "since birth."

When I told her the tragic tale, she shared in a way that changed my perspective. She told me about how his mother left him for two months right after he was born with a nurse so she could go to Hawaii. Several horrendous stories followed of the pathological environment in which Jim had been raised, which also shed light on the eldest brother's suicide. I can't reveal these matters, but what she shared with me gave me compassion and forgiveness toward Jim I hadn't thought possible. She told me the fact that he had gotten so far was a miracle, given his history. That day changed my life.

Today, I keep a picture of Betty Ford with my mother-in-law in my office as a reminder of the importance of forgiveness and compassion.

18

➤ Look Homeward, Angels

The golden aspens of fall turned into a sparkling winter white in Colorado, and we loved being in the mountains. Three families we knew from Florida had purchased homes in Vail, and the flow of our lives continued naturally. I dated steadily for a while, but deep down, I didn't want anyone involved in a serious way with We Three. It felt as though we were just getting used to a peaceful existence. We felt a sense of belonging in Vail, so much so that on our return to Florida for the winter break, I decided to list for sale my cherished house there.

After 9/11, people were taking their money out of the stock market and investing in high-end homes to retire to in Florida. The winter season sent the snowbirds flocking, so my timing was advantageous, and the angels were with me. By the time we returned to Vail in January, there were two offers from buyers in Florida, both for full price in cash, netting me a high profit.

One afternoon in Vail, while coming out of a movie alone, I slipped on black ice, breaking my foot. I was in a cast and couldn't drive, but the neighbors who showed up to help amazed me.

Still in a soft cast, I nevertheless needed to fly back to Florida for the closing on my house and to remove all of the furniture; flying presented difficulties. Then when the movers arrived to put my treasures into storage until I decided on a home in Colorado, I slipped on the marble floor and re-broke my foot. It was a tough few days, but thirty-thousand pounds of belongings were crated, packed, and stored. I was happy to get it over with. I took pictures of what to me was architectural perfection, and said goodbye to the house I had built on top of such fragile dreams; a wonderful place that never truly became our home. I closed the book on my life of more than seventeen years in South Florida.

I wasn't able to ski all season, which left me time to select and plan the renovation of a new home in Vail. During that time, my realtor in Canandaigua called, saying he had a tremendous deal. A sale had fallen through at the closing table.

"This place has your name on it, Ellen, but I've got forty-eight hours to replace the buyer at this same undervalued price or it goes back on the market for its original listing."

The timing wasn't ideal, but I'd wanted to own a home there ever since attending the wedding there. This was my dream. The only way I could really swing two houses at once was at a bargain price like this one. I had to have a look-see. Luckily, a girl in her twenties whom we met while renting in Beaver Creek, was still available to stay with Jane and Brit.

I flew to Rochester the next day, and the realtor drove me to the lake. I absolutely loved the place, and after a single walkthrough, signed the purchase papers and hired a construction crew. Back in Colorado, I renovated it via phone and fax throughout late winter, spring, and early summer with the help of my longstanding friend Virginia. I kept everything a surprise for Jane and Brit.

In June, I started on the Colorado home and got a bit sidetracked. My darling boy had gotten a little mouthy with me that year. I called my therapist Sarah, with whom I'd continued our sessions every other week by phone after I moved to Colorado. We discussed the importance of a boy taking responsibility for his actions and experiencing the consequences or rewards of his own choices in order to develop as a young man. I told him: he could shape up and remain with his buddies for half of the summer, or a-marching he would go to a summer leadership program at the Culver Academies Military School. His behavior didn't improve, so we flew into South Bend, Indiana, and I drove an hour from there to Culver, privately questioning my decision. However, when Jane saw the brochure on the program, she begged to go too. She loved structure along with leadership and was able to continue the horseback riding she'd started in Vail. She competed with the Black Horse Troops that were used for the Presidential parades, and in Jane fashion earned several first-place ribbons. Brit learned about team building and personal responsibility, and I hoped the experience would make the difference he needed.

And then it was time to show them our new summer home in Canandaigua. My dad flew in from Florida to meet us there. Jane and Brit were astonished when they walked into our very own lake house, and I loved seeing their surprised faces. It had a cottage feel with hardwood floors, wainscoting, and hues of yellow, blue, and shabby-chic décor. We had a tremendous view of the lake; and in my customary fashion, it was completed right down to the family photo collages in the frames and perfectly hung on the walls when we arrived. I had a six-foot floating trampoline set up over our dock, which the children thoroughly enjoyed. Brit helped me pick out a twenty-six-foot boat and an electric hoist was installed.

My childhood friends, Virginia, Ann, and Sue, along with cousins and all their children, flocked to the lake almost daily. I loved entertaining and baking there, taking everyone out on the boat, and seeing all my former clients as well. Jane and Brit were forming friendships with the children of my lifetime friends, along with knowing their extended family, and that pleased me greatly. The summer was reminiscent of my childhood on Lake Ontario at Grandma Pink's and Grandpa Fred's, and it felt good to give my children the continuity and memories I had known and cherished. I couldn't believe a longtime dream of mine had come true.

I took the kids to see Mom and Pete—which was the only way she saw them. Mom and Pete were busy with their own lives, and I was happy for her. Somewhere along the way, my old resentments had fallen away for the most part, and forgiveness had quietly replaced them. Yet for her, there remained a strain between us. I felt as though she couldn't let the past go, even though I had.

At summer's end, we returned to Colorado to find the construction on our house wasn't going to be completed for another week, but the lease term on the rental house in Vail had ended. The kids were worried about a place to stay. I was in touch periodically with Frank from Boston whom I'd met in Vail seven years prior—the great guy who took me out to dinner and with whom I had chemistry, but also had a gut feeling telling me to put on the brakes. I was still a few years away from learning the true story. In his mid-fifties, Frank hadn't yet married. I saw him a few times a year when he came out to ski. We continued to attend our yearly gala together where I enjoyed hearing tales of his quest for the perfect mate.

"*Mi casa es su casa,*" he said.

We stayed in his beautiful three-bedroom townhouse in Vail Village—the same one I had watched him nervously sign a check for years earlier. He was no longer nervous about anything at all—with the possible exception of me and what he didn't want me to know—because his business was doing so well. Jane and Brit loved the place, and then loved our new home even more.

My dad visited us in Colorado several times a year. I had built a separate one-bedroom in-law apartment for him with laundry facilities and his own garage, but he did not want to move. I didn't want the children to lose the deep connection they'd established with him.

And someone else paid a few calls. Jim tried to see Jane and Brit, but had very little success at building any kind of real relationship.

The year Jane was twelve, he phoned, asking if he could come see her for the holidays.

"No," I heard her say, "I just don't feel safe with you, Dad."

This caused him to check into Menninger's Psychiatric Center in Topeka, Kansas, to seek the help he needed. We were all hopeful that a solution was in sight, allowing him to re-enter his children's lives. Unfortunately, he checked himself out earlier than advised by the staff. A doctor called to advise that I not allow him to be alone with his minor children. I asked for some explanation, but he wouldn't elaborate. We didn't hear much from Jim after that.

That same December, I received a call from my dad in Florida telling me he was in the emergency room at the Boca Raton Hospital. He was in terrible back pain. X-rays showed that his back had fractured, and further tests proved that he had a rare form of cancer called multiple myeloma. He had friends with him for the initial testing, and afterward I arranged through my contacts for his results to be sent and reviewed by the top cancer specialists in the United States. At the time neither Sloan-Kettering in New York or Dana Faber in Boston could treat him. We were referred to the only specialists who could see him at a research hospital in Arkansas. My connections from former clients made this possible, as did getting an appointment in Little Rock, Arkansas, at the research hospital that specialized in that cancer. Sam Walton, the founder of Walmart had died of the same cancer, and had funded a research hospital in his hometown of Little Rock with the intent to find a cure.

Dad got scared and cancelled the initial appointment, and with the large waiting list, we couldn't get in again for two months, which would be mid-February. Unfortunately, he couldn't fly out to be with us for Christmas, but my brother Tom went to see him in Florida.

We Three loved Christmas in Vail, especially decorating and

baking in the new home with the backdrop of the glorious snowy mountain range. There were several parties to attend, and friends invited us for Christmas-Eve dinner at their home, the start of an annual tradition. They were wonderful to me and sponsored me into the private Ski Club on Vail Mountain. Their daughter, who was Jane's age, stayed at our home whenever they traveled. I cared for her as though she were one of my own. Her mother was ranked in the top five internationally in her field, which sometimes would tap into my less-than insecurities. Although I struggled with not having a professional title to hang my hat on, my commitment to provide all the support along with the life I never had to my children outweighed those feelings. Unlike my married friends who were parents, I was alone raising two, and that was my main focus.

In February, I met Dad in Little Rock at the Multiple Myeloma Center.

The doctor at the clinic said, "He has less than three months to live unless he has a full stem-cell treatment. Even then, there is just a fifteen percent chance of success."

I was shocked. Dad was now seventy, but physically much older because he hadn't taken good care of himself. The transplant and aftercare would take several months, during which time I arranged for our babysitter to move into the house in Vail, so I could travel back and forth weekly.

The day of the transplant, my mother walked into the hospital room. I was reminded that in spite of a history of alcoholism, infidelity, and even divorce, there was a common bond between us. My parents had been together since they were in their teens, and while Mom was happily married to Pete, she hadn't lost sight of her deep-rooted sense of family loyalty.

At the hotel that night I asked, "Mom, what made you come all the way to Arkansas to be here for Dad?"

She replied, "Ellen, honey, I'm not here for your dad. I am here to support you."

I was touched. Those rare moments are what I chose to focus on—the living amends as evidence of the underlying fiber that bound us. Both of my parents eventually showed up for me, as best they could.

We were thrilled to learn that the stem-cell transplant worked, but now Dad was only given three to five years of remission maximum. The probability was high that when the cancer returned, he would go quickly. Dad wanted to return to his roots in Rochester to live the remainder of his life, and I assisted, as did my brother. Tommy was married and had been living in San Francisco. He said he'd oversee the sale of Dad's condo and get his car up to New York. Tommy didn't have any children, and mine needed me after my bouncing back and forth for a few months.

By the time Dad completed the treatment, it was almost summertime, and the children and I went to Canandaigua to be with him. My brother eventually moved back to Rochester with his wife. Dad was able to reside with them for some time and get his strength back. Dad found his own apartment and soon resumed a normal routine. It was quite miraculous.

The next year, Jane was in eighth grade and Brit in seventh. Even our normal routine in Vail was like a vacation. On weekends, we would mountain bike, ski, or drive to Denver. Our house usually had several children spending the night. Parents knew I didn't drink and ran a tight ship, so they were comfortable leaving their children with me. I was so grateful to be in a community where I was included, as a single mother, with the other couples and families. I had always sought that feeling of inclusiveness and belonging, and the community in Vail was good to me. It felt like home. But all that was about to change.

The following spring in 2004, Jane said, "I want to look at girls' boarding schools on the East Coast."

Surprisingly, about thirty percent of the students would be doing the same. The Vail Mountain School was a wonderful education, but Jane was precocious, and her class only had ten girls. Within a matter of weeks, the three of us were in Connecticut, Boston, and Washington, D.C., to tour the three girls' boarding schools in which Jane was interested, along with similar options for Brit. Ignoring the fact that my heart was breaking at the notion that We Three wouldn't be together every night in the same household, I would rent a place for us to be together on the weekends. My commitment to give them the best possible education while being there for them overshadowed everything else. I knew this, but I had to discuss it at length with Sarah, with whom I continued to speak by phone every other week. Not returning to the Vail Mountain School wouldn't be an easy decision. Friends were sad to hear that Jane and Brit would be going east for high school. We'd be leaving our extended family.

I also consulted with Trudi Rossi, my astrologer, because by this time she'd proven right on so many things. She'd done charts on both Jane and Brit, and felt the move to Boston was a good one.

"Ellen, don't worry," she said. "Both children will flourish. Brit will become an architect, and Jane will be very successful in front of people." I couldn't help but feel excited by these prospects, now that I had learned to trust Trudi implicitly.

Jane chose Dana Hall in Wellesley, Massachusetts, while Brit fell immediately in love with a boys' school a few miles away called Fessenden. I think he really looked forward to being in a male world after living with two females. I located a place to rent between the two schools for the following fall, as did a group of Vail parents who also maintained a residence near their children for the duration. Of course, we'd fly back to Vail for school breaks.

But once again, my home was breaking up, and I was having a hard time thinking of it as an adventure. I worried about my costly real estate sitting empty while we jetted around. I yearned to enjoy a community and come home to a place that offered my vision of beauty and comfort, and I could say, Ah, I'm home.

19

➤ BLACKBALLED

I knew the decision to go to Boston would prove to be the right one, of course. Brit formed bonds that would last a lifetime with friends and families from all over the world. He became a captain of his tennis team, played guitar, golf, and was an excellent student. He'd attend eighth and ninth grades at the Fessenden School and enrolled for high school at the Milton Academy. Jane flourished immediately at the all-female high school where she was elected class president her first year at Dana Hall and played varsity sports.

I rented an apartment in Boston and attended sporting events at both schools, which allowed me to see each kid every day or so. It was very difficult for me not to have them in my home full time, but I understood that it takes a village to raise a child. So, the choices were correct—for them, anyway. Boston was a provincial town, and difficult to transition into. They say it isn't just the weather that is cold in Boston, which I found to be true. I focused on my recovery program that allowed me to plug into a new area instantly, along with being an active parent at both boarding schools. I had friends in Boston, and I connected with other parents from Vail in the area, but there were times when I was just plain lonely.

Boston was unbearable in the winter, so I decided to rent a condo at Ocean Reef from November through April. It was a quick direct flight from Logan to Fort Lauderdale. I knew families there from my investment career, along with friends from Boca Raton,

Colorado, and Boston. I felt at home there and loved the weather. I joined the Ladies' Nine Holers and often was awarded longest putt or drive in a scramble. Some weeks I would go back and forth between Fort Lauderdale and Boston twice in order to see Jane play volleyball and to watch Brit on the football field. All three of us headed south to Ocean Reef on long weekends and at Thanksgiving; and then, of course, we went home to Vail for the month of December and for the March break.

Jane kept spreading her wings to fly ever farther from my nest. She cheerfully announced she'd been chosen to go to Australia as an exchange student the following summer.

Really? Honestly? For a whole summer? So far away?

Yes.

Brit wanted to participate in an outdoor program for three weeks in the Pacific Northwest.

But … what about our cottage on Lake Canandaigua?

"No, I want to be at home in Vail for the rest of the summer break," Brit said.

"Me too," said Jane, "if there's any time left over."

So, that's what we did. Summers were perfect in Colorado. My father could visit, and we all loved the hiking, attending outdoor concerts, farmers' markets, and seeing friends. I hadn't realized it yet, but I was creating exactly the life I'd dreamed of for myself and my children, even though my survival mode focus kept me from seeing it at the time.

In the fall, after Jane and Brit were settled back at school, Virginia joined me at Ocean Reef, and it was really nice to have time alone together. We'd been friends since we were twelve. She had remarried, and between her children and her husband's, they had five between them, which didn't allow for much free time, especially because she also had a career.

One day, while sunbathing, my phone rang and it was a

neighbor in Canandaigua asking if I'd consider selling my cottage to a friend of his who was looking to buy. Properties were in high demand at that time, and mostly sold by word of mouth. I hung up, saying I'd think about it.

Virginia said, "I'd like first option! I love that place."

She'd been very involved in helping me pick the décor and loved the finished results. If I sold to her, I could invest a great deal and still have enough to purchase my own condo at Ocean Reef, which I could put in trust for the children someday. Virginia, her husband, and I agreed on terms and signed a contract.

I'd been a member at Ocean Reef for a decade, and it had provided continuity and tradition. I immediately found a nice condo and made an offer of cash without contingencies. The offer was accepted with twenty-percent down, a hefty fee. Owning property at Ocean Reef also meant upgrading social membership to equity membership—which required a substantial initiation fee in addition to the cost of the condo. The membership board needed to approve a social member advancing to equity membership, but that was a mere formality—I assumed. Knowing I had been at the club for a decade and was sponsored by original founding members, there seemed no need to make my approval by the existing equity membership a contingency to the sale—a decision that would prove to be disastrous.

I left Florida for Colorado over the Christmas holiday. The current CEO of the club also had a residence in Vail, and I was having a holiday party with the intention of introducing him and his wife to the community of which I'd grown so fond. There were more than one hundred people coming, and I was quite excited. Jane and Brit insisted on attending to see all of my friends, and I continually felt like the luckiest mother ever to watch the people they were both becoming.

We attended Christmas-Eve Mass, had dinner with friends, and went on the mountain to ski as a family on Christmas Day. I cooked and baked, and we played plenty of Scrabble games. I adored making those memories for them—and for me. It was a more restful holiday than usual, which my angels must have arranged, knowing the roller-coaster ride I was about to take.

I received an email that the membership committee at Ocean Reef would resume monthly meetings in early February, after the holidays. I wasn't closing until May on my condo there, so that was no problem. When I returned to Florida in early February, I would also be attending a fund-raising gala with another couple who encouraged me to purchase a ticket and join them. The husband was the president of the Ocean Reef Foundation, a private philanthropy group. I would be seated with them at their table for the black-tie event. I would probably be the only single woman there, but I knew eight of the ten scheduled to sit at our table and most of the other four hundred attending. I planned to wear a long, black, fitted gown, with my shoulder-length hair partially up, and the family-heirloom diamond jewelry I so rarely had occasion to wear.

At breakfast that morning, I ran into the couple I had entertained in Vail, who were perfectly cordial. Afterward I had a pedicure and my nails done in preparation for the evening gala. As I returned to my condo, my phone rang. It was the head of the membership department.

"I must inform you that you have been declined as an equity member," he said.

"Declined?" I could feel the blood drain right out of my face. "How could that be?"

"I'm sorry," he said. "Goodbye." He ended the call.

Without any explanation, the club was turning away additional revenue from an existing member? I was in shock, and it made no sense. I called an attorney friend who owned a home there.

"The club has no obligation under its rules to disclose a reason," she said, "but a member must have petitioned for denial of your equity membership."

Had I been blackballed? Next, I phoned my friends. Surely as CEO of the club that year, he could assist.

"Yes, Ellen," he said, "I did know about the decision, but I make it my policy not to interfere with my committees who are simply doing their jobs."

I was shocked and furious, ending the call abruptly.

I made a few other calls to friends on the Reef.

"Yes, I was very surprised when I heard that a few people decided to prevent you from buying," said one woman. "The intent was apparently to get you out totally, but the club has no grounds for that."

I felt betrayed, only I had no idea by whom. I felt sick.

Legally, they could block my equity membership, preventing my purchase. This meant I'd lose my twenty-percent deposit, as there was no provision for reclaiming that. No one had ever been turned down for application to rise to equity status. Of course, neither had a single woman ever applied to purchase a condo and become an equity member.

My insides roiled with frustration and anger, but I had no intention of missing the gala. I headed for the gym to get the tension out of my body. I had only a few hours before I needed to look my best and be at the fundraiser, acting charming with my head held high. On the treadmill, there was no one around me, so I was able to get calm, meditate, and pray; but I felt all over again the way I had as a kid, not being wanted or fitting in. I asked God for strength and clarity to move forward. *And Lord,*

I added, *send one of my former clients in his big jet to get me out of this mess.*

Actually, I think my angels were taking notes.

The event started at six o'clock, and I mingled with people I knew as I made my way toward my assigned seat. I prayed no one could tell how much of a wreck I was on the inside. I was the last to arrive at the table. As I took my seat, I felt like the same baby in my highchair who was in the wrong place. Would I ever find my fit? I glanced at my dinner companions around the table: the master of ceremonies for the evening, who was a Miami news anchor, along with his beautiful new wife; a man who was a retired artist, formerly CEO of Federated Stores, and his wife, whom I knew well and liked; another couple that I knew from recovery; the hosts of the event, who headed the foundation; and a man and woman speaking French—the only ones at the table I didn't know. At first sight, I felt a sense of familiarity, but when the gentleman's gaze met mine, I looked away quickly to avoid the obvious chemistry I felt between us. He did, after all, have a woman sitting next to him.

As the evening progressed, I felt more at ease—accomplished through my very own coping skills and nary a drop of alcohol or even the desire, though it flowed quite freely around me. That in itself made me feel stronger.

There was a live auction, and the familiar-looking man was making the whole room buzz.

"We have a record-breaking solitary bidder this year," the emcee announced, "by Mr. Ron Joyce. Thank you, Mr. Joyce."

So, his name was Ron Joyce. Why did that ring a bell? Even for this group, this was a fabulous sum. I knew that if I looked at him, he'd be looking at me instead of his date, so I became fascinated with the floral centerpiece and then glanced around the room.

Other eyes were on me as well. At the next table sat that evasive CEO, the president, and the chair of membership along with the wives. They all glanced my way repeatedly, as if talking about me. By then I'd learned all too well the skill of shutting off harsh judgments that came from being pigeon-holed.

Suddenly, I heard a voice say, "Where's your husband?"

Startled, I turned. *Oh, my God, it's him.* He spoke English without an accent.

I replied, "I don't have one."

He then said, "That's the best news I have heard in thirty-five years!"

I believed him.

He took my hand saying, "Let's get out of here."

Ron and I rode over to the marina by golf cart to board a hundred-foot fishing yacht where we chatted nonstop into the early morning, as though we had known one another our entire lives. Ron joked that it cost him a small fortune in bidding that night to try to get my attention, and I still hadn't looked in his direction.

"You seemed to have the attention of your lovely date," I said.

"Oh, she's an employee," he said, smiling and flirtatious. "I'm a bachelor."

He shared that he'd come from Nova Scotia, was raised in poverty, and had never finished high school. He became a police officer in Canada in the '50s. After meeting a professional hockey player who became his best friend, they decided to run and name a coffee shop as partners. Ron took that one shop to a massive franchise of more than twelve-hundred stores, which he sold in the early '90s to Wendy's after becoming friends with the founder. It finally hit me where we'd met before. It was in the parking lot of a men's golf course in Florida in the early '80s, and I was there getting a signature from a client who was Ron's golfing partner. It was obvious to me Ron hadn't recognized me, something I decided to keep to myself.

"I'm a very instinctive guy," Ron said. "Ever since I got here, people I don't trust have been coming at me from all directions."

"I'm not surprised," I said, knowingly. I had no intention of telling him my woes.

"You, I trust," he said.

I thanked him, and he proceeded to ask for my assistance over the next few days helping him choose a property to purchase at the Reef. One might think him impetuous, but he was simply a confident man who could trust his own instincts.

"I'd be so grateful if you would help me out."

He was grateful? It was I who needed saving, and his arrival and request seemed like an answer to my prayers. What I didn't know was that he intentionally was engaging my brain, time, and attention—me.

One evening turned into three days, ending in a bid on an eleven-million-dollar home for him with a vast ocean view. He needed to return to Toronto for a board meeting, and left me in charge of negotiations. He called daily and was back by Saturday, insisting I join him in Barbados for a meeting regarding his plan to form a bank with five partners there.

Before Ron returned, the president of the club called, asking to meet with me.

"Well, I'm booked at the moment," I explained a bit gleefully, "but I'll be back the following week." I set up an appointment.

"Ah ... does Mr. Joyce need any special assistance?"

Ohhhhh, so that was why the club wanted to meet with me. The single largest contributor to the Ocean Reef Foundation, and potentially largest equity homeowner, was noticeably in my back pocket. I decided to focus on being of service to Ron, but I was enjoying myself immensely in the process.

"Well," I said, "it would be a great help to Mr. Joyce if you could arrange special clearance for his jet to land by making exception to the club's airport restrictions."

I happened to know the rules were only because of the noise factor, as the runway did accommodate the size of his aircraft.

"Oh, certainly. No problem."

When I told Ron of the arrangements I'd made, he thought I was a genius. He still had no idea whatsoever of the club's rotten dealings with me as he was planning to deepen his commitment there. In fact, my Ocean Reef-membership dilemma seemed almost a distant memory with all the excitement of staying in a beautiful stateroom on Destination, his one-hundred-and-thirty-five-foot yacht for the sail to Barbados, not to mention all the mental stimulation around the high-stakes business deals that now included my input.

After the fabulous Barbados trip, he dropped me off two days later at Logan Airport, as he continued on to Canada. I would see the Wednesday sporting events of my children, catch up with them for a few days, and then he and I would meet in Florida the following weekend.

We spoke daily about the Barbados deal, negotiated back and forth with the sellers for the Reef house, and discussed numerous other situations. He was a remarkable man, and had my full attention. I learned air travel was also a part of his growing empire. In the early years, he realized he needed to fly from location to location around Canada, and got his pilot's license. He turned that into a charter company with a large fleet of aircraft and more than a dozen full-time pilots. When he found landing challenges at the executive airport in Toronto, he purchased the land and opened his own Jetport to maintain control of his travel interests. Where he once picnicked on barren land as a child with his mother on the coast of Nova Scotia, he now had built his own version of an Ocean

Reef Club with a private landing, a gorgeous golf course, and resort homes. It was a resort that housed philanthropy meetings, boating and golfing events, and which drew several U.S. presidents, private dignitaries, and even Tiger Woods for a celebrity golf fundraiser. The small town that had supported him on welfare as a child now enjoyed commerce from his resort. Everything Ron touched flourished in an immense magnitude. As the single largest stockholder of several publicly traded companies, he sat on several boards. He chaired a half-billion-dollar initiative and had already financed part of the hospital, the entire performing-arts center, and the university football stadium where he resided outside of Toronto. I loved the way he gave back after being so phenomenally successful.

When I returned to Florida, he'd been delayed due to unexpected business. My father was coming to visit, followed by Jane and Brit for Presidents' Day weekend. Ron asked if I would host his best friend and his wife until he could get there in a few days. I agreed happily, and welcomed them to the Reef for their first visit there. She was warm and down to earth, and he had served in high positions under both Prime Ministers Trudeau and Turner. His business profile was similar to Ron's in its scope and success.

I spent several days with them, showing them the Reef as they pondered a multi-million-dollar condominium—duly noted by the club president and my other detractors. Dad joined us for lunches and dinners, and it was a fabulous time getting to know these lovely people. Ron was returning before my children came from Boston, and, true to my firm policy, I wasn't interested in mixing the two visits at that point. Ron had seven grown children, but I didn't have any experience yet with what he was like as a father. I rented a large home for Ron and his friends to stay together the next few days, and I also arranged a small cocktail party at the house for all the Canadians who were at the Reef. Ron gave me *carte blanche* and trusted me to entertain as he would.

We were absolutely at ease with one another and often finished each other's sentences. We were falling for each other, and we both knew it.

Because of all this whirl of activity, I'd postponed my meeting with the club president. I met Ron as he jetted in from Calgary. We were headed toward his place when my cell phone chimed. It was the membership head.

"I was hoping I could join your party for lunch," he said.

I turned away from Ron. "I'm sorry, but I can't speak to you right now."

Ron knew how to read me by then. "I've noticed there's something a bit off. What was that all about?"

Inside his rented home, Ron eventually coaxed the story out of me about the way the club had treated me. He listened and became very quiet. Nothing further was said about it.

Ron and I were scheduled to meet with the owner of the main real-estate firm on the Reef to solidify his home purchase. We drove together in the golf cart, and he surprised me by holding my hand. Ron was a handsome man, thirty years my senior. He smoked occasionally, which I hated, and drank vodka all day the way I drank water. His behavior rarely changed, and since I was unaffected, I was able to accept his habits as being his to deal with. Funny how it is when the heart calls, the list of deal-breakers disappears, and are no longer considerations. I was about to witness why I adored him.

"Stay with me," he said, as we entered the private office of the broker that owned the real-estate company that represented the eleven-million-dollar property in question.

As this man began to explain the agreed terms, Ron held up his hand.

"I will not be purchasing a home on the Reef—not now and not ever."

"But what happened? Why … ?"

"Ask your CEO, president, or head of membership why I may have had a change of heart—and while you're at it, let them know I won't be renewing my social membership or donating any further to their foundation either!"

With that, we walked out, at which time I leaned in and gently kissed him on the cheek. No words were necessary. I had just witnessed everything I needed to know about Ron Joyce. Without Ron buying at the Reef, his friends backed out and bought in Naples, Florida, instead. None of them ever again returned to Ocean Reef. Fifteen-million dollars in real-estate deals went down the drain because of the Reef's shabby behavior to me.

Eventually, I did receive a letter of apology from the club, requesting I reconsider purchasing and offering me my social membership at no cost—which I accepted as partial compensation for the money lost on my down payment, even though my visions of a future there had drastically changed. I saw what had happened as a sign that it wasn't meant to be, and I also knew they wanted my access to the Ron Joyces of the world.

As their high-school years passed, Jane and Brit progressed beautifully, and the migrations between Colorado for holiday breaks and Boston continued. Over the next year, I met most of Ron's close friends, and was involved with several business dealings. I saw his homes and met a few of his seven children and several grandchildren. He was a formal man, which I appreciated. He never wore anything less casual than a sports jacket, and we fit well together because I preferred to be dressed either in a skirt or dress. We would talk for hours into the night and share our pasts along with future dreams. He was a passionate, affectionate, caring man. And I was so impressed that despite his intense business and social schedule, Ron had faithfully flown to be with his mother every few weeks for an evening of dinner and cards. And then in May of 2007, her life drew to an end.

Brit and I had scheduled a Memorial Day-weekend golf trip, but Ron's mother's service would be that same weekend in Nova Scotia. Ron said the course at his resort was playable, so Brit and I flew up there from Boston. I didn't want Ron or anyone involved too closely with my children, so Brit and I stayed in our own suite. My devotion to them was a point of contention with him.

I was intensely proud of how beautifully Brit blended in with the powerful, successful men that were there—blended so well that I retired for the night as my fifteen-year old stayed up playing cards, and talking politics and art with the men. I think I fell asleep beaming up at the ceiling and on through to the heavens.

The next day, Ron said, "You have more in half of that boy than I do in all seven of my children combined. Your commitment to him has really paid off."

That was a high compliment from him given that he had made it clear in the past how he saw me as a hovering mother who cared too much about her children. I was moved.

Brit was proud too, and astonished. He'd never witnessed the level at which his mom had been working with such successful men. My son and I golfed, went skeet shooting, rode bicycles, took walks, and enjoyed talking over the next few days.

On the last day, I hadn't heard from Ron. I heard the engines of his jet fire up. He'd taken off without a goodbye. That was really odd. Brit and I returned to Boston, and I still hadn't heard from Ron. I called him, and he was cool to me.

What in God's name had happened?

20

➤ A Heart Divided

I didn't brood over Ron's change in attitude because summer was approaching. That would mean a lot of planning and time in airports accommodating Jane's and Brit's complex summer plans after completing their sophomore and junior years of high school. Jane was going to New York for the "Women in Leadership" summer residential program at Barnard College, and then to Bentley College in Boston for volleyball camp. Brit was going to Peru for three weeks, where he'd be part of building a school for the underprivileged, residing with a Spanish-speaking family, and afterward sightseeing and climbing Machu Picchu. Brit had taken Spanish most of his life and spoke it quite well. I'd only get to see them in Vail after their programs. Brit would be back a month before Jane, and I was looking forward to some initial time alone in Vail, and afterward, the one-on-one time with my son. He'd gotten a job as a bag boy at a private golf course in Vail, because golf was his passion. When Jane returned, we'd have one full month together as a family. I booked flights, arranged connections, and supervised packing, insuring each had the appropriate apparel. Nice tidy plans—which were about to veer wildly astray.

The times in Vail were wonderful. I outdid myself in the kitchen. I talked to my dad every day on the phone. Often, I would call him from the grocery store to get the ingredients to a recipe he would later dictate to me over the phone. He had become my total go-to person and greatest confidante.

Brit landed into Vail at midnight after being delayed from Peru. He looked exhausted, and with one look in his eyes, I knew something was wrong. We loaded the car, and on the drive to the house his responses to my questions about the trip were brief.

"Mom," he said, finally, "I've been smoking pot. I think I have a problem."

My heart stopped beating, and I took a slow, deep breath to keep from gasping. "Okay. ..."

"And something else. ..."

Dear God. ...

"I'm really scared I have inherited some of the mental illness from Dad's family."

Far worse than drugs if true. The mother calm took over; the instinct that knows what her child most needs is for Mom to seem in control—not panicked out of her mind, not hysterical, but calm and reassuring. "Okay. ... You were right to tell me. You're really tired, honey. The most important thing to do is get a good night's sleep."

He did, but did I? I lay awake for hours, prayed like a woman slipping at the edge of a cliff with a baby in her backpack, and then hit the Internet. In the morning, I was on the phone to Sarah, Dad, and others. In two days, Brit and I would catch a flight to Los Angeles. There was an adolescent center located in Malibu that came highly recommended and that also provided full psychiatric testing. The expense for six weeks was astronomical, but Brit was willing, thank God.

The early mountain morning was clear on the day of our departure, and I hurried out to the garage, suitcases in hand. A jewel-toned hummingbird flew right up to my face and hovered there a moment. I froze so as not to frighten it. *Know that life is beautiful,* it was saying to me, *and all is well.* A sense of serenity—that's the only word for it—spread through me, readjusting all my settings. Brit and I could do this, and God would be with us ... now and always.

I stuffed my fears for the moment and all the attendant feelings. I could easily make pragmatic decisions, and any emotional aftershocks would have to wait.

At the treatment center, I signed the admitting papers and said goodbye to Brit. He'd just turned sixteen. Dad and Sarah comforted me on the phone, but I was a mess. Despite my faith, all my years of being sober, and having the twelve-step knowledge I possessed, it's another story when your own child is in trouble. My mind turned with questions: If I'd done something differently, could he have been less at risk? Was the lack of a father figure hurting him? What was I missing that I could be doing to make him better?

And all my plans. ... This was not my idea of the month alone together. I called the golf course where he would not be working. I got myself situated, and that night I drove straight back to Malibu for a support meeting.

The room was dimly lit with candles. As I sat down, a man said hello. I couldn't make out his face, but I knew that voice, even though I couldn't quite pin it down. When the leader asked if there were any visitors, I raised my hand and shared the circumstances that had brought me to Malibu and how scared I was. When the meeting ended, the lights were turned on, and the man seated next to me was a well-known movie star who'd had three of his children attending the same adolescent treatment center. He offered his phone number and assistance. His kindness, his experience, and his generous spirit helped me through a very tough time, and I appreciated it.

Over the next four weeks, I flew back and forth, spending long weekends in Malibu and participating in the family program. In Vail, Jane had a temporary job at a retail store after her summer programs, but she joined me for a weekend, and it was good to have We Three together, even though it was for family-therapy sessions. I'd called Jim, asking him to participate, but he refused. Neither would he allow his own records to be released for Brit's benefit. His lack of cooperation angered me, and it hurt Brit, too, but he was in the right place to deal with it.

I attended many meetings while in Los Angeles, and I really liked it there. The recovery community was friendlier than anyplace I'd ever been, and very populated. It was almost chic to be in twelve-step there, whereas in Boston it was still taboo.

Brit's psychiatric tests were complete, and he proved to be just fine. He was greatly relieved, as was I. We spent a few weeks together as a family in August to enjoy the mountains and regroup. I realized it hadn't occurred to me to call Ron during this trying time, and that he hadn't contacted me either.

I returned to Boston with my teenagers in the fall and decided to stay there for Brit to drive him to his support meetings. I continued to watch Jane play volleyball and then have dinner with her afterward. I loved hearing the stories of how happy she was at school. The next day, I would be on the football field with Brit, and then have dinner with him, too. I joined a committee to help raise funds at Brit's school and made some great, lifelong friends. New England was beautiful in the fall, and it was easy to take a shuttle flight to Rochester to see my family and Virginia.

Finally, I heard from Ron.

The week before parents' weekend—the same at both Jane's and Brit's schools—Ron called. I didn't hide my pleasure at hearing from him.

"I'm hoping you'll join me and fly down to the yacht with me," he said, "to meet a few couples and then sail through the Panama Canal." Just as if everything was normal.

The mystery was killing me. "Ron, why didn't you call all summer?"

There was a silence. "… because Ellen, I didn't appreciate being snubbed. I was deeply hurt and offended."

"What are you talking about? I would never snub you."

Another silence. "That last morning, I arranged a tour in one of our helicopters for you and Brit. I did not enjoy telling the pilot *never mind* after I'd made a big deal of setting it up."

"And how was I supposed to know about all this?"

"I left a message in your suite. You didn't get it?"

"Of course not! We'd have loved to have taken the tour."

Ron was laughing. "Can't believe it," he said. "I was so sure you'd decided you didn't need an old duffer like me that you just couldn't be bothered."

"How could you think such a thing of me?"

Actually, I knew. Ron had been very direct about his fear of being hurt by getting involved with me, and I knew he was sensitive. Yet he also knew that he'd been the only man since Jim that my heart was entirely at home with, or that I had woken up to.

"Failure to communicate," he said, laughing again.

I laughed with him.

"So?" he asked. "The Panama trip with some very interesting people?"

"You're such an amazing man, Ron," I said, "and you know just how to tempt me, but I simply can't miss parents' weekend."

"Oh, for God's sake! They're not babies anymore, Ellen. This trip is more important than some PTA meeting."

This one hit a nerve. He hadn't even called during the whole crisis with Brit, and with no idea of what was "important" to me, he was being dismissive.

"You *are* important to me," I said sadly. "But my main devotion is to my children. I wish you could accept that. I *am* sorry."

I knew when I hung up he wouldn't call for a long while. It made me sad because Ron taught me what it feels like to be loved without a hidden agenda of rage, to be loved because of who I am, with respect, and most especially, unconditionally. And yet, I couldn't visualize any permanency between us. And he felt that keenly.

Thanksgiving and Christmas were coming up—family time for me—and I had no intention of sharing it with him. We Three would fly to Vail, and we were looking forward to it. The holidays proved glorious as always. Dinners in the formal dining room with china and crystal, games of Scrabble, ski days together, seeing friends, and enjoying traditions together. This was my bliss, and I loved it profoundly. If anything, Brit's rehab had drawn our circle even tighter. He and Jane were very close and always had been. It meant the world to me that they had each other. When I picture them in my mind, they are always hugging—as toddlers, growing up, and even now when they greet each other.

I arranged a dinner party for Jane's eighteenth birthday in March that included a group of girlfriends and would be held at a trendy restaurant in Boston. Brit surprised his sister by showing up for dessert. At almost seventeen, he was a handsome boy, and Jane's girlfriends liked him very much. Brit's and Jane's extraordinary respect for each other makes me feel blessed every day, and I know that prioritizing our time together helped to create this precious bond. Consistent parenting, nurturing, and love produced the opposite of my own sibling relationships, which was my goal.

Jane had applied to several colleges; however, she had her heart set on only one. After touring major East-Coast universities and campuses in Colorado, the only school she wanted to attend was one of the Claremont Colleges located one hour east of Los Angeles called Scripps College. It was a women's liberal-arts school, and she had no desire to go anywhere else.

I consulted my astrologer, Trudi Rossi, who said, "She'll find the perfect school. I think it's in the South, and she'll wear flip-flops to school."

I thought this was bizarre because Jane wasn't looking at any schools in the South at all, unless she meant Southern California. Then I saw on the college website a list of the top ten reasons students attend Scripps College. One reason was, "… you can wear flip-flops year 'round."

So, I was surprised when Jane's early-admission application to Scripps was deferred. Jane refused to take *probably not* for an answer. She called the dean of admissions, stating her strong desire to attend Scripps and the contribution she felt she could make to the school.

Another notification subsequently arrived from Scripps. Jane whooped for joy. "Mom, get used to me in flip-flops at school!"

I was thrilled for her, and we all celebrated.

Ron called again in February to invite me to join him in St. Maarten and St. Barth's islands. He raced his mega sailing yacht each year, which was not something that interested me.

"Ron, I'd love to see you, but sailing is just not for me."

Enjoying the intimate companionship with Ron made me more interested in having a permanent relationship with a mate. I knew realistically it wasn't going to be Ron, but I still missed him often and couldn't quite end our relationship.

While Jane and Brit were in school during the week, I enjoyed watching Jane play lacrosse and Brit play golf. Or I made quick flights to Rochester to lunch with Dad or to have dinner with Mom and Pete. When Easter arrived in Boston, the flowers were beginning to bloom, and the kids didn't want to fly anywhere, so we had brunch at the Four Seasons, went to Fenway Park to see a Red-Sox game, and saw a movie. We loved it; but increasingly, Jane and Brit were making their own plans, and I looked ahead to the empty nest. I made more of a point of socializing with my Boston friends, and in that way cleared up an old mystery.

I'd met Mimi in Vail, as a mutual friend of Frank, whom I hadn't seen for several years. Mimi was a partner in her own investment firm while also being a dedicated mother to two sons, now grown. I adored catching up over lunch in Boston.

"So, have you heard from Frank?" I asked.

"Our lovable old bachelor is finally getting married," Mimi said. "He wants a family, if you can believe that."

He was in his late fifties, so I was surprised.

"Frank's fiancée is a good person," Mimi said. "She insists he make things right with his past before they can get married."

"His past?"

"Frank's daughter."

"Daughter?" I echoed, as if the conversation had drifted into incomprehensible Japanese.

"He didn't tell you about his secret love child?"

A feather could have knocked me off my bistro chair.

"The daughter is now twenty-one," Mimi said.

We did a little math and figured Frank had found out about her existence right about the time he and I first met in Vail. I told her a little of my own history.

"Oh, my God," Mimi said. "No wonder he didn't say anything about her."

"Yet, it was there between us," I said. "I just had no idea what it was. He knew I was a love child from the get-go. Mimi, I knew there was some weird thing connecting us. The feeling was so strong, it almost made me itch."

I phoned Frank at some point after my lunch with Mimi, but he was not the type to open up. I couldn't get over the revelation of our common denominator fifteen years later. When I think back to my conversations with Frank that first time we met, I couldn't have imagined the extent to which we were also having a conversation with each other's lifelong baggage and a projection of the future based upon it. Because of that conversation and its hidden agendas, we didn't wind up together, but oddly, we both made the right decision. Didn't we?

With Jane's and Brit's increasing independence, I was alone more ... and a bit lonely.

Friends set me up on dates from time to time, but nothing that showed potential for a serious relationship. I got my hopes up over one very good-looking guy my age that was also sober. He called me and I agreed to meet for dinner. Did I have any weird connection with this man? I did, in fact. He played hockey for the Dream Team that won the gold medal at the 1980 Winter Olympics where I'd worked during college and which I'd found so thrilling. The improbability of our connection made me wonder about fate at first, and we had a nice time. He did have two middle-school-aged children, however; and younger children were not what I wanted in my future at that point.

I had walked across the Boston Commons to meet my date at the restaurant, and he offered me a ride back to my apartment. He parked his car in front of my place. In the back seat lay his clothes for the following day. This guy had planned to get lucky without even knowing me. I was mortified, and let him know it. He departed mad, but I was relieved. I would never adjust to the age of casual sex that seemed to accompany current dating. I liked my traditional values that meant sex was a consummation of love.

It made me miss Ron.

When he called to invite me to visit him in Toronto, I agreed. I was safe with him, and he sounded anxious to see me. It was a one-hour flight from Boston, and I assumed he'd send a car to pick me up; but, surprisingly, he came himself in his new Rolls Royce.

Usually he would come in by helicopter, so, for him to transport himself without a driver was rare. He arrived looking refined as ever, and climbed out, holding a large bouquet of flowers. I thanked him with a kiss and stepped inside the vehicle.

"Glad to see there aren't any holes in the floorboard," I said, referring to our running joke of the time when I arrived in Barbados and was met by a beat-up old van with numerous perforations.

He laughed. He wanted to show me around and took me first to see his charter company adjacent to the airport. Afterward, we drove downtown and pulled into the Four Seasons.

"Morning, Mr. Joyce," the bellman greeted him.

We got off the elevator at the penthouse floor where he'd just purchased a three-bedroom suite with a panoramic view of Toronto. The décor was exactly my traditional style, and I felt at home. We walked around Yorkville and went into a café for lunch. Although we hadn't seen one another in months, it was as if no time had passed. After lunch, we visited an art gallery, went window shopping, and later met one of his financial managers for a drink. I loved that he included me in his business. We returned to the penthouse to make calls, freshen up, and then we went out for a marvelous dinner. Ron and I were never at a loss for words. We shared the same Irish quick wit and really understood each other.

The next day, we went into Burlington to his home, which was more contemporary. The rooms were vast and open, with modern furnishings and fixtures. The housekeeper, driver, and cook had their own separate quarters on the property that faced Burlington Bay, which fed into Lake Ontario. Ron liked to swim for exercise, and the home was equipped with an indoor Olympic-sized pool. My things were taken to one of the guest suites, as we understood each other's need for personal space. Whether we were on his yacht or at one of his residences, we each seemed to know when the other needed to retreat for alone time. I found great comfort in that. We both were avid readers, so it was common for us to sit in silence together and read. Our exhilarating intellectual exchange made it seem as though we'd been on the same wavelength an entire lifetime.

There was a dinner event that evening for which Ron had told me to pack a cocktail dress. He didn't mention that the occasion was to honor him, and the room was filled to capacity. He accepted his award humbly, saying he was just doing his duty and should be congratulated for having me with him. He embarrassed me to death by saying, "Ellen is the only woman I know who is smarter than I am!" We danced and had a wonderful time. He always made me feel as though I was the most beautiful woman in the room, something I'd never have imagined after years of Ellen Melon or Crater Face resonating in my consciousness. Socially, I could hold my own wherever I was, and the stares that accompanied being with a man so much older than I were nothing new. His family, business associates, and closest friends knew he was in love with me, and that I never took a penny from him, knowing women flocked around him only for that reason. I was self-supporting, and fiercely independent, and he respected that.

Back at his home that night, I asked him to give the staff the rest of the weekend off, so I could cook breakfast and dinner on Sunday. He agreed and accompanied me to the grocery store, into which he hadn't set foot in decades. We returned home to football on TV while I cooked and baked. After dinner, he began to tell me about his first two wives, his joys, and regrets. He went into detail about his children and their histories together. I listened intently, knowing he was sharing his emotional life with me, which wasn't easy for him. I already knew all of the details, but this time the story revealed his heart.

"I have only really loved three women in my entire life, Ellen. Two became my wives, and the third is the woman in front of me."

I looked at him, full of tenderness and kissed him. "I love you too, Ron."

The next day, I finally met his best friend, who was also his second cousin, over a lovely lunch. Afterward, Ron took me to see one of the summer camps his foundation had established for underprivileged children. Named after his cherished partner, the pro hockey player, it was like a five-star hotel, in true Ron Joyce fashion. There was a massive telescope at the camp, one of only ten in existence. Ron and his partner had purchased a parcel of land together with the hopes of building side-by-side summer homes for their families, but after his partner's tragic death in his early forties, Ron built the first camp on the land instead. It grew from there to the current eight facilities.

Monday morning, I awoke at five o'clock in the morning. Ron was still asleep. I suddenly needed to return to my safe cocoon. Ron fully understood my sudden requirement when things became too emotionally close—the need to retreat back into myself. I went online and purchased a seat on the seven-thirty flight back to Boston.

Before I left, I leaned over Ron who was still sleeping, and kissed his cheek. He stirred and opened his eyes to hear me whisper, "I need to go."

He nodded and said, "I know. It's fine."

This time I had a strong sense I wouldn't be returning. On the return flight, I mulled things over, the lovely feeling of unconditional love, and tried to project it over the long haul. For me, there were physical limitations associated with his age that I as a younger woman would grow to resent. I knew how rare it was to find such mental and physical chemistry as I had with this man. Yet, it just wasn't right. Was I simply too afraid of the vulnerability that went with true intimacy that I didn't know a good thing when I held it in my hands?

I needed something more, and feared that was impossible.

I arrived in Boston in time to hit the gym and was happy to be walking across the Boston Commons toward the Ritz Carlton for my workout. While stretching my leg on a bench, I saw a pair of men's glasses on the floor. A female trainer prodded her male client on an adjacent mat.

"Do these glasses belong to ..." I looked at the guy, "… him?"

He looked up and our eyes met. Lots of songs are written about such moments. They usually mention bolts of lightning or heat waves or fireworks or volcanoes—maybe all of the above.

"Nope. Not mine," the man said.

Instantly, I took off. Actually, that was one of the few times I'd ever experienced a raw physical attraction like that. What did such a power surge mean? It left me scattered—and scared. I hated feeling out of control, but he was definitely one of the most handsome men I'd ever seen.

I called Mom on the way home from the gym to discuss the details of her upcoming trip with Pete to Boston for Jane's graduation from high school.

"You seem distracted," she said.

I told her about the guy in the gym. Without going so far as to mention that the experience had blown my socks off, I just said, "He's the best-looking man I've ever seen."

"Really? That's only the second time in your life I've ever heard you say that about a man."

I didn't remember saying that in the past.

"So, who is he?" she asked.

Exactly my question.

21

➤ Mixed Messages

Over the next few weeks at the gym, the handsome man would position himself on the weight machine right in front of the treadmill on which I would be running. It unnerved me, so I kept my eyes fixed on my television screen and pretended not to notice him. I told myself that I wasn't functioning at a junior-high level, it was simply that no one was very friendly at that gym, and people I didn't know rarely said hello or acknowledged me. When he would finish and walk away, I checked him out thoroughly. I loved his dark, thick hair; I nicknamed him *Great Hair Guy*.

With Jane's graduation the next day to be followed by our special vacation, I got in a final workout before all our family plans swept me up entirely. Sweaty afterward, I stepped into the elevator, and Great Hair Guy got in after me. Several people occupied the elevator, as usual, and no one spoke.

Then, I heard him say to me, "Hello."

I turned to him. "You must not be from Boston."

He responded, "What makes you say that?"

"Because I have been at this gym for a year, and no one has ever said hello to me!"

He smiled. "I'm actually from Los Angeles, but I live here, too."

"Oh! I'll be renting a condo in Malibu." I smiled back. "My daughter will be in college nearby, and I wanted to try living in L.A."

"My name is Charles, and yours?"

"Ellen," I said, having difficulty keeping eye contact.

As the elevator doors opened, he said, "Well, I'll see you next week."

"I won't be here," I replied. "I'm taking my children to Bermuda, then home to Vail for the summer."

"You could always email me."

Why did he *assume* I would want to send him an email? "Where might I send it?" I asked.

"Well, Charles at ..." And he gave me the name of his business website.

Who was this guy or who did he think he was?

Jane's senior year ended, and graduation was lovely with all of the girls in the traditional white dresses and fresh-flower wreaths on their heads. I was so very proud of her. My brother Tommy and his wife had driven Dad over from Rochester to attend, but Dad was taking a new and powerful medication in his struggle with cancer, and it left him extremely weak. It meant so much to Jane that he had come. Dad and Tommy left immediately after the ceremony, while Mom and Pete joined us at the Four Seasons.

After a wonderful day, Jane, Brit, and I gathered Jane's things from the campus, dropped them at my apartment, packed, and flew to Bermuda. The golf courses and beaches were divine, and We Three thoroughly enjoyed ourselves.

Jane and Brit had gone ahead to the beach, where I joined them after a workout at the hotel's gym.

"Mom," Brit said, "Next year, with Jane no longer in Boston, I want to be a senior at Milton without anyone hovering over me. What's the point in being at boarding school if your mother is up the street? Okay?"

He was a healthy, handsome young man, and I felt reasonably sure I could trust him to stay committed to recovery meetings. He had a good head on his shoulders, and I planned to visit him once a month or so while giving California a try, because I was looking ahead to the time when they'd both be in college.

"I'll think about it," I said.

I actually attended a support meeting later that day, where I met with a good friend of Ron's from Canada. What were the odds of that? We spent four days in Bermuda, and then returned to Boston.

I went to the gym one last time before leaving for Vail, and Charles walked right over to say hello. He seemed quite nervous.

"Be sure to email me," he said.

"Sure." I could hardly breathe. I rushed off before losing my composure. A butterflies-flailing-in-honey feeling in my tummy stopped me. *My goodness gracious, what was happening to me?* I realized just how much was missing between Ron and me. A physical attraction this strong couldn't be a good thing.

Could it?

Back home in Vail at the end of June, the wildflowers were blooming in the mountain meadows, and it was wonderful being there as a family this last summer before Jane entered college. Jane was working at the fitness center to save money, and Brit started caddy training at a nearby golf course that was the sister program to Augusta National. My children were growing up so quickly, and I didn't want to miss the precious time We Three had left together. I planted my own flowers that year, saw friends, cooked and baked for the children, attended local events, and I was very happy.

It was mid-July while cleaning out files on my computer, that I found an email from Charles' personal email address in my spam folder. It read simply, "Hi, Ellen, how is L.A?" I wrote back that I was still in Vail and wouldn't be there until after the summer. This started our daily interchange, sometimes multiple times per day, depending on what was happening in each of our lives.

"So, Mom," Jane asked, "who are you emailing so often with such a twinkle in your eye?"

"Oh, he's a guy from the gym in Boston."

"Does he have a name?" Jane probed.

"Not one I intend to share." I winked. "Let's just say he's my email friend."

"We'll call him Cyber Guy then." She giggled.

As time passed, Charles became an ongoing object of amusement.

"What's new with Cyber Guy, Mom?" Brit would tease. "Any Cyber passes?"

Even Dad, via phone, got in on the fixation of my email relationship with Cyber Guy. It was almost as if Cyber Guy had become a family pet. He was amused and entertained by the ongoing email saga. Dad was always telling me that he felt I deserved the best and reinforced what a remarkable mother and woman he thought I was. This was a long way from the man who'd been by turns emotionally unavailable and horribly abusive during my childhood. I felt so grateful that the patience we had both shown with our relationship—after that most stunning revelation that we were not biologically related—had paid off in a way we never could have imagined.

Because that was likely to be our last full summer together as a family, it was a good thing we were all so jolly. I had a tough time sending Brit off alone to Milton Academy in Boston. I wouldn't be constantly looking over his shoulder and would just have to trust him. I knew I couldn't stay alone in Vail all winter, which made me decide to lease the condo on the ocean in Malibu for six months. Brit and I were happy to take Jane to Scripps College and help her get settled in her dorm.

We shipped both Jane's and my vehicles to Claremont, California, with hers packed full. After we landed, we helped get Jane's car unloaded, shopped for all the incidentals needed by a first-year college student, and said goodbye. Brit caught a flight directly to Boston, where we had shipped his things ahead of time. My Malibu condo was nicely decorated in Tommy-Bahama and Ralph-Lauren furnishings. The ocean view was gorgeous. I hung a hummingbird feeder outside, and arranged several family photos, my favorite throw blanket, and the linens I had shipped from Colorado. The hummingbirds arrived daily on the balcony, and I watched the beautiful sunsets and listened to the waves. Oh, it was glorious. I reconnected with the many friends I'd made during Brit's summer rehab, starting a full life of social events and gatherings.

Charles continued emailing almost daily. He worked all over the United States, so I never knew where he was, and I didn't ask. By now I'd learned he was famously successful in his career on the West Coast, and not so insignificant on the East Coast after all.

I joked and called him his partner's sidekick, and he comically echoed it in his endearing, self-deprecating manner. One day over the phone I told Mom about his business association.

She gasped. "Ellen, oh, my gosh! I know exactly who he is! Don't you remember? I was reading a tabloid while visiting you in Florida almost eight years ago. You ripped it out of my hand, looked at the photo of the man, and said, 'That's the best-looking man I have ever seen!'"

I had apparently said that to her twice in my life, but I had no idea it was about the very same person. That couldn't be a mere coincidence, I thought. Were the Fates at work here?

Less than a month into the school term, Brit sent an email that was out of character, and I was concerned. My gut told me something was not right. I called his advisor and was directed to his football coach. There was concern over the crowd he was hanging with, and that explained the tone of the email. I decided to fly to Boston unannounced for a few days to see for myself how he was doing. I let Charles know I'd be there, and we arranged to meet for coffee at the café in the gym.

I landed in Boston and went directly to Milton's campus. I knew the minute I saw Brit's face that something was not right. After talking with him, his coach, and advisor, it was agreed I should be there with Brit at least part of the time during the first semester. I contacted friends who were also parents and got the name of a real-estate agent in Milton. Within a day after arriving, I'd rented a house near Brit's campus, rented the furniture, purchased the kitchen incidentals, and made arrangements for my SUV to be transported to Boston from Colorado. I set up a therapy regimen for us to go to every other week all year as I commuted between L.A. and Boston. Brit seemed to be a good sport about it, but I admit I watched him with secret concern.

My new place in Boston conveniently allowed me to keep my gym membership, and I would see Charles at the gym when he was in town. The very next morning, after working out and showering, I met Charles in the gym café for coffee. I was so attracted to him that I stammered and made no sense. He also seemed to be all over the board, responding very oddly, as if nervous and uncomfortable, but eventually the conversation took a more personal turn.

Charles talked about ending a highly publicized relationship in a way I found to be rather cold, and I couldn't figure out why he was telling me. Did he want to prepare me, an indirect warning that he was capable of treating me the same way? The conversation skipped all over, without a flow. It was in that moment I recalled the 9/11 morning broadcaster lipping the name of a man she was concerned about. It had been him! I left the café wondering what had really transpired between us and what it was that attracted me. He was an odd man, yet people spoke of him with high professional regard. My head said run, yet my heart wanted to get closer.

I did some vetting and found he had dates with girls half his age. What was he doing with me? I made some immediate judgments about him, thinking he was yet another bachelor who was powerful, rich, and a total player. I had no intention of being just another notch on his belt!

In October, New England offered its rich, autumnal palette, a thousand shades of crimson in the maples of the Boston Commons and the Esplanade ablaze with gold and bronze oaks along the Charles River. I loved watching Brit play football, breath billowing out like smoke, as I cheered with the crowd. Brit conceded it was fun to be able to spend the night occasionally at my house and have me cook for him. He appreciated my driving him to support meetings when needed. I was adjusting to the bi-coastal trek every other week. All that mattered was that he needed my support, and whatever happened in terms of my relationships paled alongside my maternal determination.

I still saw Charles at the gym, and he continued to email regularly, which I found to be just plain weird. If he wanted to communicate with me, why didn't he call or ask me out to dinner? Why couldn't he step up to the plate? If he wasn't interested, why the steady stream of emails? Nobody else in my life behaved this way. It felt like a lack of respect, as though I was something that had to be kept secret—a notion that pushed all the snaps to the emotional baggage I thought I'd shed after my diligent work. Actually, there was a mighty residue still lurking in a box like that nasty one Pandora opened. On my forty-seventh birthday, his business achieved a tremendous milestone. When I woke in the morning, I found an email from Charles that read, "Happy birthday to you, happy birthday to you. I wish we were together right now, happy birthday to you."

It was sent at 2:30 A.M. Was this guy drunk? Did he think he could hint at a booty call and I'd be flattered? If he really meant it, he'd have sent a limo to come and get me. Did he just assume I fantasized about him, and as a birthday gift, imply a late-night itch, thinking I'd be thrilled? With each suspicion, and preconceived notion that ran through my mind, I grew angrier. Later that same morning, I saw him at the gym and marched right up to him. His face lit up as I approached. That didn't stop me; I was breathing fire.

I let him have it, something along the lines of *What gives you the right ... ?* and *How could you be so insulting? ... The kind of men I attract would never ... .*

I was so forceful that his response was, "Uh-uh, Ellen, you are scaring me."

I really didn't want his games in my life, but I really did want him.

Down the road, I would be shocked to find that I had told off the shyest guy on the planet, who didn't drink much, and made a habit of waking every night to work for an hour, and he was really only flirting with me. I was attracted to him, and acting emotionally retarded because of it. Or was I simply terrified to trust love from a man?

The next month, I was in Boston cooking pancakes for Brit on a Saturday morning after he had spent the night. Ron hadn't phoned in more than two months, and while I did miss our conversations, I didn't want to allow myself to care. His call that day came as a surprise. Ron wanted to know whether I could join him in Fort Lauderdale for dinner. His close friends were there, and we'd stay on his new one-hundred-and-sixty-four-foot motor yacht. It was being featured at the Fort Lauderdale International Boat Show, which I'd attended in the past and enjoyed. Brit was going back on campus for the rest of the weekend for activities that didn't include Mom, so I figured, why not?

I arrived early in the evening to find a car waiting for me. I was always happy to see Ron; however, something was different, and the difference was Charles—he'd become a distraction. Seeing Ron's friends and my clients who were regulars at the annual boat show made the night especially fun, but when Ron asked me to return to Toronto on his plane with him, I agreed. I wanted an opportunity to talk with him alone. He always traveled with an entourage of a personal assistant, an attorney or financial advisor, and a friend or two. I'd always cherished the times we'd be alone at his home or in flight to be able to talk.

I needed to tell him things had changed. In Ron, I'd come to know the powerhouse businessman, but I also knew the sensitive, caring man who was afraid to have his heart broken. That fear was our common ground when we first met, and we were mutually respectful of the other's vulnerability. We had arrived at the moment, though, that Ron had always known was inevitable and mutually accepted as our reality.

"What's on your mind, Ellen?"

His reading of me was always accurate, and I couldn't withhold anything from him.

"Ron, you know how much I care for you and respect you. You deserve to know what's happening with me."

I saw no anger or shock on his face, just a sense of calm acceptance. "You've met someone."

"Yes. We're just friends at this stage, and it may very well stay that way, but I feel something for him that is strong, and I respect you too much not to be honest. I know that isn't fair to you, because you deserve a woman's wholehearted love."

"Wholehearted love … " his hand covered mine, a gesture of assurance, "means wanting what's best for the other person. I'm too old to marry again, Ellen, and you deserve the whole package from a man who can give it."

Oh, this was a wonderful man! I teared up a bit, loving his maturity and his ability to express his emotions so beautifully. We parted with our mutual trust and admiration intact, and the conversation proved to be worth the trip. I knew we'd be lifelong friends.

And had I heard from the person I found so fascinating? The person who'd rather undeservedly endured my indignation? Not for quite a while. Charles' name finally popped up in my email inbox over the Thanksgiving holiday. We Three were together in Vail, and I'd roasted and baked and feasted. We then visited over long phone calls with Dad and Tommy and the rest of the family. I sat down to my computer.

"Look, Brit," Jane said. "Mom's got that look in her eyes again."

"It must be Cyber Guy!" Brit said in his dramatic TV-announcer voice.

I laughed inside, and was secretly pleased the communication flow had returned.

After Jane and Brit left, I stayed in Colorado to get the house decorated and to prepare for Christmas. The emails from Charles kept coming. He'd be taking his children to Cabo San Lucas and on to Park City, Utah, over the Christmas break. I came to see that he was a devoted, wonderful father. I often asked his advice on parenting. He made me laugh, and as he was letting me know more about himself—his inner self. I shared much with him, as well. How could it hurt? I thought. We'd probably never see one another in person again.

Christmas in Vail was unbearably cold that year, and I decided to take Jane to Cabo, while Brit stayed with friends snowboarding. Jane knew that the mysterious Cyber Guy had told her mother about his trip there, and the best places to go to eat.

I continued to enjoy the relationship by email. Charles began to share more of his emotional self, and his communications filled a void. In some ways, it was perfect because I still didn't want a man involved in my family unit. What I didn't see—and this concerned my counselor Sarah—was that it also recreated a pattern I'd had from the time I was very young with my dad, the dysfunctional mixed messages. There, but not really there. Over time, this would prove to be a very dangerous game—for both of us.

22

➤ A Real Boy

I had no reason to think there was anything remotely special about the date, February twenty-first, 2009. Yet, the occasion would prove to be almost as momentous as the day I looked at Dad's and my DNA test results. I was in California after the winter break. I'd assisted Brit with applications to colleges with strong architectural programs, and then flew to L.A. for parents' weekend for Jane, right at the time of her nineteenth birthday. Shifting from Mom duties, I drove to Santa Monica for a few days to see friends, and later decided to take a stroll on the Third-Street Promenade, which was packed with people on the weekends. There were street dancers, musicians, performers, and vendors. As I strolled along, I locked eyes with an older woman across the promenade who was setting up a table. I felt a connection, some kind of vibe between us, so I approached and said hello.

The woman set something on her table, nodded, and spoke. "I'm a psychic," she said without any trace of embarrassment. "You have spirits protecting you with a bright aura."

This sounded far-fetched, but my astrology sessions with Trudi and my regression massage had taught me not to simply dismiss the paranormal. I approached closer, while remaining skeptical.

"On one side of you are two spirits, a couple with old-style names. The man is Vincent," she said, "but you knew both of them."

That got my attention. Grandpa O'Neill's first name was Vincent.

"The woman with him was his wife," she said. "They are protecting you."

Grandma O'Neill? Her name was Mildred. This was such a wonderfully comforting thought that I stayed to hear more.

"Have you been unsuccessful in love with an adult partner?"

"True enough," I said.

"There is a male spirit alone on your other side. He is tormented and hanging on, preventing you from having true love."

Okay, that's it for me, I thought. I'm sure the look on my face told the woman I was suspicious.

"If I'm correct, this very day is the man's biological birthday, and Sally Ann will tell you more."

I'd heard enough nonsense. I certainly didn't know any Sally Ann. The woman didn't ask for any money from me, and I was surprised, but I brushed off her comments as crazy talk and went on my way. I would soon learn that she was the real deal.

A week later, I was back in Boston working on a project for a client, when a feeling came over me. I thought of my biological father and felt a strong sense that I should look him up on the Internet. It had been sixteen years since I'd spoken to Jim Bayley. This was the first time I'd thought of him since then. I certainly hadn't imagined him to be the tormented spirit who was hanging onto me and preventing me from love. Google pulled up his obituary, saying he had passed away in October three years earlier. When I saw that his birthday was on February twenty-first, 1913, I felt chills that had nothing to do with the snow outside. February twenty-first was the very Saturday I'd met the psychic on the promenade in Santa Monica. I could hardly breathe.

The obituary also said he was survived by his wife, and one daughter, Sally. Could that be the Sally Ann the psychic mentioned? When had a daughter come into the picture? He and his wife never had children. After consulting with my counselor Sarah, I tracked this Sally into Ohio via the Internet. I waited a few days to get the courage and then called. A woman answered.

"Is Sally Ann available?" I asked.

She asked me to hold on and picked up on another extension. "I needed to go to a quiet room to talk," she said. "I'm very curious to know how you know the name Sally Ann. Only one person in my life ever called me by that name, my father."

I started to explain, and then we spoke for two solid hours. Sally was in her sixties, a product of an early marriage between her own mother and Jim Bayley when they were just out of high school. Sally hadn't met him until she was eighteen. My new half-sister told her story, portraying Jim Bayley as being remote and uninterested in Sally's six children and thirteen grandchildren. I began to realize that my perceived Dad had actually wound up being the better father of the two. I felt a wave of relief spread through me, the same serenity as when I listened to Betty Ford's revelations that day in Vail. I couldn't wait to tell Dad about it.

Ever since we had the DNA testing, I'd often wondered what my life would have been like if my mother had left him and married my biological father. Now I had the peace of mind that things did work out for the best. Dad and I had become best friends, and he was the only other person who was emotionally invested in Jane and Brit. He loved them dearly.

Dad and I still spoke daily, sometimes twice. There were times when he'd bring up his resentment toward Mr. Bayley for having the affair with my mom. A few years back, he shared a dream where he asked Bayley to reimburse him for the expense of my childhood. At that point, I told him he needed to take his grudge elsewhere. "It's not appropriate to share that with me," I said. He never brought it up again, but I knew he still carried anger over being deceived by Mom and the boss he'd thought was also his friend.

Luckily, I'd been given the opportunity to heal the relationship with Dad, and that was a gift. I cherished the fact that we had arrived at a clear space together, something for which I had always longed. He was emotionally available to me now, loved my children, and that was all that really counted. I'm also grateful to the street psychic, who in such a brief moment, added this healing turn to my life.

My emails with the inscrutable Charles continued. His many hats took him all over the globe, but in late February, I was back in Boston, and he emailed for me to phone him.

"Oh, I just wanted to know what you've been doing ... ," he said when I called.

Funny, I've just been wondering that myself, I almost said. I told him about my recent project.

"So, who are you dating these days?" He seemed vague, possibly distracted.

I never knew what he was thinking and was too afraid to risk asking. "Oh, just a few casual dates occasionally," I said.

Silence. Then, "Could we get together in a few weeks ... when we're both in L.A.?"

"That sounds good. I'll look forward to it."

Finally, an actual real date. *What took you so long?*

I was definitely buying a new outfit!

That night I had a blind date in Newport, Rhode Island. I was less than sparkling for the poor guy. The prospect of a date with Charles dimmed any chance this date might have had.

Sarah was increasingly concerned about this pattern with Charles. His communication over the last year was positive but periodic. She felt this was preventing me from putting my energies into someone who could be consistent and really available to me.

"You're still stuck in a situation that has the same effect on you as did your dad when you were growing up," she often reminded me.

I knew intellectually that my dad's and my biological father's inability to take responsibility for me was essentially the reason I couldn't seem to find a normal, loving relationship with a man. Neither ever validated my existence as a loving father to his daughter. I had to fight for my sense of legitimacy. I'd first chosen an abusive man—that energy felt normal because the man who raised me was abusive instead of being a loving father. Later, I'd turned to a loving father-figure in Ron—which didn't quite work. And now, with Charles, I was hoping something desirable and illusive would turn into something real, a dynamic that carried the same frustrating struggle as when I was a child. So, if Jim Bayley's spirit felt responsible and tormented, as the psychic had claimed, maybe the feeling was appropriate. I made a secret offer to this so-called spirit hanging on to me. Tell you what, Mr. Bayley, if you will help me find a loving mate, the real deal, you'd score some big forgiveness points.

As if to underscore Sarah's point about Charles, he sent an email cancelling our dinner date in L.A., saying he had to be out of town unexpectedly. I found it odd he didn't reschedule, yet he continued to email regularly.

I was still in Boston, and Brit was with me. "You're like Geppetto, Mom."

"From Pinocchio?"

"Yeah. That Cyber Guy needs to turn into a real boy!"

I didn't know if I should laugh or cry.

I was actively dating, though there was no one serious, and was out several times a week with different men. So while I discounted Sarah's advice and pursued the vicarious relationship with Charles, I did not forget her comment. My instincts told me there were lessons I needed to learn from this man, and ultimately it would be worth the effort. In the short term he would definitely prove helpful to Jane.

Three weeks later, Jane's lacrosse team played in competition matches in Florida during the March break, so I flew there to meet her and Brit for a long weekend at Ocean Reef. We Three were happy to be together, and Jane's lacrosse team did well. Jane wasn't clear about what she might like to do over the summer, considering her interests and potential college major. She loved sports and was thinking of media studies, so during a routine email exchange, I mentioned this to Charles. He suggested Jane email him. I told Jane he was a consulting client of mine and gave her his contact information. He was kind enough to give her further direction.

"Mom! Who is this guy to you? A client?" Jane asked. "You've always kept us apart from your business and social life. Now you're letting someone important like him help me?"

"He's a good man, honey, a father himself, with good intentions." I remained vague.

Before I knew it, Jane was set up to interview for an internship at one of the companies he owned in the media field for the summer in Boston. Perhaps helping my sweet Jane was his form of making up for his unpredictable behavior toward me, I thought. I trusted him with Jane's best interest at heart—except then he made another move I didn't understand.

His email said he was happy she got the internship and added, "Surely, somehow you could find a way to repay me."

Aha. I knew it. He had another agenda. I'd have to set the record straight immediately. I phoned his cell with my guns drawn.

"I would have to withdraw Jane's internship if there are any sorts of expectations or strings attached on your part," I said.

"Ellen. No. No strings," he said, stammering, and abruptly ended the call.

I could hear the echo of Grandpa Fred's voice as if he were right there next to me. He'd have said, "Poor bastard, he doesn't know what hit him with you!"

Now I knew he was really just trying to be helpful to my daughter and simply flirting with me. I wouldn't have known flirting if it was served on a silver platter; flirtations the size of two by fours couldn't break my armored helmet. I was the one who was ALONE. If I didn't look out for myself, no one else would. I had to be the provider and the protector with my sword drawn like a man.

A few days later, I was in California to be with Jane, and Charles left me a voice mail to call him. Calls between us were unusual. Given that it was April first, I thought it might be a joke. When I reached him, he carried on small talk at first.

Then he asked, "Are you dating anyone?"

"Not at the moment. Someone wants me to join him for the Aljar Awards in D.C., but I am hesitant to go."

"ALGER," he quickly corrected my pronunciation, going on to say, "Well, you're too dangerous for me."

"Oh, you have nothing to worry about, because I know you'll never even try to cross that line with me."

A brief silence, then, "What if I did?"

I barked, "You won't."

I often think of this moment. In hindsight, it may have been the last chance I'd ever have to encourage him to take our relationship to another level. If I'd considered the possibility that he was almost as defensive as I was, and if, in that moment, I'd felt womanly and reassuring and sexy and flirty, might our lives have changed direction? All I could feel were my defenses rising. *More games*, I thought, and I was tired of them. The question was, were they his games or *mine*? I also had to focus on the fact that he was helping my Jane; I just couldn't see my part in creating any confusion at that point. She was growing fond of him and, for the first time, experiencing professional guidance from a very successful man who would support her best interests. That meant the world to me, and to risk a fleeting romance and put that in jeopardy? I wouldn't dream of it.

With Jane in California, Brit and I spent Easter alone in Boston, and my son was so kind to me. He had started a tradition of writing me poetry for every holiday, and it warmed my heart. Though he stood six feet, two inches at seventeen, he agreed to pose with the Easter bunny for a photo at the Four Seasons where we had brunch—which I posted on Facebook. I relished seeing his consideration and caring for me. We'd gained so much ground in therapy together as I commuted between L.A. and Boston, growing closer than ever. The difficult year had proven to be worth the effort. I could detect his inner lack of confidence and the pain he still felt being abandoned by his father, though he hid it well. The irony for me was that both of my children grew up without a father, as I had. My main consolation was that Brit knew he could always have one person to count on, no matter what. Me.

He was a superior student and had been awarded a small academic scholarship at the University of Miami School of Architecture. We visited two of the colleges that had sent Brit letters of acceptance during the final weeks of school, taking a red-eye to the University of Arizona, followed by a day-trip to Syracuse University. University of West Virginia was also an option. All offered excellent programs in architecture, but Brit wanted a program that gave first-year students solid studio time, so he could discover as soon as possible if architecture would be his true calling. I loved listening to his fascinating thought processes, fully aware that I had to let go and allow him to make his own choices. I had to cut the strings to allow my son to become a man.

Just after Brit's senior prom, Jane finished finals in California and prepared for the lacrosse tournament on the East Coast. An outstanding athlete—unlike her mother—she'd soon compete in the NCAA Division III Lacrosse Tournament. Her team was one of the best on the West Coast, and I was excited to see her compete at this level. As it turned out, her team made it to the final round.

As Brit's graduation drew near, my life became a frenzy of packing, moving out, shipping, returning rental furniture, moving in, and back and forth. My mother and Pete were coming in from Rochester, but Dad's medication continued to tax all his strength, so he could not attend. Jane, back in Boston, was increasingly excited to begin her internship there and to occupy the summer rental I'd found for her in Harvard Square.

The day of graduation was beautiful and sunny and perfect for the outdoor ceremony. Brit announced he'd decided to go to Miami. We all proceeded to the Four Seasons, just as we had for Jane the year before. I couldn't believe it when I spotted Charles sitting a few tables away with his business partner. He was constantly in my force field, and for the life of me I couldn't figure out why. Was it that small of a world, or was there more to it? We both pretended not to see one another.

Despite a few lingering insecurities, Brit had charisma, class, and carried himself well. He was passionate about golf and loved being in Vail to caddy in the summertime. He enjoyed earning money even more and made incredible tips, though he was the only teenager among the thirty-and-older professional caddies. Throughout the summer, he made tremendous contacts on the course with men who flew in from all over the country just to play at their club.

Several weeks prior, my dear Ron had called and invited me to bring Jane along for the Fourth-of-July weekend aboard his yacht in Marblehead to watch fireworks, and I accepted eagerly. Brit would stay in Vail for the busy golf weekend.

Once in Boston, Jane and I picked up Ron at the private Signature gate when he flew into Logan. One of his crew carried a box the size of an ice chest, which Ron told him to put in the back of my Range Rover. Jane asked what it was.

"Mostly ice," he said, smiling mysteriously. "I've just come from Prince Edward Island where I went fishing. I know your mother loves salmon, and I heard that you love crab. Men are supposed to be hunters and providers, Jane."

Jane's eyes grew wide, and I grinned at her sudden grasp of Ron's gallant grand gestures. We drove toward Marblehead, with Ron in the passenger seat, instructing me where and how to drive.

"I didn't know you two were in love!" Jane blurted from the back seat, where she sat alongside Ron's eldest son, who happened to be my age. "I thought you were a client of Mom's. I've never seen her like this. It's nice."

We laughed at her essential insight, and I was pleased to see them hit it off immediately. I had gotten to know his son Steve, and liked him very much.

We arrived at the yacht club, and the tender from Ron's yacht was waiting to take us to board his anchored vessel that sported a main sail seventeen-stories high, and required a crew of fourteen to race. By the time we settled into our huge staterooms—two of four—Jane was enchanted. There were also quarters for the captain, his mate, the chef, and servers. We were served a five-star dinner, and Ron had a pastry chef on board to impress Jane, knowing she loved chocolate, just like her mother. Later, she beat him at dominoes, which no one before ever had, and he loved every second of it. I was pleased to have her interact with an adult male she looked up to, and to witness me being treated so lovingly by a man. All these things mattered to give her a different life than I had.

We went for a wonderful sail the following day and enjoyed fabulous food. The Fourth-of-July fireworks dazzled us from the water, and by the time the weekend was over, everyone was sad to see it end. Ron's and my solid and continuing friendship delighted me.

For the remainder of the summer, I continued alternating between Boston to be with Jane and then hopping back to Vail, which would always feel like coming home. I loved the peace and tranquility I felt in my home in the mountains.

One day, Charles emailed me, sounding excited as he shared about a project that would be part of his legacy. He then phoned, and I listened with great interest about what he had in mind to help others in need. I respected the way he was using his resources to give back, and instantly I envisioned ways that the project could come to fruition in half the time and double the resources. If I could contribute, perhaps he'd benefit, because I wanted to assist Charles in what was important to him, just as he had helped with what was important to me, my Jane, and her future. If this plan could ensure the success of his legacy program, I would be reciprocating.

I decided to do some research to make sure of my plan's feasibility. I didn't want to come on like gangbusters. An involvement on this meaningful endeavor was my idea of thrilling and possibly a chance for him to turn into a "real boy" in my life. Was he meant to be only a professional relationship for me and my daughter? Just thinking about it all hooked me on visions of collaborating with this brilliant, handsome man, along with the opportunity to contribute to something that mattered to him.

23

➤ Limbo

After Jane's internship came to an end, we played another game of musical chairs and belongings between Boston, Miami, Vail, and L.A. At the University of Miami, Brit hugged me tightly and told me how much he appreciated me. I tried to hold back the tears, as I left my baby behind at college. It was time to move on. Flying back to Los Angeles with Jane, I started thinking about what lay ahead. I was excited to be able to stay put in California, compared to the last few years commuting. Now that I was comfortable with where both of my children were in their lives, perhaps I could begin to focus more on my own. Because I loved the weather, and I'd met so many new friends through my recovery groups in California, I decided on Santa Monica.

When I pulled up and the valet unloaded my car, I felt like I was moving into my own Four Seasons. The rent was high, but I loved the first-class building and the furnished apartment even more so. All I needed to do was put away my clothes, and I was home. A friend suggested I call a matchmaker she knew. I'd never considered that as a possibility and decided to follow up.

The matchmaker was a woman in her early fifties and very private, only taking clients by word of mouth. I liked the way she sounded and made an appointment to meet with her for coffee. After seeing her male client base, I hired her. Within a week I was scheduled for my first date, which, while pleasantly entertaining, failed to spark the right chemistry.

I joined a nearby gym, sticking to my predicable routine. What I didn't expect was for a certain someone to be a part of it. Upon hearing the familiar voice, I looked up from my exercise mat.

"Jane proved to be a stellar intern in Boston, I am told," he said.

"She loved it, and is so grateful to you for the opportunity and your guidance."

As Charles worked with the set of weights on the machine next to me, he continued on, "Does she want to go back to Boston?"

"Actually, she's wondering whether she'd rather get into your line of business on the West Coast."

"Have her email me."

As usual, we walked away from one another awkwardly, without a word.

He was so kind to Jane, and there was no mention of any possible way to express my appreciation, flirtatious or otherwise. I considered my gratitude to be in the form of my business plan to expand his project. Charles was the top in his field with national and international recognition. Jane couldn't have asked for a better mentor, and I appreciated the way he was there for her. I just couldn't understand why this busy, bi-coastal man with three grown children of his own would make the time for us. It baffled me.

The next day Jane called and said that Charles had emailed her.

"He invited me to shadow him at work next week. I get to see how a show comes together from start to final taping! Isn't that wild? I'm beyond excited."

By the end of the month, I was missing her, so I drove to her campus due east, as I did every few weeks to take her to lunch or go shopping. Jane still didn't know who Cyber Guy was, and I started feeling as though I needed to give her some warning. I worried how to keep my friendship with Charles—I hate to burn bridges—yet not get my heartstrings tangled in a knot, all the while staying close enough that Jane could approach him again.

Over lunch, Jane shared exuberantly about her experience, so I decided to hold off explaining about Cyber Guy.

"Mom," she said, "watching the process of how a show is created was phenomenal! I was able to sit on the sidelines and even watch the negotiations with the network suits, and that hooked me."

"Well, great! You will do well at whatever you put your mind to, honey. Are you absolutely certain you'd rather be behind the camera instead of in front of it?"

"No, Mom. I'm thinking of a dual major in media studies and maybe English. I have a dream now and clear goals. I'm so lucky he's your client and so nice to me."

"Right. …"

"You're still on good terms with him? …"

"I hope so. I mean, probably … sure. I am."

"Mom?"

"Things are fine." They would have to be. I'd make them fine. No matter how odd he was with me, I was grateful my daughter had him in her life as a positive, successful role model. Nothing could mess that up.

Although we were only an hour apart, I hated leaving her. She had self-confidence, goals, self-respect, beauty, friends, and was athletic, too—all the things I lacked at her age.

Jane and Brit Skyped weekly by computer, sometimes including me, and I loved the modern technology that enabled them to see one another and talk. Skype kept We Three together. Brit loved his architecture and knew he'd made the right choice. He'd connected at UM with friends from Culver Academies—the military summer camp we'd sent him to—a football camp in Denver, the Fessenden School—his middle school in Boston—and from a summer camp in Upstate New York. He also mentioned a new female friend.

Limbo—the place of sighing; not hellish, but definitely not heaven. I hadn't heard from him and wanted out of the Charles limbo. I turned my energies elsewhere, especially toward several new friends in my apartment building. So many interesting, successful, and even some famous people resided there. I occasionally used the gym in the building if I didn't feel like going out. One day, a man in a Michigan T-shirt struck up a conversation about Charlevoix and where he'd lived. He was the CFO of the Getty Trust, so I asked if he knew my investment friends in Boston and elsewhere. We had several friends and acquaintances in common. He wondered how I knew so many movers and shakers, and my answer led him to offer a brilliant idea—usually my bailiwick. In one short hour, this stranger had given me direction as to how I could better frame and package my consulting business.

With a new website, logo, and coordinated business cards and stationery, I sent an introductory letter to hundreds of my associates and clients. Within a week, there was a response. I'd just finished a two-week assessment for a client, when a call came from a high-profile man who had a visionary concept that could make history. He needed a middle person to bring some of the parties together to accomplish it, and I had access to the people he needed. I always found it interesting that people so successful felt uncomfortable making calls to strangers, when anyone would be honored and excited to meet them.

The meetings required a trip or two to Washington, D.C., and I was excited about it, as Thanksgiving approached. I phoned a friend, Bob, who lived in that area to see if he'd like to have dinner while I was there. Bob was the CEO of a national men's clothing company and wintered in Palm Beach. We had mutual friends and had seen one another at Ocean Reef from time to time. Bob and I had been set up on a blind date years back, and we weren't a good match, but I'd introduced him to a few women I thought he might like—none of whom clicked. Sometimes Bob would call just to talk when he was lonely, and I especially loved his remarkable business sense—he'd been named in Forbes magazine numerous times as a top-performing CEO.

Bob contacted me via text, "I'm not in D.C., but I have a friend named Ed who lives in Maryland. I think you two would hit it off."

He talked up Ed. The man had expanded his father's small local business into a national success, and was a prominent philanthropist.

"I've heard stories about Ed from mutual friends at Ocean Reef."

"I think he's a great guy," Bob said, "but he's just come off a one-year error-in-judgment marriage—all of us told him not to do it. Anyway, he'd welcome an evening with a gorgeous woman."

I trusted Bob's judgment. "Why not? Give him my phone number."

Ed phoned the next day, and the conversation flowed naturally between us for more than an hour; when I mentioned my upcoming business meeting in Washington, he was eager to set a time and place to meet. He was straightforward, assertive, and open about his feelings of embarrassment after his recent divorce. Clearly, he hadn't given up on love. I looked forward to our upcoming date.

So my head and heart were in a good place a few days later when I ran into Charles at the gym. There'd been some progress on his initiative. He talked about how it was developing, but he was concerned over its capacity to be successful. My idea bubbled up out of the visions I'd already mulled over and researched. I shared my thoughts with him in a general, conservative way, and he said he'd like to discuss the concepts further.

"Great," I said, thinking, *What, over email?*
"Are you dating anyone?" he asked.
The question always perplexed me. "I've met someone interesting that I like," I said.
"Where does he live?" he probed.
"D.C." I said.
"Well, that's too far," he responded.
"Too far from what? I can be anywhere."
His friendly tone changed. "Well, I'll be in touch about your idea."
I sensed that I shouldn't hold my breath. Fortunately, I was excited about the trip to D.C.

Ed arrived at the hotel where I was staying in Baltimore and met me at the lobby café. We'd spoken so often by phone, I felt as though I knew him already. I assumed he was the same age as his friends who were around sixty, but he was tall, with a broad, slender build, and very fit-looking, almost in a scary kind of way—more like a thirty-year-old that worked out daily. His eyes were cobalt blue, and there was instant chemistry. The day went into night, as we talked nonstop for hours. I had been on at least a dozen dates over the last few months since hiring a matchmaker, but no one grabbed my attention the way Ed did. He was smart, accomplished, conservative, family-oriented, extremely successful, and engaging. He kissed me goodnight tenderly, and I was definitely attracted to him. After my meetings the following day, I changed my flight in order to spend more time with him. We strolled around Annapolis, holding hands romantically, and had a wonderful lunch before he took me to the airport. I thought about our time together, and the passionate goodbye kiss we shared, on the flight back to Los Angeles. Wasn't this how love was supposed to begin?

I finally checked my messages. Charles had called, but I waited to return it until the day after I got back.

"So," he said, "let's hear about this idea of yours. Over breakfast?"

"Actually …" Was he thinking this was an actual date? Or are we two casual friends chitchatting about business? I had a business proposal for him. I did not want be another name added to the long list of women he'd dated, especially not when I wanted to be taken seriously as a professional. Just hearing his voice, though, tempted me. "I think your office would work better." My tone was firm.

He sounded reluctant, but he agreed.

Charles' office was understated, and his assistant was very nice, as she led me in to wait for him. I was looking at the framed photos of his family on the credenza when I felt the warmth of his body very close behind mine. He reached around me to point out a particular picture, one that clearly showed him in a private plane with his grandchildren, but he stayed close. Chills skittered up my spine and then back down again.

Did I turn to him then and gaze into his eyes? Subtly shift my weight in an inevitable gravitation toward whatever primal tension might connect us? Break through all my fears and just give the guy a chance?

Hah! No, no, no. Oh, no. I assumed he was trying to impress me, and that was *A Terrible Thing* because the outer trimmings were not what lured me to him, but the integrity he exemplified, and the dedicated father he was. Right? Of course it was. I could smell him, and felt a little light-headed. I gritted my teeth and willed myself not to shiver at the thrill of standing so close to him.

I still hadn't dared to take my eyes off the photos. "You have a wonderful family, Charles," I said, and then made my way to the sitting area in his office.

I was safe, pride intact, dignity staunchly defended. It never occurred to me that he might feel utterly dejected about my failure to respond to him in any womanly way whatsoever. I say *might* because I'll never really know. I'll never know if I nicked his ego to the extent that he turned offensive—or if he was actually simply offensive.

As I sat facing him, I got a good look at him for the first time that morning. He looked disheveled.

"I had a *late* night with friends and …" He named a famous female journalist. "You've heard of her, right?"

"What? Knowing we had our meeting, you're hung over and not on your toes? Am I wasting my time here?" I was disgusted and couldn't keep the sneer out of my voice.

"No! I only need a few hours sleep. I'm fine."

At that point, his assistant patched in a call on speakerphone from another famous friend, a film producer who obviously had been out with them the night before. Charles definitely wanted me to hear of his nocturnal escapades.

"I could only get a cheek kiss from her whenever I aimed for her lips!" He laughed heartily along with the voice on the speakerphone.

I wanted to throw up. What was he, twelve?

I'd probably gone a bit pale with shock, but I refused to break my composure. He got off the phone, and I became brisk. "Charles, about your legacy initiative. … I'm excited about ultimately growing it into a national program. …"

"National? We aren't even established regionally yet. I go slow, Ellen. Baby steps. …"

"Okay, okay. I'll chill, but stay open to the possibility."

"So, how was your weekend with … Ed?" seemingly trying to avoid my idea.

I told him about Ed, and he picked up a pencil as I spoke, fidgeted with it, and snapped it in two, and then did the same thing again.

"I'd much rather talk about my ideas. ..." I started talking and spoke for about three minutes.

"Okay," he said, holding up his hand in a gesture that meant *enough*. "This is very detailed. Leave it with me; I'll look it over. I've got another appointment."

I was dismissed.

As I drove away, I wondered why he'd scheduled a meeting in the first place. Charles was a complicated man, and he acted like a very confused person. Thank goodness I could speak with Ed every day, and wasn't waiting for him to make a move.

Thanksgiving in Vail was wonderful with Jane and Brit, and I arranged for portable oxygen for Dad, so he came and had no trouble with the altitude. He was still a great cook, and we roasted a beautiful bird and cooked fancy fixings. When the email signal pinged on my computer, all three teased that it must be Cyber Guy.

"I guess it's time to tell you who Cyber Guy is." I looked at Jane. "It's Charles."

Jane's mouth dropped, and she looked distraught. Brit's laughter came close to braying. Dad whistled.

"Mom!" Jane exclaimed in the same tone one might use to announce that the house was on fire.

"Honey, don't worry. Charles will keep his connection with you separate from me," I said.

"You better make sure of that! You email him and ask to be sure. For my sake! I need him, Mom!"

I calmed her, though I was feeling less and less confident about my ability to find the delicate balance in what bound me to Charles. Though we'd been emailing for two years, I felt the weight of all the things that could go wrong. Forecast: disaster potential—moderate to high.

24

➤ The Brain that Flew too High

In Washington, D.C., I finished my last set of meetings for my current project, and Ed was about to pick me up at my hotel. Excited, I wore a classic wrap dress, stiletto boots, and my sheared black mink to fend off the winter frost coating everything in the capital. Ed arrived, standing tall and elegant in his navy cashmere coat.

"Wow," he said, and immediately pulled me into his arms, kissing me passionately.

I loved it, and I needed the affection more than he could imagine.

We drove a scant hour to Baltimore, and Ed showed me the sites of some of his philanthropy in action, which greatly impressed me and underscored the compatibility of our values and political views. We drove up the driveway of his beautiful estate on several acres of waterfront to a stately brick colonial mansion that included three guest homes and staff quarters off the pool and above the six-car garage. Inside, I was amazed at how close our taste was in design, right down to the Dutch seventeenth-century art. I had reserved a hotel room nearby for the night, but after seeing his seven guest suites, I felt comfortable enough staying there with him. I went into his gourmet kitchen to ask the housekeeper for a cup of coffee where a large tin of dark chocolate on the center island tempted me. I liked him more by the minute.

We went out for a lovely dinner that evening and returned to a crackling fire. We cuddled, kissed, and talked until we had to retire in order to be up early. Ed was speaking on an entrepreneurial panel at a local university in the morning. He asked me to join him, but I wanted to get in a workout and take things at a slow pace with him. He understood and showed me his exercise room on the lower level of his home, which was larger than my commercial gym in Santa Monica. No wonder he was so fit.

We went out for lunch before he took me to the airport for my return to Vail to prepare the house for Christmas.

"When can I see you again?"

"Maybe in Vail right after New Year's? You're coming out to your place in Aspen, right?"

"I don't think I can wait that long," he said.

I was happy he liked the Rocky Mountains as much as I did, and I looked forward to seeing more of him. In many ways, he was a dream come true; though Ed had children, I could tell they weren't the priority mine were to me. I sensed there was something missing between us that kept me from wanting to rush into anything. Still, I'd be a fool not to pursue the relationship.

I was back in Vail when Charles called.

"Ellen, I want to have you on a conference call with a member of the board for my program," he said.

Hooray, things were finally starting to move.

I knew this board member's wife from my women's support group in Boston, but didn't want to break that anonymity.

"I'd prefer to speak with him alone first. You trust me, don't you?" I asked.

"I don't understand why you won't allow a proper introduction by me, but if that's what you want, then go ahead and make the call yourself," he said.

I was very pleased that he was confident in my abilities to the point of allowing me to fly solo with such an important man.

"Report back to me," Charles said.

I quickly prepared for the afternoon call. Upon realizing I had more than two decades of recovery, there was immediate camaraderie, and we got several balls rolling, which I relayed to Charles the next day.

"This sounds good, Ellen," Charles said. "Would you be willing to share your ideas with the director of the foundation?"

We discussed and agreed on my trip to Boston to meet with her on December twenty-ninth.

I formulated the specifics of the fundraising, which spelled out how to raise three times the amount they had pledged to fund the program in half the time. As usual, once I carried an idea into planning and execution, I was focused and determined. The strategy cited twenty-five specific companies and their CEOs with a marketing plan for participation from each.

I'd already phoned several of my venture-capital contacts, knowing they had funded some of the companies listed in the plan, which meant they held a seat on each company's board. There were other contacts in Boston who could make introductions for me to meet the corporate heads also listed on the plan as participants. The response was very positive with willingness beyond my expectations.

Knowing Charles went at a slow, methodical pace, I decided to wait on sharing how far I'd gone with the preliminary commitments. He believed in under-promising and over-delivering. I didn't want to overwhelm him by being ten steps ahead, but there was no way I would present a plan in writing what I wasn't absolutely certain I could execute.

The long-standing business contacts I reached out to knew my word was my bond. They let me know they liked my high, positive energy—plus, I promised I'd host a dinner party where each could meet Charles and his partner. They were admired in Boston, and even these very successful and wealthy businessmen were eager to make their acquaintance, so that was part of the bait. Once the New England CEOs of the national companies were on board, I had further ideas on how to take the project nationally. For the time being, I would keep that to myself. I didn't want to push slower-than-molasses Charles over the edge. I knew my pace was too fast for him, on all fronts.

I jetted back to Vail for Christmas, joining my children who were already there. Somehow I'd managed to complete the business plan, making follow-up calls in between decorating the house, shopping, and baking my annual Christmas cookies. I function well with a full plate. I was thrilled it was Christmastime with Jane and Brit; I had a project ahead I was excited about, and a possible romance to boot. Life was good, but I didn't know how quickly all that could change.

Charles emailed from Cabo, where he was with his children for their yearly Christmas trip. His email reminded me why I love Jewish men:

"Roses are reddish, Violets are Bluish.
If it wasn't for Jesus, We'd all be Jewish!"

He was funny, and also a committed father and grandfather—liking to keep up on family was something we had in common. We each played Scrabble when we were with our children, too. He was the only single father I knew who held similar values and put his children first as I did. He and Dad were the only men with whom I shared what mattered to me the most in life: Jane and Brit.

Before Christmas, Charles phoned me to discuss my upcoming meetings in Boston with the director and vice-president of the foundation, to cover the parameters in order to prevent conflict of interest. Despite the Christmas rush, I finally connected with the director to confirm our meeting.

"I can't confirm now," she said coldly. "You may phone me on the scheduled day."

Excuse me? It was as though she didn't realize I was flying in from Colorado for the sole purpose of meeting with her. "Charles requested that we meet in person," I pointed out.

"Oh! I'm so sorry," she replied. "I will, of course, be meeting with you. See you at … 10:30?"

The call ended. I found it strange that this woman wasn't aware of the nature of our meeting, and had sounded quite aloof at first. I emailed Charles who brushed it off as simply her personality. He wasn't a man who liked to be questioned. I had a strange gut feeling then that something wasn't quite right.

I tried to let it go and simply enjoy our fantastic Christmas in Vail. We Three attended our traditional Christmas-Eve Mass and enjoyed a formal dinner. Christmas Day we remained in our pajamas all day, and loved the thoughtful gifts, good homemade food, Scrabble, and conversation. We called family and friends to say Merry Christmas, but I was relieved the three of us were enjoying peaceful and loving holidays. Ron phoned to say hello and said he missed me, but I was far more excited about Ed's call. I'd soon see him in New York after the Boston meetings. Jane and Brit had plans with friends and were quite happy to be staying in Vail while I was gone.

It was bitter cold in Boston the last week in December. I landed late in the afternoon, and it was almost dark, but I warmed up over dinner and coffee with a couple of friends. The next day, I met with the director. She'd been running the foundation for seven years and had pledged to raise a figure I thought was much too low for the project. My ideas for tripling the amount must have seemed like a direct threat to her.

"Well, it's nice that Charles has friends with fun ideas," she said. "But I really don't think anyone could actually deliver …"

She was clearly intimidated by me.

"Excuse me," I said, "I'm an independent consultant."

Her face dropped. This woman still had received no prior information about what Charles was planning through my participation. I backed off, gathering only the information I needed. We ended the meeting by her saying, "Let's stay in touch."

It was later that I learned the Board of Directors of the Foundation was required to vote on the hiring of any outside parties. No wonder she was a bit aloof with me then.

The shuttle from Boston to New York was on time, and Ed was waiting for me when I entered the lobby of the Pierre Hotel. He'd come by private jet an hour earlier, and had red roses in hand for me. Business was the last thing on my mind.

Charles had been emailing several times, but I told him I had a date in New York, and would be unavailable for a few days, and I'd get back to him to report about my Boston meetings.

Ed threw his arms around me and had the bellman take my bag to our magnificent two-bedroom suite overlooking Central Park. He gave me a lovely bracelet by a designer I liked, and I wished I could have reciprocated. I thanked him with a kiss. We bundled up and strolled hand-in-hand down Fifth Avenue to see the marvelous windows, famous for their decorations. The holiday season in New York is dazzling, and Ed's attention on top of that left me a bit breathless. He was a man with whom I felt safe, and I especially liked his strong attraction toward me.

We dined that evening at Cipriani, and I wore a beautiful red dress, which Ed loved on me. Over dinner, he wanted to know all about my meetings in Boston and asked questions about the business plan and the project. He couldn't have missed my excitement as I answered him. He was smart, and I'd enjoyed the range of topics we discussed, until he remarked on my work.

"I don't understand why you would get involved with something like that. You'd be much better off as a helpmate to a successful businessman like me and put your energy into entertaining and philanthropy."

I blinked at him a few times, stunned.

"Your brain flies too high for me," he added.

I think I went a little numb. The evening had been so beautiful up to that point, so I didn't want to simply back off over two comments made without any intention of hurting me. We returned to our hotel suite, but my interest in anything physical had plummeted. Ed began to kiss me, and I put the brakes on.

Reflecting on my experiences personally and professionally with highly successful men, I wasn't really surprised. Most of these brilliant men were concept guys, who hired others, like me as their visionaries. Maybe I just wasn't suited for this type of man. Would there ever be a mate for me who was mentally engaging yet not intimidated by my "high-flying brain"; a man who could see past my assertive survival mode to the vulnerable woman inside? Was alone to be my lot in life?

When I returned to Vail, there was another email from Charles, wanting to know about the meetings—and inquiring about *my date* in New York. He mentioned that he was in Boston, playing in a hockey game fundraiser event for the foundation. I would have loved to watch him participate, but I wasn't invited, even though he knew I'd be in town just a day before he arrived. I supposed it was a waste of time anymore to try to figure out Charles. That would be the same as trying to figure out why Dad acted the way he did all those years.

Thinking of him, I called Dad. After listening to me whine, he straightened me out.

"Just get over it, Ellen, and think like a man! You love the project. Work it for the work for God's sake, and forget about this guy beyond that!"

He was right, but I was still emotionally vulnerable with regards to this man, and I hated that even worse.

I was taking Jane to Cabo the next day and looked forward to being in a bathing suit after freezing in Colorado and Boston. Jane liked going back to school with a tan. Cabo was becoming a yearly tradition because of Charles' initial suggestion, but I would not be thinking of him on this trip. I planned on enjoying my time alone with my daughter, and we had a great time together.

When we returned to L.A., I found out that Charles was not accustomed to being ignored. He had left several voice messages on my cell phone that was off, and emails, too. I called Charles, who was aggravated that I hadn't made him a priority, because he wanted to meet about my ideas for his project. I agreed to meet the next day at his office.

The following morning, I walked into the main reception, and because there was no one there, I headed toward Charles' assistant's office, which was adjacent to his. Charles stepped into the doorway to his office, and when he saw me, moved toward me to greet me with a hug. Unfortunately, my head was nowhere near being on straight. I was even more upset over the Boston incident than I knew. I just reacted—I extended my hand to shake his. That would have been bad enough, but I had to top it off with sarcasm.

"I'm not sure you deserve a hug."

His assistant had to have overheard, and by the look on Charles's face, I knew I had made a big mistake and humiliated him.

"Wait in my office, and I'll be right there."

I sat on the couch and was a nervous wreck.

When he came in, he closed the door behind him, and simply said, in a very curt tone, "Well?"

"Charles, I think we should discuss our personal relationship to avoid any confusion with the project because …"

"There's no confusion here. I don't know what you are talking about." His tone was curt and almost mean. "What happened with the guy in New York? Did you break his heart?"

What did that have to do with anything?

I brushed off the question, and he opened the door. The remainder of the meeting was a waste of time. Charles didn't want to discuss the plan I had put together and was obviously upset. When I left, I knew things were not good, I just didn't know how bad I had made them.

25

➤ Loss

That night, I had dinner with a dear friend, Kate, who was in town from Boston. When I got back to my apartment, I decided to call Charles to apologize. It was late at night, and he answered immediately.

"Charles, I know how inappropriate my comment was. I was wrong, and am very sorry."

"Okay, it's fine," he said, "but I need to get back to another call."

The next week, I was finishing the final details on the business plan for the project and the foundation and had several conversations with Charles on the phone. We decided I would have the initial meetings with the foundation, which would commence the first week in April. I set up appointments to meet with several of the staff members, along with Charles in Boston that week. I also arranged appointments to meet with the CEOs of the companies in New England I had targeted to sign on, as the point person between them and the foundation.

Given that I would be back and forth between Boston and California, I would need to move to a less-expensive place in Santa Monica and find a place to rent in Boston. Jane was returning to Boston that summer to intern again at the broadcasting company, so we'd need an apartment there anyway. Brit was finishing his last summer in caddy training in Vail. I was able to find an apartment over the phone with a real-estate agent in Boston at the Ritz

Carlton where I belonged to the gym. Having no other projects in the works, I needed to earn income and we agreed verbally that I would take the standard percentage of capital raised. It would be some months before my efforts would generate monies, but I knew the front-end cash outlay was an investment worth making for my housing and to get a vehicle transported to Boston. It would pay off in the end.

During my daily call to my dad on January thirty-first, I was filling him in on all of the exciting details of my new work ahead, and being bi-coastal again.

"I'm really happy for you, Ellen, and proud ... but I have some bad news."

The dread in his voice told me I didn't want to hear what I knew was coming.

"I've come out of remission," he said, "and the doctor said I have an option of daily shots that might give me six months ... otherwise, my time left is quite limited."

"Oh, Dad. ... This is terrible. You will definitely try the shot plan, though, right?"

"I don't want to make daily trips to the hospital, honey, and the side effects are pretty horrific."

"Dad, you've been independent: driving, attending support meetings, cooking, and seeing friends. ... Why wouldn't you want to do this?"

I eventually spoke with his doctor, and was able to talk Dad into trying the shot treatments. I phoned him daily all week while I proceeded with planning my work in Boston.

Six days later, before I could make my daily call, Dad called me.

"I'm not taking any more shots, Ellen. They make me feel horrible. It's time to let the creator take over."

I teared up and couldn't talk.

"I don't want to have a poor quality of life, no matter how much time I have left."

"Okay, Dad. ..." I said finally. I didn't know what else to say, but I knew I needed to respect his choices about his own life.

When I checked in with him the following morning, a nurse answered the phone. Apparently, Dad had fallen during the night, and he was being moved to an extended hospice-care facility. I phoned the airlines, as well as my brother Tommy. He went directly to Dad's place, and my flight would arrive by dinnertime. That was February fifth, 2010, only six days since he said he was out of remission, and I was in shock to find myself en route to Rochester, New York.

Although Janet was six years older, and Tommy was close to Dad, I seemed to be the camp director in the family. Each of us had separate relationships with him. I'd had to work through so many issues that my brother and sister didn't have to work through, but as a result he'd been a best friend to me over the past sixteen-and-a-half years since finding out the truth. Maybe that happened because we were no longer imposed upon one another. He would confide in me in a way that he couldn't with his own children, and he had depended on me for support since Mom divorced him.

I arrived in time to follow the ambulance that insurance required transport Dad to the hospice center. Dad was admitted to critical care, which had a maximum stay of one week. We'd discuss an alternative facility with the social worker on Monday. After he was settled, I left and checked into my hotel to get some sleep. The next day, I arrived to be with Dad in the morning.

As I entered his room, he said, "Hey, Ellen Melon ..."

"You are kidding me, right? You want one of your last memories to be of me whacking you?" I chuckled, leaning over to kiss his frail, vulnerable face.

We prayed together and read from his spiritual-recovery book.

He turned to me, quite seriously. "I want to share some things with you, Ellen," he said. "First of all, I'm not going to last a week, so don't worry about arranging moving me to extended care. Can you get flights for Jane and Brit to come say goodbye?"

I was stunned, wanting to fight the inevitable.

"If I lose my faculties, please don't allow Tommy or Janet to witness that. I want to go out with dignity. Promise me," he said.

"I promise."

And then he asked, "Would you be willing to stay in the pull-out bed here if I lose consciousness? ... I don't want to die alone."

"Oh, Dad. Yes, of course," I said.

He smiled then and thanked me for all of the marvelous travel we had shared, the way I had provided for him, and he praised me as a mother and said how remarkable Jane and Brit had turned out. He told me he found me to be remarkable. My eyes welled up.

"Here's the main thing, Ellen. Once I'm gone, you get on with your life. What you had to endure because of your mother's affair was not your fault. You should leave Rochester and never look back."

My chin began to quiver but I forced myself to remain stoic as I nodded and held his hand. When the nurse came, I stepped out.

I went out to the family lounge to arrange flights for my children, took one deep breath, and sobbed. He had been the only person I had in my life to go to, and I couldn't bear the thought of my life without him at the other end of the phone every day. I began to feel really scared and very, very alone.

Janet and Tommy came and went over the next few days, as Dad was slipping rapidly. The family lounge offered an area where I could talk with privacy. I kept my scheduled phone calls with Charles and the president of the foundation, so I'd have a focus outside of losing Dad. The entire situation felt surreal. No one prepares you for losing a parent, especially when he's your best friend too. I was scared and lonely, wishing I had someone to be there for me.

By Sunday, Dad told me it was time to bring my things to stay with him.

"I'm scared, Ellen," he said.

From that point on, I stayed with him. Janet and Tommy came and debated what kind of service he should have.

When they left, Dad joked, "You should leave as soon as possible, so you don't get stuck with the whole bill for whatever they come up with."

I shot right back at him, "Hey Dad, by the way, can I have that Kindle I just gave you for Christmas?"

He laughed, saying, "Giver-taker!"

Monday night, Dad was in extreme pain and couldn't speak very well. His body trembled.

"Do you want me to hold you?"

He nodded yes, and I climbed onto the bed next to him. I held him tight for hours, as he continued to have mini strokes throughout the night.

Jane and Brit arrived Tuesday evening. Dad was on the maximum morphine allowed and was just coherent enough to nod and even grin at them. After that, he never spoke again, but he held on as everyone stayed with him.

Friday, February twelfth, was Jane's twentieth birthday. Dad took his last breath with my children and me by his side, holding his hands. I was relieved he didn't have to suffer and that we were able to say goodbye—goodbye to my friend, my dad who was not my father, and goodbye to all the past he represented that kept me from claiming my own identity.

It had only been twelve days since the call when Dad said he was out of remission, but to me, it felt like a lifetime. Brit seemed to retreat inside of himself, and I was worried about him. Jane was very verbal, and spoke to our counselor Sarah by phone during the week for support. This was a first experience at death for Jane and Brit, and my dad was their "Papas," the only male role model they ever knew. I thought the sooner they returned to their routines at college, the better off they'd be, and I intended to fly back with Jane.

My sister and brother couldn't agree on when or how to have a service for Dad, but he had wanted to be cremated. All the dysfunctional dynamics were loud and clear between us. I ordered a large flower arrangement for the Mass, went to see my mother and Pete, and left for the airport with Jane and Brit. I hoped to never return. While I'd forgiven my mother, I no longer felt a part of the family. Dad's passing represented a time to close the book on what had been a lifetime of defending my existence.

After getting Jane back to school, I found an apartment a few blocks away from my luxury place on the ocean that was one-third of the expense. I hated leaving that building because I'd made so many friends, but I couldn't afford to stay there and have a place to live while working in Boston, too. I was totally focused on succeeding with the project, and for Charles as well, which meant another few years of bi-coastal living.

Charles and I had one more meeting in early March at his office. He barely mentioned my dad's passing, but he was turning sixty in a month and was a bit freaked out about it. Maybe that was preoccupying him. I teased him about needing Ginkgo Biloba and suggested a visit to the chiropractor with me in Boston. Surprisingly, he agreed to both. He gave me some additional names to call at the foundation in Boston, but once again, it was awkward, and I wasn't sure why he'd called a meeting by the time it ended.

When I got back to my apartment, I made the calls immediately. I was moving the next day and wanted to tie up all loose ends. I think I was in perpetual motion to avoid facing the pain of Dad's passing.

When I called the foundation, I reached the assistant of the executive with whom I needed to set up an appointment. She had expected my call, and after we did our scheduling, she wanted to put me in touch with the partner's wife.

"She's planning a surprise party for Charles's birthday, and you should be there."

"Oh, thank you, that's a nice offer, but I'll get in touch with her myself."

How nice to be included, I thought; however, I wondered to what extent Charles had shared that he was hiring me as a consultant. The partner's new wife was also on the board of the foundation, and so this point was important. My involvement needed to be announced by Charles. Unfortunately, I couldn't be in Boston for the date when his party was planned.

I had an idea. I decided to send a private message via Facebook to the partner's wife who was planning the party, since we were both a "friend" of Charles on the site. I would offer to send a funny poem with inside jokes. She replied immediately, and I explained that I had been in his office the day before and had known him since my children attended schools in Boston, and that I had done some work for him. There was a gracious interchange back and forth, and we left it that she would look forward to meeting me and receiving the poem that she would deliver at his party.

The next day, while I was in the middle of moving, Charles phoned, and without even a hello asked, "Why on earth would you email my partner's wife?" his voice just below a shout. "You've never even met her!"

I winced. The wife must have phoned his assistant in L.A., asking who I was.

"Why would you do something so *inappropriate*?" he roared. "This is a personal violation!"

He obviously knew nothing of the surprise party. "Now you've put me in a position of having to explain who you *are*!" he shouted and ended the call.

I was aghast. A knife had pierced my heart. Of all the things he said, *putting him in the position of having to explain who I was* seemed to be my worst offense. That remark cut deepest. I was the inexplicable one, the one who shouldn't be there, the one who had no right to approach those who belonged. Charles saw me as illegitimate.

I felt I'd been reduced to my childhood horrors of being the outcast, the one who represented a hidden truth that must not be told. I felt the stabbing pain of my origin all over again and felt helpless to pull out the knife.

A few hours later, he sent an email: "I am pulling the plug on your participation in my project."

26

➤ Happy Birthday, Dear Char-les...

For me it was an emotional mugging, first a skewer to the heart, and then a blade rammed into the gut. I reeled and went straight into shock, but I forced myself to continue reading.

"I can't possibly have you representing me if you have no concept of what is appropriate," his email said.

Final blow: a twist of the blade.

I couldn't believe what I was reading. The man who routinely asked me about my love life during business meetings thought I was the one who didn't know how to be professional and appropriate.

I refused to be discounted like this via email. I replied, insisting he call me by the end of the day. I was so upset it was hard to complete my move to the new place. I understood it sounded questionable that I would use Facebook to contact his partner's wife, but he had no idea about the surprise party, and I wouldn't think of ruining it for him. Certainly, he must have known I knew how to exercise prudence.

At 6:30 that night, he phoned. "You tell me why you would need to email my partner's wife," he yelled.

"I was trying to arrange something for your birthday as a surprise," I said.

"You know both of my assistants for God's sake!" His voice crackled with outrage. "Why wouldn't you contact one of them? Why my partner's wife, whom you have never met?"

Quick on my feet, I replied, "I wanted to have a sign reading

'Happy Birthday' flown overhead during the outdoor concert playing on your birthday. I knew your partner or his wife were the people to arrange the air space."

There was a dead silence, followed by Charles yelling, "If you think I'd want thirty-seven thousand people to know I am turning sixty, then you really don't know me at all!" and he hung up.

I tried to reach out to him again but knew until the actual party took place, there was no point. It would be a long five-week wait until the date came and went to be able to tell him the truth. I was heartbroken and had no idea what to do. I always seemed to know what to do, until now. Between Dad's death and this, I was in shock.

I stared at all the boxes around me in the tiny apartment that in no way resembled home as had the luxury building on Ocean Avenue. That place was like living in a luxury adult coed fraternity with wonderful camaraderie. If I were there now, I'd go down to the private lounge and recharge with a latte from our Starbucks machine and possibly run into someone I know or work out my frustrations at the private fitness center. I'd felt so safe there because tenants could only access the floor on which they resided or the rooftop pool and common areas. The twenty-four-hour concierge would greet me by name each time I returned home, and I felt protected and not so alone.

I eventually got the little apartment sufficiently squared away, and then lay awake all night in a strange new bed, mulling over and stewing about what had happened. I'd have to explain to all my Boston friends that I would not be back there for business, and this alone was bitter. Far worse, I'd have to contact all the participants in the plan to explain that everything was cancelled. What would this do to my professional reputation? And of course, there was also the income source I was relying on that now wouldn't be coming in.

My sweet Jane. She was looking forward to returning to Boston as a second-year intern. Internships were hard to come by and an important part of the college résumé. March was too late in the year to find another internship because most students had started looking and interviewing in the fall. I couldn't afford to house her there if I wasn't earning what I had expected.

I couldn't turn off my high-flying brain, so it was a relief to get up early and pack my clothes.

On average, I rarely went five days without a trip to the airport. This time, I headed for Florida to meet Jane and Brit for the remainder of their spring break. I was grateful for a seat in the first-class cabin to try to get some sleep on the flight from Los Angeles to Fort Lauderdale. But as the plane took off, the reality of the events over the past twenty-four hours hit me all over again. I sobbed uncontrollably. It felt like my whole world had fallen apart.

"You really don't know me at all. ..." Charles had said. Did he actually think I was capable of any malice toward him? I could have blown the whistle on the birthday party to protect myself, but I couldn't be that self-centered. After all, this was his sixtieth-birthday surprise. I tried to hang onto my faith, believing that everything happened for a reason. I prayed and looked forward to having a two-hour therapy session with Sarah in the morning.

When I landed, I headed straight to Boca Raton, and slept well that night at the hotel near Sarah's office. The next morning, Sarah stooped a little to embrace me. She was tall and lean with short, simply-styled blonde hair. She wore no makeup, with a natural, classic elegance. She was highly academic and had been in family practice for more than two decades. I respected and had come to love her. It was so good to see her.

"You look dreadful," she said, "very stressed out." Sarah was always honest with me and able to ask questions that helped me come to my own conclusions.

As we went over how I had come to work with Charles and the details of the business plan, I had a revelation. I hadn't been committed to the cause so much as I was supporting what mattered to the man. My commitment was to him, so much so that I hadn't protected myself with a written contract outlining my compensation. I was acting totally out of character.

"Oh, my God, Sarah," I said. "Much as I didn't want to face it, I've been in love with Charles all along."

"Even though you were aware that his emails and infrequent encounters were a rerun of the random positive reinforcement you experienced throughout your childhood."

I nodded. "Yeah, I knew I was getting the same old mixed messages, so I didn't want to love him. I guess I'm stuck in a cycle that is both familiar and unhealthy for me."

"Awareness is the start of the willingness to change," she said.

Right. I had some work to do on myself. …

I left Sarah's office with some relief, and looked forward to seeing Jane play lacrosse, as I drove north to West Palm Beach. Oddly, Dad's death never came up, but I knew it would in the future. I longed to be able to call him right that minute and hear his take and calming reassurance that all would be well. I prayed instead.

I watched Jane compete in her tournaments, and then she came with me to pick up Brit in Miami. When Jane and I arrived at his dorm on the UM campus, I was taken aback to see that he'd shaved his head. He hadn't even begun to pack. Something was happening with him, but I didn't have the emotional energy to pursue finding out. I was blind to a serious situation that was right in front of me.

Even though I spent time with Jane and Brit in the sun and played golf, I was not emotionally present; I was hurting. How could Charles yank the carpet out from under me on a moment's notice? Did he have something to hide? What was he so afraid of?

I couldn't accept his abrupt and devastating reversals. A memory returned that I'd suppressed, that of our first coffee date when he admitted to "dumping his girlfriend of four years via an email." My ears had somehow gone deaf to that blatant message, only to have him do the same thing in business to me. So, why was I so surprised?

I questioned the capacity of his character, and my pain morphed into anger and then fury. I would bill him for what I'd initially offered freely out of my deep appreciation. To be certain of an appropriate fee, I reached the VP of a top marketing firm based in Boston, and described the proposal and follow-up I'd done.

"Your plan for a dozen companies to participate would be billable by us for six figures," said the company VP. "But you detailed a plan to implement, with twenty-five companies, so we're talking double that."

That was what I'd calculated. Instead of enjoying my son and daughter, I carried on email exchanges with Charles, asking for compensation—at least for the plan I had written. It wasn't pleasant communication by any means, and he essentially attempted to regain friendly footing, but had no intention of paying me for my time. What was I going to do now?

After taking Brit back to school, and getting Jane off to Los Angeles, I flew home to Vail. I wanted to be in the mountains where I could reflect, heal, and sleep in my own bed. I was happy to be in my home, but found myself crying daily. I phoned Sarah, who suggested I bring up my crying at my doctor's appointment. Full blood testing on me revealed hypothyroidism, which was known to cause depression. I thought it was Dad's death combined with the job loss. My doctor told me that after a few months on the synthetic hormones, I should begin to feel better. I looked forward to not crying daily or having to continually pretend to be happy.

I stayed in Vail for almost two weeks without going anyplace, and finally settled down enough to think about Brit. I knew I should fly back to Florida and figure out what was going on with him. I would certainly have the time given that I would not be in Boston for my scheduled meetings with various foundation staff members. Charles and I had stopped communicating, and his birthday party was still a long two weeks away. I had plenty of time to see Brit. So off I went. We hadn't had any time alone together since Dad had died; and losing his only male role model had affected my son more deeply than I'd realized.

Once at Ocean Reef, Brit and I had a nice dinner and retired early so we could golf in the morning. I couldn't call Dad anymore, and I sorely missed my late-night emails with Charles. I dreamed about him that night, and when I woke up, I sensed that I was on his mind, too. That had happened previously. Early the next morning, I stepped out to get coffee, and there was a hummingbird outside my door. I went back inside and wrote an e-note to Charles. I said I was very upset inside, and the entire situation was unfortunate. I asked if he was able to just push it under the rug, or was I on his mind, too? Within minutes of hitting send, my phone rang, and it was him. He wanted to know how I was and asked if we could talk when we were both back in Los Angeles. I agreed, and in spite of all that had happened, I was pleased to hear his voice.

Golfing with Brit was fun, but he seemed unusually withdrawn. Normally, he would be talkative on the course, but that was not the case that particular day. He wasn't even teasing me about my swing either. I encouraged him to talk about losing his grandfather, but he refused. I finally told him that the Boston job had fallen through, and the wall around him collapsed. He immediately became concerned and protective of me, which I loved about him. I knew he really loved me, and also that he was troubled inside, not having the strength to address it. Yet I couldn't interrupt his studies to deal with things, I thought. I told myself he was going through a normal developmental stage for an eighteen-year old. I was saddened to leave him once we got back to UM.

I needed to get back to Los Angeles and be with my support group and friends. This ordeal had taken its toll on me. With the date of Charles' party approaching, I decided I would simply unload my side of the story and then be done with him.

Jane played her last home games and finished her second year of college. Thankfully, she was able to find an internship with a small production company in Los Angeles for the summer, as well as a part-time paying job at a children's store a friend of mine owned. I decided to commute between L.A. and Vail during June and July. Brit would be caddying there, and I wanted to be able to be with each of them, while also allowing them some freedom at nineteen- and twenty-years old. Being at home with a parent after living at college was not easy, and I knew it. Even though I had guided and protected them, I also knew to give them space to show that I believed in them, too.

The night Jane first stayed at the new condo was damp and raining. She didn't mind the four-block walk to the beach and said she'd be comfortable living there all summer. Although we had grown accustomed to temporary housing, the three of us seemed to be at home wherever we were, so long as we had each other; but the place was a far cry from Ocean Avenue. I was trying to practice acceptance.

The night of the party arrived, and I sent my email at midnight EST. By that time, the happy-birthday song would have been sung, the toasts toasted, the champagne imbibed. The guests were leaving. I'd composed it carefully, explaining why I'd called his partner's wife. I shared how hurt and insulted I was. I'm afraid I also was a bit psychologically analytical. Charles' response came through within minutes.

"Ellen, I apologize for any unnecessary harm I caused you, but

I stand by my decision to remove you from the project. It wouldn't be right to bring our personal confusion into a project that is in its infancy. But, I really don't appreciate, nor do I intend to address your extensive psychological assessment of me. I hope you can forgive me, and if my actions hurt you, again, I'm sorry."

This wasn't the sincere apology I'd hoped for. I felt used and discarded, even though it was my fault I hadn't insisted on a contract between us or told him the extent to which I'd lined up participants for the plan. I put the personalities before my principles, which is always a recipe for disaster.

As a spiritual person, I had to accept that this had all happened for a reason, but I couldn't ignore my heartache and disappointment. *Thrown under the bus* was the phrase that came to mind, but I had to focus on my responsibility in creating the situation and not carry resentment over it.

In addition, the loss of my dad was about to take me by storm when I'd least expected it.

27

➤ Losing Home

Out of embarrassment over losing the Boston project, I had stopped contacting most of my friends and colleagues there, and I wasn't responding to their emails questioning what had happened. I was known for always living up to my word, and I wanted the whole fiasco to just disappear, as though it hadn't happened. For the first time in my life, I couldn't face things. Since Dad had passed, I was finding it uncomfortable in the solitude I once cherished. I was lonely. Sudden tears still ambushed me, often at awkward times. So when Jane and Brit came to stay with me right after their college terms, I felt excited and happy. Being together with both of my children was just what I needed.

It was hard to believe Brit had finished his first year at architecture school. He was an excellent student and loved what he was studying. As soon as I saw Brit when he landed at LAX, however, I knew his moods hadn't improved from the time when we saw each other at Easter. In fact, things were far worse. The next several days were simply horrific with him. He was rude, unkind, and disrespectful. *How much more can I take*, I asked my angels. I wished I had Dad to turn to.

Brit's uncharacteristic behavior became so unbearable to both Jane and me that I got him a ticket and flew him home to Vail. I couldn't quite handle him at the time. He was turning nineteen, and while I loved him dearly, I was too fragile to help. I was scheduled to go to Vail in a few weeks anyway, and I'd deal with him then. Hopefully, I'd be stronger. Jane quickly settled into a routine with her production-company internship and part-time job, so I turned gratefully to the support of my recovery friends in L.A.

By the time I left for Vail, I felt real trepidation about being home with Brit, because his rudeness was foreign to me. He was my loving son who danced in the kitchen with me, wrote me poetry every year for gifts, and carried my grocery bags. I didn't know what was happening, and had no one but Sarah to talk to about it. I was scared. Originally, I'd been able to live nicely on my consulting work and the interest from my investments, but for the last few years, I'd been living off of my principal and on the seasonal rental income from the lock-off in-law apartment in Vail I had built for Dad. I felt that I would soon be hemorrhaging financially. Somehow, something would happen, and I had to have faith in that.

I looked forward to being in my own bed again. June in Colorado meant planting flowers, going on hikes, and seeing friends. I needed to get out in nature, hike on the mountain to clear my head, and find my joy again. Brit was out of the house early each morning. He was promised a car for graduation from high school but had decided to wait until he could have it on campus in Florida, so car shopping was on the agenda. I would need to figure out how to swing it financially. I spoke with Jane nightly, and she sounded content. At twenty, she was more than capable of being on her own, but I missed the last two weeks of being with her daily.

I decided to cook and bake, which I loved to do in my kitchen with the panoramic view of the Rocky Mountains. Daily the hummingbirds would arrive outside the window around the deck. I was making food in large quantities, so I could freeze meals for Brit to have during the periods when I'd be back in L.A. I wanted him to have my homemade food even if I wasn't there. I made spaghetti and meatballs, meat loaf, lasagna, chicken dishes, along with his favorite cookies and brownies. The first visit of two weeks went fairly well between us with only minor disagreements. He still didn't seem like himself, and he agreed to see a local psychologist while I was away.

I returned to Los Angeles. While I hadn't had any contact with Charles, I still continued to ponder and analyze all that had happened.

In one of my weekly phone sessions with Sarah, she assured me my sadness was normal for having lost my dad only three months earlier.

"And frankly," Sarah said, "I'm relieved that the contact with Charles has ceased. I strongly encourage you to let it remain that way."

"Intellectually, I know this," I said.

She rehashed the toxicity of people who employ random, positive reinforcements. "Falling for them is like getting hooked on gambling," she said. "You're waiting for the next positive results, and not noticing how much is being lost in the process."

"Wow," I said. That one really got to me.

"Ellen, you've been trying to 'grow' from this relationship for more than two years," Sarah observed, "but it's a pattern that is taking you down rather than facilitating your growth. You can now only grow by breaking the pattern."

I think I got it. Well, maybe.

During my next trip to Vail, I knew that Brit was in trouble. He looked high when he was home and had severe mood swings. I tried to discuss it with him, and he said he'd been depressed over losing his grandfather.

"I don't know how to handle it," he said, head down, not looking at me.

I didn't know how to handle it either. After the first session, the psychologist had prescribed antidepressants for him, and he scheduled an appointment weekly. His attitude and anger toward me didn't change, but I was relieved to see him getting help.

I wasn't getting any better, and tried to conceal my daily crying from both of my children. I felt numb and isolated. I had no drive or motivation. I was starting to feel hopeless, scared, and desperate to find a solution. I had been praying daily, but so far I couldn't seem to stop crying on my own.

The tenants in the in-law apartment notified me that they were moving out. There had been more than one incident where they'd lost sleep due to the disturbance from Brit and his friends he had visiting while I was with Jane in L.A. As professionals, they both were up early for work and couldn't tolerate the late-night noise. It was upsetting to have this as a result of my son being inconsiderate, and more evidence of how out-of-character he was being. We had agreed that while I was gone he would only have one friend over at a time. I relied on that rental income. Financially, with the job loss, I knew I wouldn't be able to maintain renting in Los Angeles on top of the massive expense of this wonderful home.

Confident Jane was just fine, I extended my stay in Vail and saw my primary physician. She suggested I start taking antidepressants right away. I was totally opposed, associating medication with someone not being able to handle life, or as a sign of weakness.

"You just lost your father," the doctor said. "This is the first year of empty-nest syndrome; you're processing another sudden loss of the job. It makes sense to give it a try."

I felt some shame about taking antidepressants, but crying every day was not what I wanted. I was not a depressive person, but hopelessness was setting in, and I needed to get myself and my life together. I started on the medication.

A few days later, a couple interested in renting our house contacted me. I was open to the idea of renting, given that friends referred them. This could be the break I'd been praying for, but my home kept me grounded. Without it to return to, I was afraid I'd feel homeless. It was my practice to pray and meditate on decisions prior to retiring at night. I pondered whether I was better off alone at the house in Vail working on writing, or in Los Angeles where I had developed a vast support system. I fell asleep with that question lingering.

My answer came the next morning, but not in any way I expected. I woke unusually early and proceeded down the stairs. An empty plastic freezer bag lay on the landing. I thought perhaps Brit had gotten home late and took some of my baked goods up to bed, accidentally dropping the wrappings. Then I noticed the front door was ajar, and I had a bad feeling in my gut.

I continued into the kitchen. It was totally ransacked. Some sort of animal must have been in the house. The hair lifted on my arms and neck, and I ran upstairs to wake Brit.

"Brit!" I shook his shoulder. "Hurry into my room!"

He followed, wide-eyed, but not quite awake. Frantically I locked the door behind us then phoned the police.

"The animal might still be in the house," the operator warned, "so stay put until an officer or ranger alerts you to come out."

Within five minutes, I could hear voices downstairs, and shortly thereafter, a yell.

"You can come down now!"

The ranger held a rifle and the police officer carried a gun.

The officer said, "A large bear broke in through the front door. The deadbolt wasn't locked, and the front door handle was easy to claw open for a hungry bear."

I didn't see many scratches on the wood door or on the refrigerator where he had come in to help himself. There were open food wrappings all over the floor, and shredded cheese scattered everywhere.

"You were lucky," the ranger said, "not to have property

damage. Seeking food, bears usually pull off the doors of appliances or cabinets."

There was no damage, just a mess to clean up. The officer called animal rescue to bring a cage to catch the bear.

"That was a six-foot cub, and it will be back within a day when hunger sets in."

After the officers left, Brit thoughtfully helped me without my asking.

"You know, I had just prayed for a sign about whether to stay in Vail at the house alone."

Brit smiled at me in his peaceful knowing way and hugged me. "I guess you got your answer, Mom. I'm so glad you weren't hurt in the process."

"The bear ate all of the food I made you," I said teary eyed.

Brit grinned, kissed my cheek, and responded, " Well, Wo-Man, chop-chop then! Get cooking and baking!"

Once again, I thanked God for this blessing of a boy. I saw a glimmer in that moment of his inner essence, something I hadn't seen in him since before Dad died. He was a tender soul, and I knew he loved me, but his behavior of late had been so erratic. There were mood swings that I assumed were part of his teenage years. I didn't want to believe he was capable of drifting into a marijuana addiction.

With mixed feelings about leaving the house I'd created for Jane and Brit to be their home—their place they could always return to—I agreed to lease the house for eighteen months starting in September. My Vail friends who had moved to other areas of the country were all able to keep their second homes in the mountains, and I was envious. I couldn't remember ever feeling this alone or scared. I attended my meetings in Colorado, but I didn't share on a deep level. I couldn't. Something had altered me, shutting me down, even though I'd finally begun to feel better on the antidepressants. I'd stopped crying daily, but being in the house with Brit was no longer comfortable. He discontinued the antidepressants, saying he felt worse on them. He'd be returning to Miami mid-August to get settled for his sophomore year, and it couldn't come fast enough for me. I was anxious to give Brit the space he needed and to move on to whatever would be next for me, which I hoped would mean doing some writing before packing up the house. The renters wanted the place unfurnished, so I'd take some furniture with me, especially my own bed. The remainder would be stored in the empty in-law apartment.

My luck changed a bit when I ran into a couple at the grocery store in Vail whom I hadn't seen in a year. They owned the local jewelry stores and were expanding. They were looking to increase their estate inventory.

"Do you have interest in selling any of your pieces Ellen?" they inquired, having seen me wear jewels at various fundraisers in Vail.

That made me think. As I drove home, I knew that my angels were pointing the way. Over the years, I'd collected family-estate jewelry that was worth a considerable amount of money. I'd never had the opportunity to wear most of the pieces, including an exquisite platinum Edwardian bracelet with a total diamond weight of twenty carats; a five-row choker necklace of small four-prong-set diamonds equaling thirty carats; a seventeenth-century emerald bracelet; a ruby-and-diamond set; and a Harry Winston diamond necklace from the 1930s. I phoned the owner of the store, and he agreed to come by the house the next day. It made me sad to let go of things I had planned to pass down to Jane, but it seemed like the smartest thing to do. I did keep a few items for both of my children and still generated a generous six figures by selling the rest. I was so grateful to have the assets to be able to sell. Now I could get a car for Brit.

We bought him an SUV, which he'd need because he'd be living off campus in Coral Gables. He packed it full, and the carrier picked it up a few days before Brit flew back to Miami. We did have a pleasant few days together. As we hugged goodbye at the airport, I teared up, concerned for this young man I loved so dearly, while watching him become a stranger before my very eyes. I was powerless and could only hope and pray he got through this time safely. If I had known then he had actually been feeling suicidal, I never would have sent him on his way.

I flew to Los Angeles, and as soon as I landed, I began to feel enthusiastic, thinking of finding a new place to fill with my own things, and having scheduled the movers to be in Vail the following week. I'd lived in turnkey rentals with other people's furniture for the past seven years. I was also looking forward to some time for day trips I'd planned with my sweet Jane. I found a wonderful three-bedroom condo in Brentwood on the second day and signed a lease. It was in a location where I could walk everywhere, and the building had a nice pool and secured underground parking. It had all been remodeled, and my things would fit nicely. I was excited for the first time in months.

Two days later, I didn't know what hit me.

The text came from Brit's girlfriend. "I am worried" was all it took for me to call her immediately. Brit had been inside his house with a roommate for days without seeing her or responding. I tried phoning and texting him without any response. I knew he was in trouble and phoned Sarah. She contacted a woman in Miami to assist. My adrenaline kicked in as I went online to book flights to Miami and texted Jane to pack a bag.

The only seats available on the redeye a few hours later were priced astronomically high. I wasn't letting Brit know we were coming, and Jane was a darling to join me. I missed not being able to turn to my dad, and would have felt really alone if she weren't with me. I was on automatic pilot in survival mode—something I had come to master.

We landed early on a Sunday morning. Although totally sleep deprived, we rented a car and went directly to his house. He was obviously stoned and had been partying hard. We got him into the car and checked him into a hotel and had him shower. I called the interventionist Sarah had scheduled and arranged to meet at her office. I was in a total fog. We arrived at 10:00 A.M. at her office, and the next time I looked at my watch it was 6:00 P.M. Confronting Brit and trying to break through his denial and defenses was excruciating. He was angry and mean, blaming me for everything imaginable. I knew I was looking at a stranger and not my son, although my heart was breaking. The hours ran into days.

I needed to hold it together. Somehow, I was wired to be pragmatic rather than emotional at important times like this. Emotions would hit later, like the aftershock of an earthquake. I made a few calls to my support friends when I could. By Tuesday, we had been through endless hours of tough love, as my son was convinced I was the anti-Christ. At one point, he ran away overnight. I had barely slept in three days but somehow had the soundness of mind and faith to stay strong. I emptied his bank account, contacted the Dean of Student Affairs, and had his access denied on campus. Classes were scheduled to start the next day. I gave him a choice to either go into a residential program for help, or I was leaving him on his own without support, or a car.

By that afternoon, he agreed to enter a wilderness program in St. George, Utah, that was suggested by the interventionist. There was a late-afternoon flight to Utah that day, and he would be met by the program counselor when he landed. As I walked him to security, I felt his fear and anger. Jane was waiting in the rental car, and I couldn't help but fall apart as I tried to hug his angry, stiff, six-foot-three, thin body. We both were spent from all of the emotions and exhaustion. I hadn't eaten very much since Saturday and realized my movers would be at the house in Colorado in thirty-six hours.

I booked flights for the next day from Miami to Vail for Jane and me, and we slept for ten hours that night at the hotel, which we desperately needed. I received a text that Brit had arrived safely and was in good hands. At least I knew he'd be safe and substance-free where he was. Powerlessness overcame me. I wasn't capable of helping him through his troubles, and he was in God's hands.

Jane never complained that she lost her week off before having to go back to college. We landed in Vail at night, and the movers arrived the next morning. Packing was one day and loading the next for the contents of a five-bedroom, five-bath home. The movers pulled away as my cleaning crew arrived. Jane and I went to the airport, heading back to L.A. for a day of rest before she had to get back to school and my movers would arrive with all the furniture. What a fiasco.

It felt as though time had come to a standstill for the past eight to ten days. I knew my son was safe, and I had to trust that he'd be all right in the process, but I couldn't quite let go and do nothing. He'd reported having been suicidal to the counselors. It was uncertain whether Brit was experiencing a mild post-traumatic-stress syndrome, reliving the loss of his father from losing my dad, or if he was an actual addict. Before the last six months of my life, I hadn't ever felt truly lonely, but under duress, I found it impossibly demanding to be the total support to two offspring with no one to support me. That was when I decided to email Charles for help. I knew this was an emotional slip, but he had become my automatic default when I was afraid or felt alone. Especially when it came to my children, I could count on him. The heart and the head don't always stay in sync, and I was powerless over that with him.

Charles responded to my email immediately with the direct

phone number of the top psychiatrist at Massachusetts General Hospital who was awaiting my call. Thanks to Charles, a brilliant expert would monitor my son's progress and testing. That was the kind of behavior on Charles' part that tugged at my heartstrings. I shared it with Jane who emailed him a thank you. He responded by saying if she needed anything, he was there for her as well. They continued an interchange. I was unnerved knowing I had slipped back into my pattern. Sarah was going to be furious.

Moving forward with our lives meant, for Jane, starting her third year at college, and, for me, a new place complete with my hummingbird feeder outside. The sweet little birds began visiting me right away. I resumed the discipline of working out, and eagerly moved back into the center of my herd of friends. And I made new friends, starting at a new hairdresser's in Beverly Hills. I met a lovely woman, who, like me, was also sober more than twenty years. Our meandering conversation revealed that her boss had been Charles' roommate in Harvard. Would side detours and connections to Charles ever stop popping up in the obstacle course of my life?

With my new haircut and improved spirits, I made an appointment with a matchmaker who set me up on a date for that very weekend. One friend suggested I see a metaphysical healer to remove all negative residue from my body. I was past skepticism in view of the fact that similar encounters had proven so life-changing in the past. I agreed and saw the woman the day before my date.

This healer was also psychic. I just listened as she read me. She said I would be meeting a man that weekend that had a love-child connection. She also told me she was a love child, too, and shared her story. She knew things about what my son had experienced, as well as my life, and had me mesmerized. As our session came to a close, she asked me an unnerving question.

"Why did you leave out the dark-haired man who is playing 'Big Daddy' to your daughter?"

She knew about Charles and our connection, but I dismissed it.

"I haven't seen him in months," I said.

"You will, within seventy-two hours."

That made me nervous. I was looking forward to dating and having him as part of my past. He may have been a good mentor for my daughter and graciously put me in touch with a wonderful doctor, but that didn't diminish the fact that he was trouble for me.

28

➤ Hummingbirds

The next night during dinner, sure enough my blind date, Len, spoke of his eldest daughter and how he found out through blood tests when she was ill that she was not his daughter. His wife had passed years earlier, and it was a total shock for him to learn that his first-born of four children was not his. He was a nice man but not a romantic match for me. I was astonished that the healer had been so accurate.

The following day was Sunday, and I was leaving a grocery store after attending a support-group meeting. As I walked out of the store, I noticed a couple with a small child coming toward me. I thought, *What a lovely family.* As I glanced at the dark-haired man on one side of the child, I heard my name. The woman and child went ahead, as I realized it was Charles coming toward me. We embraced, and I was tongue-tied and shocked all at once. I hadn't seen him since that last meeting in his office six months prior.

"How've you been?" he asked, "And your son?"

"Much better, thank you. Is that your new family?" I asked, trying to ignore the gut-wrenching pain in my stomach.

"Hardly."

Did I detect a note of sarcasm? "Well, good seeing you." I rushed away toward my car.

As I turned on the engine, uncontrollable tears ran down my face. I didn't understand this involuntary wave of emotion that came over me. Of course, I rushed into an analysis. Were these simple tears, mourning all the lovely possibilities that had died, the secret dream of my heart that had been crushed? Or were these complicated tears, mixed in with the salt of older tears from childhood and from Dad's death? I was two-and-a-half decades sober, had undergone years of therapy, and wondered if this old pain would ever stop repeating itself.

My birthday had arrived, and Jane celebrated with me. We had lunch at the Polo Lounge at the Beverly Hills Hotel, one of our favorite places for lunch.

"Hey, Mom?" She asked afterward, amusement in her eyes. "Would you be willing to get a matching tattoo with me?"

Relatively conservative Jane and thoroughly conservative me with tattoos? My jaw dropped but I shut it immediately. How lucky I was that my twenty-year old wanted a permanent symbol of how close we were.

"That sounds perfect," I said.

Laughing, we went to a place on Sunset Boulevard patronized by a friend of mine who had several tattoos. We each got a one-quarter inch open black heart in the same spot on our ankle. Over the years, whenever we signed our names to each other, we'd draw a small open heart in closing, so this was symbolic for us. I was so grateful Jane had wanted me to do this with her.

Just when we each were finished, Jane asked, "Can I have a second one? I want the word three on my ring finger, small enough to be covered by a narrow band."

I was floored. This fabulous young woman was expressing the love and value she put on our family, *We Three*. It was a wonderful, unforgettable birthday for me.

Brit sent me a letter from Utah, asking me to come for a

two-day visit. He was a month into his wilderness program, out in the middle of nowhere, surviving off the land, and getting in touch with who he really was. He'd been writing me weekly, and his counselors called me weekly, aiming to help rebuild our relationship as part of his therapy. I responded to each letter. I would go, of course, but I was a bit nervous about being in the wilderness without outside contact or modern facilities. I'm a city girl who prefers heels and dresses; but nothing meant more to me than my children—especially now that my son needed me.

Wilderness—such a simple word for what Brit was experiencing. We had sleeping bags and a backpack. No central lodge, not a shower in sight, nor even a tent. Brit had to dig a hole for me to use as a toilet. If I generated any trash whatsoever, I had to carry it in a bag until the weekly trash truck came. We ate jerky and berries and cooked oatmeal and noodles or rice over the open fire. At first I actually worried about broken fingernails, but when I heard a faint scratching noise beside my head one night and saw a tarantula digging a hole, my priorities shifted drastically. The time with Brit there in Utah was precious and indescribable. We bonded on a level that rekindled the deep understanding we'd always shared. He agreed to come to Los Angeles for his aftercare for the remainder of the semester because he'd taken a medical leave of absence from college. We got to know the essence of each other, and I left knowing he would ultimately be fine.

I was able to exhale after months of worrying about him, and after one heck of a long shower, I looked forward to moving into what was next for my life. As I was dressing, catching a glimpse of the small heart tattoo on my ankle, I realized between that and tarantulas, I had indeed come a long way.

Back in L.A., I began writing and also started a blog entitled *Secret Love Child* in the hopes of inspiring others to share similar stories. I hadn't a clue what I was doing or why, but, intuitively, I knew I needed to do this. It has proven to be a very satisfying process.

After two months, Brit finished his wilderness program and flew directly to LAX where I picked him up. It was hard for him to adjust to the stimulus overload of a vast city after being in such a remote area. He still seemed vulnerable. I took him to the aftercare facility immediately, which was only thirty minutes from me in Brentwood. It was located in Woodland Hills and looked like an educational building from the busy street. When we arrived, we were taken into the admissions office, where I needed to make the initial payment for his care and set up weekly counseling sessions. I was grateful he was into the solution after such a tough time.

There was a window behind the desk of the woman we met with, and it faced a busy street. To my amazement, there was a hummingbird at my eye level, whirring steadily for several moments before disappearing. It seemed like a reminder, telling me I could open up any time to an immediate connection with a loving presence, something greater than me; I was reassured. I also sensed the presence of my dad. Even now, I can think of this moment and find my serenity.

My blog was almost ready to be launched, as I entered articles and comments on forgiveness and the dynamics of being a secret. I had hoped that this would inspire me to get writing the book that lived inside of me, but it hadn't. Something was holding me back, and I couldn't put a finger on it. Then, the answer came.

One day, there was a private message in my Facebook mail from an unknown "Joseph" asking if Dad (by his name) had been my father. I replied in the affirmative, asking why he was inquiring. Nothing could have prepared me for his response:

"This may come to you as somewhat of a surprise. And I am deeply sorry if it gets you upset. But I am your half-brother through your father. I just found out today that he had passed, and I regret not ever getting to know him. I'm not looking to bring any heartache or tarnish the image of your father at all. But I am looking to maybe find out a little more about him. If you are open for a discussion, please let me know. Thank you for your time."

29

❧ LOVE CHILD

A half-brother?

I flashed back to the lawsuit in which my father had been involved that was brushed under the carpet in the late seventies. Of course. It had been about paternity and Mom was upset, I vaguely recalled.

How could Dad have kept this from me? After all the work we did to heal our wounds, he was guilty of the same crime that was committed against him? It was mind-boggling, I mean, REALLY? Both of my parents had secret illegitimate children while married? Unfathomable. This was almost too much to wrap my head around.

When I saw Joseph on Facebook, there was no question that he is my dad's son. I showed his photos to Mom, who concurred. Poor Joseph, what he didn't know was that we were not related at all. He, in fact, was like me, the secret love child, but unlike me he was brought into the world by Dad, my not-father. I felt empathy and compassion, knowing just how he felt. I asked for his phone number, and as I proceeded to call him, I knew for sure that the time had come to write this story.

Joseph and I first spoke by phone, following up with his written story. His mother worked for the same company, as did Mom, Dad, and Mr. Bayley. She was on a business trip when she uncharacteristically drank too much, and had a one-night stand with my dad, producing Joseph. She was unmarried at the time and later married Joseph's stepdad. Joseph carries his mother's last name.

In the late 1970s after his birth, his mother sued my dad for child support; however, the case was thrown out of court. All documentation mysteriously disappeared. That was when Mom accompanied Dad to court.

His mom was always open and honest with Joseph, and he did not reach out to find my dad until he was eighteen. When they spoke the first time, Dad was defensive, and the conversation did not go far. During a subsequent phone call, Dad was apparently more open, but Joseph chose not to meet with him or further pursue him. It was hearing of Dad's death that prompted him to contact me. To date, I marvel at the coincidence that of the three children Dad raised, Joseph would choose to contact me. Not related, but, in essence, we are the same.

We met in Rochester for coffee, so I could provide him with the information he sought, as Sally Ann had so graciously made available to me.

Janet and Tommy refuse to acknowledge him, and I had to let go of it and move forward in my life.

My sister Janet has multiple sclerosis, but initially managed it well with very few symptoms over the years. For privacy reasons, I did not elaborate on her in my story. She has had other unresolved demons that have manifested in her life, and she and her husband divorced long ago. He is a wonderful father to her two children now in their late twenties. Seeing her struggle has been difficult, and the entire family had given up on her getting help for her addictions. However, perhaps Dad has been her angel from above, as she entered a recovery center in Los Angeles and is on the upswing. I am happy to facilitate assistance, and have a special place in my heart for her.

Tommy and I were never close. We drew together when

necessary for Mom or Dad's health, but otherwise, there simply is no relationship. He was pained to hear about the existence of Joseph, feeling deceived by Dad, no doubt. I, more than most, understand.

My Mom and Pete are the love of each other's lives. Pete is forty-two years sober, and a wonderful support to me if I call him. He loves my mom, which is what really matters. She finally forgave herself for her sins around me, but far too long after I had forgiven her. However, my mom now has Alzheimer's. I visited her in Rochester this past fall while she still remembered me. Pete takes good care of her, and I'm grateful she has him and his undying love. Mom is carefree without much to dwell on, existing purely in the moment, and I am sad to see her slipping away. She shared her deep love for my biological father during the visit, her guilt for the deception, then she smiled and said, "You know, Ellen, I always thought of you as my special love child."

By the following spring, Brit came to the other side of his difficult time. I believe he did relive some trauma of the abandonment by his father when his "Papas" died. This trauma, coupled with a young man becoming an adult with only a mother to rely on, was more than he could handle amidst the natural push and pull that takes place in that process of separation. I was his only go-to person left, and he saw me fall apart for the first time ever, at a time that he needed my help.

He finished his spring semester and stayed in Miami for a summer session to make up for the credits missed the first semester. He was able to join me in California for a few weeks at the end of the summer, when We Three visited Monterey, Carmel, Pebble Beach, Sausalito, and spent a few days in San Francisco where we took an architecture tour. We returned to Los Angeles where the two of us took a walking tour of the city, and recently met in Chicago to do the same.

He is currently successfully continuing in his architecture program, is happy, and remains a wonderful son to me and brother to his sister. He has informed me of his intention to attend graduate school either at Harvard's Design School or Columbia University.

Jane is a senior at Scripps College and worked for Warner Brothers last summer, where she continues to work once a week during her school year. She is the resident advisor in her dormitory, and will serve as captain of her Division III lacrosse team. Charles remains her friend and mentor, and I couldn't be more proud of her. I have no doubt she will continue to find her way.

Both of the children forgave their father this year, agreeing to be at his wedding. When Brit had concern over dishonoring me by doing so, I assured him that he couldn't honor me more deeply than by choosing to exercise forgiveness.

Jane said she wasn't sure she wanted to attend at the age of twenty-one; however, she was concerned that at forty she may have regrets if she didn't go. Their attitudes and decisions to attend have validated for me that my commitment to parenting has definitely paid off.

When I mentioned to their father the content of this book, he was fully supportive. He encouraged me to write every detail, hoping that if it were to help one father reconsider some of the choices Jim made and his behaviors, and prevents repeated conduct, it would be worth it. He is with a woman who loves him, and I'm happy for him.

Regarding my personal life, I am hopeful that now I'm finally open to love. I'm so enormously grateful to everyone who has helped me get to this place.

Virginia, my best friend since we were twelve, is a tremendous support to me. Speaking with her almost daily is a true blessing in my life.

Ron and I remain dear friends, connected by phone and email, though I haven't seen him in more than two years. He sounds well, and remains very active in business. I adore him, particularly for being so supportive of my writing this book. "Be sure to use my real name," he said.

And I'm grateful to Charles on so many levels. For a shy, awkward man when it comes to attractive women, he had in his own way risked letting me know him. Unknowingly, while doing so, he held up a mirror that forced me to face my own fears around intimacy and childhood wounds. I am grateful to him for being a catalyst that catapulted me forward.

I phoned him right about the time the Schwarzenegger-Shriver news hit (he knows them), which happened to be the exact day I completed my first draft, to inform him he would be in my book.

He responded, "Just don't use my real name. I trust you. What's it about anyway?"

I replied, "Do you remember me telling you I found out in my early thirties I was not quite who I thought I was?"

"I don't know whether I knew that," was what he said next, "but I recall you came from a checkered past."

Checkered past. I felt like I had been hit by a stun gun. I thought I'd worked through all manner of baggage with Charles, and that he couldn't possibly hurt me anymore. Yet I couldn't even reply, I was so taken aback. I quickly ended the conversation.

I was sure that when Charles had read my history via emails, he couldn't be bothered remembering the details, filing my confidences into a catchall bag of undesirables. His words, "checkered past," hit every nerve ending in me over being a secret my entire life and the shame I carried. I also think they propelled me into my final phase of healing.

In predictable fashion, I followed up with a very nasty, accusatory email, questioning whether that was why he had kept me a secret. Was he ashamed of me? Had he gotten too big for his own britches? Who did he think he was? Did I need to remind him that even billionaires put their pants on the same as the average Joe?

My recovery program has a saying: "If it's hysterical, it must be historical," which certainly applied with me with Charles, infinitum. We are also told to "pause when agitated," which I did not adhere to when hitting the send button on my computer. Oh, dear, there I was again, with all my wounds front and center.

Charles' response? "I'm tired of feeling punished by you. Please remove my email address from your records."

I did some serious soul searching, dealt with it in therapy with Sarah, and a few weeks later, wrote him a long email. He was right to feel that way. I had been punishing him—every time he attempted to get close to me or unintentionally hit a nerve. I took full responsibility for my part, apologized, citing exactly where I had been wrong, and specified how I ought to have handled myself during various interchanges with him.

He appreciated the words and forgave me. I never found out why he had abruptly cancelled the job the way that he had, although his head of the program contacted me to pick my brain about my national expansion plan. His side of the street is his business, while I remain eternally grateful to him for being a guide and support to my daughter.

I ran into him in October last fall after not seeing him for a full year. And where? Of course, the gym.

When I saw him waving and heard his "Hello," my eyes lit up. I waved and smiled sheepishly, resuming my exercise. After showering and dressing, there he stood as I was leaving. He opened the door like a gentleman as we walked out together. He pushed the down button for the elevator leading to the underground parking, making small talk. As the doors closed, I thought of our first hello in another elevator across the country in Boston. Here we were, alone with our eyes locked on each other, gazing in a way that confirmed the physical attraction still existed. As a tingle ran through my spine, I wasn't sure if the elevator would explode, or I would implode before the doors opened. When they did, I exhaled as if coming up from underwater for air. Cheerfully, I threw my arms around his neck.

"I loved seeing you," I said sweetly.

Could he tell that I thought him just as handsome now as I had the first time we'd spoken in an elevator? At the same time, I also felt proud of myself that I could respond to Charles purely as someone who'd played an important part of my life, and not with any lurking baggage waiting to pop open and ambush me. It was just this dear man and me. I had spent a lifetime void of a man's love, and Charles was wed to his work. His values and commitment to his family were compelling attributes, but I wanted a man who was available both emotionally and physically for a true intimate relationship. I also need a man who knows what he wants, which will include me. He is a good person, and there for my daughter, which is why I will always have a soft spot for him in my heart.

Hummingbirds continue to appear regularly to me, especially during my times of worry or concern. I recently read: "Legends say that hummingbirds float free of time, carrying our hopes for love, joy, and celebration. The hummingbird's delicate grace reminds us that life is rich, beauty is everywhere, every personal connection has meaning and that laughter is life's sweetest creation."

I began my blog, www.lovechildstories.com, a year before hearing from Joseph. I hadn't intended to write this book then, and couldn't have imagined what would transpire from the blog. Before ever writing this book, I was solicited by a daytime-television show to appear as a guest, a writer of a major magazine, and an agent to represent me. It's as though I put intent on it during my meditations, and it organically manifested. That's how I knew there was a message that could help others. I have dozens of emails of stories from others like me, and launched "Ask E" online as a forum for questions to be answered by me from anyone who needs help on all that surrounds the secret love-child dynamics, family secrets, and how to overcome the obstacles life can present. I want to stress healing and dignity, along with the notion that even if we were a secret, we stand in the light deserving to be cherished as any other human being. It is only ignorance of society that attempts to exclude a person from the legitimacy of family, community, and God's grace.

➤ *Ellen Who?* Book Club Discussion Questions

1. What role did the author's childhood play in shaping her business skills? Her life skills?
2. Some of the author's coping skills developed in childhood were a double edged sword. What were these skills and how did they both help and harm the author?
3. How did being "illegitimate" shape the lens through which the author views the world and people's attitudes towards her? In what ways does she overcome this?
4. The role of forgiveness plays a large role in this story. What were the results and benefits that came to the author when she forgave her father? Her mother?
5. How did the author's past shape her parenting?
6. The author had a very close relationship with her siblings as a child: in many ways, her sister raised her and she raised her brother. Why do you think the author and her siblings became somewhat estranged? Was this necessary for the author's sobriety?
7. Synchronicity plays a large role in this story. What were some of the surprising synchronicities?
8. Why do you think the author became closer to her father than either of her siblings did?
9. What did the author gain by contacting her biological father?

➤ Questions for further personal reflection

10. What role has synchronicity played in your life, if any?
11. What do you make of the psychics' predictions?
12. How does our society view and treat "illegitimate" children? After reading this book, does it change how you might think about "illegitimacy"?
13. What do you make of the author's nontraditional career? Does it inspire you to take risks or be creative in your own work?
14. The author places a high value on integrity and family. What are your values and how has your past helped to shape them?